Matchless

Matchless

*Joyce Wethered, Glenna Collett
and the Rise of Women's Golf*

STEPHEN PROCTOR

First published in 2025 by
Arena Sport, an imprint of
Birlinn Limited
West Newington House
10 Newington Road
Edinburgh
EH9 1QS
www.arenasportbooks.co.uk

Copyright © Stephen Proctor 2025

The right of Stephen Proctor to be identified as the Author of this work has been asserted by him in accordance with the Copyright, Designs and Patents Act 1988.

All rights reserved. No part of this publication may be reproduced, stored or transmitted in any form without the express written permission of the publisher.

ISBN 978 1 913759 19 3

British Library Cataloguing-in-Publication Data
A catalogue record for this book is available from the British Library

Typeset by Hewer Text UK Ltd, Edinburgh

Papers used by Birlinn are from well-managed forests and other responsible sources

Printed in the United States of America by Integrated Books International

For Ruth Ann,
my inspiration in golf

CONTENTS

CHAPTER ONE: EMPRESSES OF GOLF	1
CHAPTER TWO: LADIES ON THE LINKS	5
CHAPTER THREE: AUNTIE MABEL AND THE CZAR	18
CHAPTER FOUR: SHE IS FIERCE	32
CHAPTER FIVE: AMERICA'S ANSWER	47
CHAPTER SIX: CORONATION AT PRINCE'S	62
CHAPTER SEVEN: THE GREAT GLENNA	80
CHAPTER EIGHT: INHUMANLY GOOD	95
CHAPTER NINE: LEVIATHANS AT TROON	106
CHAPTER TEN: THE ETERNAL PROBLEM	122
CHAPTER ELEVEN: MATCHLESS	137
CHAPTER TWELVE: THE GRAND STAGE	153
CHAPTER THIRTEEN: SWAN SONG	169
CHAPTER FOURTEEN: ENDURING LEGACY	183
CHAPTER FIFTEEN: AFTERLIVES	196

NOTES ON CHAPTERS	209
BIBLIOGRAPHY	225
ACKNOWLEDGEMENTS	235
INDEX	239

One

EMPRESSES OF GOLF

EVEN before they struck their first shots on that spring morning at Troon in 1925, Joyce Wethered and Glenna Collett surely must have sensed that something extraordinary was about to unfold over that ancient links in Ayrshire. During the years since the Great War, on opposite sides of the Atlantic, the Englishwoman and the American had played such overpowering golf that they set a new standard for the women's game, sweeping aside even the breakthrough players who had preceded them. Wethered and Collett had become the talk of the golfing world, and fans everywhere were desperate for a match between them. Ten months earlier, the American magazine *Golf Illustrated* had demonstrated the extent of that hunger with a full-page presentation titled 'Empresses of Golf'. It featured studio portraits of Joyce and Glenna looking their loveliest. Wethered, 23, sits in an armchair, wearing a sleeveless dress over her willowy frame. Collett, 21, stares serenely at the camera, her elbows propped up on a table, her chin resting on her folded hands. The caption notes, simply, that: 'A meeting between these two stars is a treat that is in store for the golfing world in the near future.'

Now, at 10.20 a.m. on 25 May, that moment had arrived as the two women prepared to tee off in the British Ladies' Championship. Both wore a cloche hat, a calf-length skirt and a sweater over their blouse – Wethered's a cardigan, Collett's a Fair Isle she bought in Scotland to ward off the chill. Everyone attending that championship had hoped the draw would place Wethered and Collett in opposite brackets, setting up the delicious possibility that this first meeting between them would come with the title on the line. It was not to be. Fate brought them together in the third round, raising fears that the rest of the championship would be a let-down. The golf Wethered and Collett played certainly lived up to its billing. Before they reached the turn that morning at Troon, both Joyce and Glenna were keenly aware that in one another they faced the most formidable opponent they had ever confronted in a match, or ever would.

Playing over that windswept links along the Firth of Clyde – a genuine championship test at 6,415 yards – they arrived at the ninth tee all square, with scores approaching level fours, the standard in that age for flawless golf. Wethered was one over, Collett a stroke higher. Scores that low were unthinkable for women in 1925. Two years earlier at Troon, playing from the same tees, Arthur Havers won the Open Championship by playing all four of his rounds in a shade over level fours. Wethered and Collett were, frankly, astonished by the game they brought out in one another. 'I played as perfect golf as I ever will play,' Glenna marvelled in her memoir, a notion Joyce repeated in hers, almost to the letter. That afternoon at Troon marked the beginning of a sporting rivalry that would captivate the golfing universe for a decade and establish a lifelong bond between two very different women, one born of respect for a competitor whose brilliance inspires your own.

Four years later, the competition between Wethered and Collett would reach its heart-stopping crescendo – this time, fittingly, in the final of the first Ladies' Championship to be conducted at St

Andrews in a generation. Both women would live to a great age – Collett to 85, Wethered to 96 – but neither would ever outlive the legend they created that afternoon on the Old Course. Their match eclipsed even the glories of Troon. Bernard Darwin, golf correspondent for *The Times*, was so dumbstruck by what he witnessed at St Andrews that the greatest of all golf writers found himself, for once, at a loss for words.

Wethered and Collett would meet on nearly a dozen other occasions in the afterglow of that championship – at the 1932 Curtis Cup and during Joyce's 1935 tour of North America – generating a level of respect for women's golf that would once have been unimaginable. Their accomplishments represented nothing less than the realisation of a goal women had been striving to reach since the earliest days of golf. Ladies began taking to the links as soon as their husbands began donning scarlet jackets and heading to the club for a game. They did so with the single-minded intent of proving that they, too, could master the sport that had so beguiled their men. That quest took on a deeply symbolic meaning because it unfolded during a singular time in history, an era when suffragettes around the globe were fighting stubbornly, sometimes violently, to establish their rightful place in a patriarchal world.

Even as women founded their own golf union and launched their own championship in 1893, their fight for the right to vote was gaining momentum worldwide, with the final victory achieved just a year before Wethered and Collett engaged in that unforgettable duel at the home of golf. With the suffrage issue dominating headlines in the US and Britain, the supremacy Wethered and Collett achieved in golf stood as living testimony to the point women fought to make. Given a fair chance, they could develop a level of skill equal to any man's. The women's rights movement, however, was not the only history that coloured the rivalry between Wethered and Collett. There was golf history, too. Their matches were played during the years when America was building what Darwin described as its 'great golfing empire'. Season after demoralising season, the most cherished of British trophies, the Claret Jug, was spirited away across the Atlantic.

By 1929, when Wethered and Collett met in that epic final over the Old Course, the truth was that there was only one player left in Britain who had not been vanquished by an American – Joyce Wethered. It is, perhaps, one of the ironies of history that the upshot of the enormous recognition Wethered and Collett brought to the women's game was something neither Joyce nor Glenna wanted, as women who believed firmly in the prevailing ideal of their age – that golf was its best when the game was played for love and not for money. Less than a decade after they left the field – Wethered at the conclusion of her triumphant US tour, Collett for the sixth and final time as America's champion – women would take their first steps towards establishing a professional golf tour of their own, once again striding confidently into a world that had previously been the sole province of men.

Two

LADIES ON THE LINKS

———•••●••———

READERS of Edinburgh's *Caledonian Mercury* awoke to news so shocking on 24 April 1738 that it would be reprinted in papers as far away as London and the American colonies. 'Early last Tuesday morning,' the report read, 'two married women of the city stept out to Bruntsfield Links to a concerted match at golf, followed by their husbands carrying the clubs. Curiosity led thither a great crowd, who were charmed with seeing the half-naked viragos tilt the balls so manfully, and their dexterity in holing. Considerable wagers were laid; but Charming Sally carried the prize.' The mind reels with questions about this curious report. How did men in that male-dominated society come to be carrying clubs for their wives? Had they lost a bet? What was meant by half-naked? Had those two domineering women – virago, after all, means 'female warrior' – played without a corset or a proper hat? Truth is, not much can be known with certainty, beyond that women playing golf in public was rare enough in 1738 that the story would be picked up by the *Daily Gazetteer* and *Read's Weekly Journal* in London and across the Atlantic in the *South Carolina Gazette*.

This much can be safely inferred: women had wanted to play golf from the moment men took up the game. It is worth noting that the match reported in the *Mercury* took place six years before the Gentlemen Golfers of Leith staged the first formal competition in 1744, playing for a silver club donated by Scotland's capital city. Reports of women playing golf continued to crop up regularly through the years. The *Statistical Account of Scotland* mentions women and children playing over the links at Musselburgh during the 1790s. In December 1810, members of the Royal Musselburgh Golf Club voted to donate a prize for a competition among the town's fishwives. Evidence of women playing over the links at St Andrews surfaced early on, too. In 1855, Mrs James Wolfe-Murray, daughter of the Royal and Ancient Golf Club's revered leader John Whyte-Melville, scandalised the town by boldly taking to the course, playing alone with two clubs.

A dozen years later, women would get the first golf course of their own, designed by the man who did more than any other person to spread love for the Scottish game, Tom Morris of St Andrews. The ladies' links he created, however, was something entirely different from courses played over by men. By the early 1860s, women in town had taken a fancy to putting, a brand of golf Victorian society considered far more appropriate for ladies than Mrs Wolfe-Murray's forays on the St Andrews links. Women played their games over a handful of short holes near Old Tom Morris's shop, which caddies had laid out to pass the time as they awaited a bag to carry. Caddies didn't appreciate women invading their space, although they were savvy enough to keep quiet about it, and gentlemen of the R&A didn't want their wives mixing with ruffians. They asked Morris to lay out a proper course for the women of St Andrews, leading to creation of the Himalayas putting green, a rollicking 18-hole adventure that has changed little over a century and a half and remains among the most popular attractions in town.

That same year, 1867, saw the formation of the oldest women's golf club in the world, still thriving as the St Andrews Ladies' Putting Club. Morris showed his commitment to welcoming women into the world of golf by doing double duty for the next 30 years as keeper of the ladies' green. The club's first competition, conducted on 5 October 1867, was a roaring success, drawing a substantial crowd of upper-crust ladies and gentlemen as well as 22 entrants, among them women with the most famous surnames in St Andrews – Moncrieff and Chambers, Tulloch and Boothby. The prizes were the club's Golf Medal and silver pebble brooch, both of which are competed for even today. Newspapers lapped it up, with fawning coverage appearing in the *St Andrews Gazette*, the *Fifeshire News*, and even the national newspaper, *The Scotsman*, which described the event as a 'most novel, interesting and excellent competition'.

Over the years, the Ladies' Putting Club came to play a significant social role in St Andrews, one that would remain part of the game through the ages. In those days, gentlemen could join the club as associate members. That provided an outlet for courting in an informal atmosphere, a rarity in the Victorian age. Men and women could play alongside one another in monthly medals. During the spring and autumn events, restricted to ladies only, men could tag along as markers or caddies. The Ladies' Putting Club also made one other social contribution that will forever remain part of the game. In a way that ancient golf societies for men had never done, it made the game a family affair, one children would be introduced to by their parents, as is so often the case today. In July 1888, the *St Andrews Citizen* announced plans for the first Children's Golf Club. It was open to boys and girls, ages five through 13, whose mothers belonged to the Ladies' Putting Club, as well as to the children of visitors who swelled the club's ranks every summer. By September, the club had been formally launched, with 134 children as members.

The experience of one famous family – the Taits of Edinburgh, frequent visitors to St Andrews – demonstrates the impact the

Children's Golf Club would have on developing young players. In 1895, a band of travellers that came to St Andrews every summer and were popular with the townspeople donated two prizes for a competition among members of the Ladies' Putting Club, a claret jug for first place and a medal for second. The best of 60 scores was the fine 105 turned in by Edith Tait, the older sister of a youngster who would grow up to be one of Scotland's most famous and beloved golfers. Her brother, Frederick Guthrie Tait, would get his first taste of glory over the Ladies' Putting Green as well. In September 1881, aged 11, Tait took first place among 42 players in a Children's Club tournament, with a score of 107. It was an early sign of the great champion he would become, with victories in the 1896 and 1898 Amateur Championships before his tragic early death in 1900 during the South African War. Even today, the Children's Golf Club remains an institution in St Andrews, hosting putting competitions that introduce new generations of boys and girls to the royal and ancient game.

UNMATCHED ENTHUSIASM

In its report on that first competition of the Ladies' Putting Club in the autumn of 1867, *The Scotsman* confidently predicted that this new pastime 'will become a favourite game, not simply among the ladies of St Andrews, but throughout the kingdom'. The newspaper's correspondent, however, would never have guessed that the next ladies' golf club would be formed not in Scotland but England, at Royal North Devon, better known as Westward Ho! Truth is, that might have been expected, given that North Devon's founders, Isaac and William Gosset, had close ties to St Andrews. The year after Tom Morris laid out the Ladies' Putting Green, Westward Ho! built one nearly identical to it on Northam Burrows. The North Devon Ladies' Golf Club was founded that same year, 1868, with 35 women as members and a number of gentlemen as associates. It was followed in 1872 by the London Scottish Ladies' Golf Club at Wimbledon, with 14 original members. Neither of those clubs would last, disappearing after a few years and being reconstituted in the 1890s. They were, however, an early sign that English women would embrace golf with unmatched enthusiasm. It would not be long before they wanted more than mere putting.

By the 1880s, English women were forming clubs that played over courses which required genuine golf. Some had links of their own, others competed over the men's course, sometimes using forward tees. So many women took up the game that they played a significant role in the great golf boom that swept England before the war, according to new research by historian Michael Morrison. By 1894, England had 44 ladies' clubs, more than twice as many as Scotland. The membership of those clubs, however, by no means reflected the number of women playing golf. Scores of men's clubs had a ladies' section, so English women actually were playing at more than 100 golf clubs by the middle of that decade. By 1889, some 3,700 women had taken up the game, one of every 10 golfers in England. When war was declared in 1914, women accounted for one of every four golfers and their number had swelled to 73,000.

It was during this frenzy of growth that a pivotal figure in the history of women's golf – Issette Pearson – would fall in love with the game and under the spell of Dr William Laidlaw Purves. Issette was born in Devon, on 2 November 1861, to Thomas and Mary Pearson. Her father was a landed gentleman, although when Issette was still a toddler, he made a bad investment that nearly ruined him. Pearson moved his family to Birkenhead, near Liverpool, and opened an insurance business. His firm proved so successful that in 1887 Pearson decided to expand in London. It was there, on Barnes Common, that 25-year-old Issette caught the fever for golf. Tall and sturdy, with a decidedly stern countenance, Pearson looked matronly even as a young woman, in part because she always wore her dresses buttoned tightly up to the neck.

Pearson quickly earned a reputation as an outstanding player, and early on she developed ambitions for the future of women's golf. Her opportunity to pursue them would arise when she became a founding member of the revived Wimbledon Ladies' Golf Club in 1890. At the club, she met Laidlaw Purves, an Edinburgh-born eye surgeon who practised in London. He was a powerful figure in the emerging world of golf, a leader at Royal Wimbledon and Royal St George's in Sandwich, the first English links to host an Open Championship. Purves and Pearson were two proverbial peas in a pod – Issette branded by journalists as 'despotic as the Czar of Russia', Purves so caustic and aggressive that he tended to alienate those whose help he needed most. They met at a propitious time. Since 1866, Purves had been campaigning to establish a central ruling body for a rapidly growing game – one that could develop and govern a universal set of rules, as well as a handicapping system that could account for the vast differences between golf courses. Purves's efforts had gone nowhere, mostly because other powerful men in the game found his browbeating tiresome. In Pearson, he discovered an equally formidable woman who saw the issues the same way he did.

Not long after the Wimbledon Ladies' Club was re-established in 1890, its members began to play home-and-away matches against neighbouring women's clubs. Pearson immediately encountered the same problems bedevilling the men's game. While most clubs followed the rules used at St Andrews, many had local variations that created inconsistencies. Worse still, each club had its own way of establishing handicaps, which were so wildly different that matches often turned out to be lopsided. Not only that, Pearson believed women needed a national championship of their own to match the men's Amateur inaugurated at Royal Liverpool in 1885.

By then, Purves had become fed up with his lack of progress in men's golf, which would not agree on how to govern the game and its rules until 1897, years after women had shown the way. He leapt at the chance to help Pearson realise her ambitions. It provided Purves with a platform to demonstrate how effective his ideas could be when put into practice. In the spring of 1893, Purves and Pearson sent a letter to women's clubs throughout Britain, inviting them to a meeting on 19 April 1893 at 2.30 p.m. at the Grand Hotel in Trafalgar Square, London, to discuss the prospect of forming a golf union. Before those assembled got down to business, Purves gave a speech in which he laid out the goals of this new union and vented his frustrations about the way his ideas had been ignored by leaders of the men's game, especially those in St Andrews. 'When the members of the Wimbledon Ladies' Golf Club sent out their proposal that a Golf Union should be established,' Purves began, 'they showed a most commendable foresight.' Without a union, he warned, competitions between clubs, international matches and championships for women would be plagued by the same 'chaotic conditions' that existed in the men's game. Conditions, Purves added, that were created by 'an oligarchy of each local club ruling over its own individual members, and a great oligarchy, of an ancient and venerated club ruling over the golfing world', a thinly veiled swipe at the Royal and Ancient. He went on to outline the stated ambitions of the Ladies' Golf Union – establishing a uniform code of rules and a central body to govern them; creating an adequate system for handicapping tournaments, and conducting a national championship for women. Before the meeting concluded, the 13 clubs represented voted unanimously to form a Union, with Pearson as its Honorary Secretary and Blanche Martin Hulton as Honorary Treasurer. Four men were named vice presidents – Purves and Talbot Fair for England, Harry Everard for Scotland and Thomas Gilroy for Ireland.

Two months later, beginning on 13 June, the first British Ladies' Championship was conducted over the nine-hole women's course at Lytham and St Annes. Most of the 38 competitors hailed from England, although a handful also came from Ireland and Pau in France. Not a single player from Scotland made the trip. Scots were slow to accept a Union they saw as strictly English, but when the Championship came to Scotland, in 1897, they demonstrated their superiority by claiming 13 of the final 16 places at Gullane, including both spots in the final. With Scots absent, that first Ladies' Championship came down to the favourites from England – Pearson and Lady Margaret Scott, the striking, 19-year-old daughter of the 3rd Earl of Eldon. Lady Margaret came from a renowned golfing family. Her brothers Denys, Osmond and Michael were all first-class players. Osmond would be runner-up in the 1905 Amateur, and in 1933 Michael would become the Championship's oldest winner, aged 55. A year earlier, Lady Margaret had demonstrated what a formidable golfer she was by winning a tournament at Cheltenham club against a field of men. In the Ladies' Championship final, she made mincemeat of a nervous, overworked Pearson, building an enormous lead over the opening nine, and finishing Issette off by going seven holes up with just five to play.

It was, perhaps, a sign of the enormous task that lay in front of Pearson and her new union that it was not Lady Margaret, but her father, the Earl of Eldon, who accepted the trophy and delivered the victory speech. As dominating as Lady Margaret's victory was, it was her scores that raised eyebrows in the press. Two rounds of the ladies' course at St Annes added up to 4,264 yards. The nine-hole record was 36, posted by the great John Ball Jr., and Lady Margaret finished every one of her Championship rounds with a score between 40 and 42. 'Judging by the play of several ladies at St Annes last June, more particularly that of Lady Margaret Scott, there would be nothing surprising if, at some future time (and that may not be very far distant), a lady is found entering for both the Open and Amateur Championships,' Alexander Doleman wrote for *The Golfing Annual.* That was a bold prediction coming from a reporter of Doleman's experience. The 57-year-old had covered and played the game with distinction since the days when Young Tom Morris was making his stirring march to claim the Champion's Belt. Could women master the game as well as men? The question Doleman laid on the table would come to be known as golf's 'eternal problem'. It would be debated in clubhouses and tested over the links from the days of Lady Margaret and Issette Pearson through the coming of Joyce Wethered, Glenna Collett and beyond.

GLOBAL SISTERHOOD

When Pearson was falling in love with golf on Barnes Common, she was inclined to think she might be the only woman who had taken up this newly popular game. 'I could not hear of any other lady who played,' she wrote a dozen years later, 'though more than one gentleman was able to assure me that there were several in Scotland.' What Issette did not know was that even as she was working with Purves to establish the Ladies' Golf Union, women were embracing the game in every corner of the globe. Long before golf moved into England, it had been played in France at Pau, a fashionable resort in the Pyrenees. The first course was laid out there in 1856, and by 1877 Pau had a separate nine-hole links for women. The Cape Golf Club in South Africa admitted women as early as 1889, not because its leaders were forward-thinking, but because they desperately needed membership fees to stay afloat. By the turn of the century, women were playing at clubs across the nation. That was true in Australia as well. Royal Melbourne Golf Club admitted women in the autumn of 1892, followed quickly by clubs in Adelaide and Sydney. By 1894, Australian women had a national championship to match the one

Pearson had launched a year earlier in Britain. Women's golf was well under way in Canada, too. Ladies' clubs had formed in Montreal, Quebec, London and Toronto by 1891. Three years later, women from Quebec and Montreal competed in North America's first inter-club match.

But it was in the United States that this global sisterhood would develop its greatest army of adherents, women who would one day join the nation's men in challenging the hegemony of the British. Beyond that, the US was the only country where the origin story of golf was not solely one of men forming golf clubs and grudgingly allowing women to play over their links. The summer before Pearson founded her Union, a woman named Frances Boit paid a visit to her aunt and uncle, Mr and Mrs Arthur Hunnewell, of Wellesley, Massachusetts, 30 miles west of Boston. Boit had just returned from a trip to the continent, including a stay at Pau, that notable incubator of golf beloved by travellers around the world. Assuming that by then this newly fashionable game had caught on in the States, Boit brought her golf clubs with her. Like most Americans at that time, the Hunnewells knew nothing about the Scottish game. It had, after all, been only four years since the St Andrews Golf Club was founded in Yonkers, New York, becoming the first permanently established club in the country.

The Hunnewells were intrigued enough by Boit's description of the game to give it a try. Seven holes were laid out over the adjoining lawns of Hunnewell, his nephew and his brother-in-law. Boit suggested sinking flowerpots in the ground to serve as holes. Among those the Hunnewells invited to watch Boit demonstrate golf were Laura Safford Stewart, the wife of textile magnate John Wood Stewart, and Laurence Curtis, the cousin of Margaret and Harriot Curtis, two women who would later make a significant mark in the game. Curtis belonged to The Country Club at Brookline, founded in 1882 and which originally focused on horseback riding and other outdoor pursuits. Curtis was so enchanted by Boit's demonstration that he talked the club into adding golf to its amenities. Six holes were laid out the following April, a generation before the club would witness a seminal moment in American golf. 'While other localities pointed with reverential pride to their "fathers" of the game,' wrote the first historian of American golf, H.B. Martin, 'Boston golf had the distinction of having a "mother".'

Later that autumn, when Laura Stewart returned to her home in New Jersey, she and her husband did for Montclair what Curtis had done for Boston. They introduced their neighbours to the latest fad in sport by establishing a golf club. Come spring, it was thriving. Even before Frances Boit showed up in Wellesley, women along the nation's Eastern Seaboard had begun playing golf, mostly at clubs established by men, notably Shinnecock Hills in Long Island. Founded in 1891, the club would produce America's first women stars. By then, golf had already become so popular in America that both men and women were clamouring for national championships to match those in Britain. In the autumn of 1894, both St Andrews in Yonkers and Newport Country Club in Rhode Island set out to identify a men's champion in events hosted over their course.

Not surprisingly, that led to bickering over whether either championship could be considered legitimate if it was not sponsored by recognised national authority. In December, the nation's five leading clubs – Shinnecock Hills, Newport, Brookline, St Andrews and Chicago Golf Club – came together to settle the matter by establishing the United States Golf Association. That first year, the fledgling USGA held only men's amateur and open championships, but women were not about to be left out. The Meadowbrook Club in Hempstead, Long Island, stepped in and hosted a stroke-play tournament it billed as the first women's championship. It was conducted on 9 November 1895, and drew 13 women, nearly all from clubs in New York or New Jersey. The winner, after two rounds over the nine-hole course, was Lucy

Barnes Brown, of Shinnecock Hills, with a score of 132. She received a silver pitcher. That first championship attracted the attention of a Scotsman visiting the States, Robert P. Cox, a Member of Parliament representing Edinburgh. He wanted to encourage America's women golfers and asked the USGA if he could donate a new trophy for their new championship.

The following October, in the first officially sanctioned US Women's Amateur, a field of 29 women would compete at Morris County Golf Club in New Jersey for what is now considered the loveliest trophy in sport – a sterling silver cup featuring an enamel thistle overlay, inset gems and scenes from St Andrews on both the front and back. Taking a cue from Pearson and the Ladies' Golf Union, a new format was chosen to determine the champion – match play. A qualifying round winnowed the field to eight finalists, who faced off in 18-hole elimination matches to identify the champion. Shinnecock Hills again produced the winner, 16-year-old Beatrix Hoyt, whose qualifying score of 95 was light years better than the score Barnes Brown had posted the previous autumn, or the score of 150 that won the first women's tournament in Canada. Still, it was a far cry from the superb golf Lady Margaret Scott had displayed two years earlier in the first British Ladies' Championship, going around the links at St Annes with scores in the low 80s.

Those early championships in the US and Canada established a pattern that would prevail for decades. Women golfers outside Britain would have their work cut out for them if they had designs on challenging their sisters in the birthplace of the game. By forming the Ladies' Golf Union, Issette Pearson had, indeed, shown 'most commendable foresight', giving the women of Britain a massive head start in a game that was taking the world by storm. When she left that meeting at the Grand Hotel, Pearson was a woman on a mission – fixated on women establishing their place in a game that for centuries had been strictly a man's world. Over the next three decades, as the global sisterhood imitated her every move, Pearson would pursue that dream with the ferocity of a tyrant, running roughshod over any obstacle that stood in her way. In autumn of 1893, basking in the glow of that first Ladies' Championship, she would befriend the ideal compatriot, a woman who was equally passionate about golf and, conveniently, possessed a gift for telling the remarkable story that was about to unfold.

Three

AUNTIE MABEL AND THE CZAR

—••●••—

MABEL Stringer was in her second year as captain of the Littlestone Ladies' Golf Club when she received the letter that would change her life and the course of women's golf history. In the autumn of 1893, the club's secretary wrote to Stringer asking her to accompany 'a certain Miss Issette Pearson' during an inspection of the Littlestone links. Never one to dawdle, Pearson had begun searching for a club to host the second Ladies' Championship as soon as the trophy was handed out at Lytham and St Annes. She and Stringer tested Littlestone by playing a one-to-one match, in which Issette's entourage was shocked to see her soundly beaten. Until that October morning, Stringer had never heard of the formidable woman who would become her best friend and partner in the enterprise that would dominate their lives. 'During the preceding months, I had been abroad in Eastern Europe, where the great news of the championship at St Annes, following immediately on the preliminaries for the formation of the Ladies' Golf Union, had not penetrated,' she explained. Travelling abroad would have been in the natural course of events for a woman like Stringer. Aged 25, she was the eldest of seven children born to the well-situated solicitor Henry Stringer and his wife, Harriet, who lived comfortably at The Elms in nearby New Romney.

From the moment she met Pearson, Stringer became a passionate supporter of Issette's vision. Over the next three decades, Stringer and Pearson would marshal a loyal army of Union volunteers to create a vibrant world for women's golf. Along the way, they would show men how to solve one of the game's thorniest problems. Eight years into their journey, a tragic event in Stringer's own life made her an even more valuable asset to Pearson's cause. In May 1901, Mabel's father was accused of theft and embezzlement in his work for authorities in New Romney. It hardly mattered that two months later Henry Stringer was acquitted of all charges. His reputation had been ruined and the family's fortunes dashed. Mabel was forced to join the 'toilers in life's garden'. After trying her hand as a ladies' companion, Stringer settled on a new life as the first professional women's golf correspondent, often writing about events as she competed in them. During the decades when the Ladies' Golf Union was coming of age, it was Stringer who told its story in *The Gentlewoman* and other publications.

Her role in women's golf extended far beyond that, however, as she recounts in her 1924 memoir *Golfing Reminiscences*. With Pearson such an imposing presence, Stringer became the Union's friendliest face – a beloved figure who took pains to make newcomers and overseas visitors feel welcome and was known to all as 'Auntie Mabel'. Stringer presents a sassy appearance in the frontispiece image of her book, a grown-up version of the self-described 'wild child' from Littlestone. Dressed in a tweed Norfolk jacket and matching skirt, accented by a white blouse, neatly pinned tie and wide-brimmed hat, she wears a sly smile with one arm cocked jauntily at her hip.

Women's golf progressed quickly from the moment she and Pearson teamed up. Two months later came the founding of the

Irish Ladies' Golf Union, followed by unions in Scotland in 1902 and Wales in 1904, with Stringer serving as its first assistant secretary. Within five years, the Ladies' Golf Union had more than doubled in size, growing to 26 affiliated clubs. By the time the Union came of age, just before the Great War, that number would exceed 500, and during the years between wars it would crest 1,000. Both Pearson and Stringer knew that a world growing as rapidly as this would require far more than an annual championship, and they set about creating opportunities for women to gather together, compete and learn to master this most difficult of games.

They began with Open Meetings, Stringer's first coming in September 1894 at Ashdown Forest, south of London. These were multi-day affairs in which dozens of women gathered for a cross between a golf tournament and a country house party. Open meetings featured a variety of competitions – scratch and bogey events, long-drive contests and more. Evenings consisted of musical entertainment, often performed by the women themselves, many of whom were gifted singers or pianists. Charming as Open Meetings were, Pearson and Stringer were keenly aware that if women were to make the progress they dreamed of in golf, developing the skills that marked truly great players, a sterner brand of competition would be required.

The idea they developed, County Golf, became the rock on which the women's game was built. Each county fielded a team of 10 golfers. Throughout the season, teams played matches against one another, leading to an annual championship. The pride of making the side and playing for one's county added the edge required to breed new and better champions. In that first season, 1900, teams were fielded by 14 counties, mostly those around London. The championship bout was between Kent and Surrey, the side that would prevail that year and one day produce the greatest champion of them all, Joyce Wethered.

A decade later, Stringer added the capstone to this new world of women's golf, forming associations that conducted their own competitions. She founded societies for women affiliated with Parliament, the legal trades and the military, as well as for veteran golfers and young girls taking up the game. Other women created associations for the medical trades and the stage. Together these developments created a schedule for women golfers as intense as any men's. 'From the beginning of March until the end of October is one unbroken series of matches, open meetings, championships, and one asks oneself, "How on earth do they do it?"' Stringer marvelled.

It was not only in Britain that women's golf was making rapid strides. American women were building their own world of golf, albeit one of slightly different cast given the vastness of the United States. Americans imitated Pearson's county golf model with regional associations that staged tournaments and matches between clubs in their part of the country. Associations formed in Philadelphia in 1897, New York in 1900 and Rhode Island in 1914. Others followed as the nation expanded westward. Regions also took to hosting their own annual championships, a line-up that would eventually include five major events. American women, however, faced one special challenge, the weather. In the Northeast and Midwest, where the game first took root in the United States, courses were snowed under for nearly half the year, making golf an impossibility. Just before the turn of the century, industrialists Henry Plant and Henry Flagler solved that problem by building railroad lines and resorts along the east and west coasts of Florida, founding cities like Tampa, Palm Beach and Miami that would become major golfing centres. By the 1920s, when American champions like Glenna Collett were coming of age, Florida had become a favourite winter haunt of northern golfers. They competed in a series of tournaments known as the Orange Blossom Circuit, which prepared them for major events like the Eastern and North and South Amateurs.

Of course, none of these developments, in Britain or America, would have had the impact they did had Pearson and the Union not tackled the central problem of competitive golf – how to assign handicap strokes in a match between golfers from different courses. 'There are two ways of doing this,' Pearson wrote. 'One is to give handicaps on what you and others think a player can do, and the other is to handicap them on what they have proved they can do.' Pearson's reference to handicapping based on what one thinks a player can do was a swipe at the way men handled the issue, with strokes assigned by the club professional or a committee. By 1896, Pearson set out to prove it was possible to handicap based on what a player had proved she could do. The issue was that each club set its own scratch score for establishing handicaps. As standards varied widely, results were utterly unreliable. Pearson's solution was to have the Union set scratch scores by having a first-class golfer play the links and evaluate the merits of each hole. Women who wished to compete in Union events were required to submit three scores made in medal competition. Those were averaged and compared to the Union's scratch score to establish their handicap, which could be used on any course they played. Women golfers in America and elsewhere quickly embraced this concept, but men were slow to acknowledge that the Union's calculations actually levelled competition. In 1911, the USGA finally admitted Pearson was right and adopted her system. Even that did not move British men to concede. That would not happen until the mid-1920s.

IN THE WAY

The response to Pearson's innovations in handicapping makes it perfectly obvious why she had to be 'as despotic as the Czar of Russia'. From the outset, the golfing world baulked at the notion of a Ladies' Golf Union. When Horace Hutchinson was asked about the prospect, his advice was, in a word, 'Don't.' Women, he wrote, weren't fit for golf, physically or temperamentally. 'The first ladies' championship will be the last, unless I and others are greatly mistaken,' Hutchinson predicted. 'The L.G.U. scarcely seems worthwhile.' Hutchinson, at least, came to see how wrong he'd been, and, in 1896, became a vice president of the Union and a strong supporter of women's golf. Other men were not so easily persuaded. Their sentiments were summed up by Henry James Moncreiff, better known as Lord Wellwood, in Badminton's 1890 book *Golf*. If women choose 'to play at times when male golfers are feeding or resting no one can object,' he wrote. 'But at other times – we must say it – they are in the way.'

American men were no different, according to Genevieve Hecker, an early star across the Atlantic. Most clubs in the US, she wrote, also allowed women to play only at 'times when it was thought that their presence would not incommode the Lords of Creation'. Hecker, Stringer and the other pioneers of women's golf were painfully aware that they were not entirely welcome, even at courses that had a ladies' club. One obvious reason was that most of them had no women's clubhouse, although that would quickly change as more and more women took up the game. Littlestone, for example, relegated ladies to two empty rooms in an abandoned Coast Guard cottage. 'Knowing no better, we were hugely pleased with our quarters,' Stringer wrote. 'What the golfing girl of today would have said to them is not difficult to imagine!'

During that early age, Stringer said many a 'ladies clubhouse' was no more than a corrugated iron hut. 'So far as I can remember, the little shanty for the use of lady members of the Hoylake club was about the poorest of the lot. It did not even seem to stand straight on its own little sandhill.' Even when women were invited into the men's clubhouse, it was made clear that they were entering a male sanctum. That was the case during the annual Christmas tournament at Littlestone. It was a mixed foursomes event in which men and women played together as a team. That format became a staple of golf because, in the tradition of the

Ladies' Putting Club, it offered an opportunity for unchaperoned courtship. 'On this festive occasion,' Stringer recalled, 'we were afterwards entertained to tea in the men's clubhouse, but on the strict understanding that we were on no account to go in by the front entrance!'

Lack of accommodations and restrictions on when they could play were hardly the only obstacles these pioneers had to overcome to achieve mastery of the game. The biggest impediment may have been the clothes that fashion dictated they wear on the links. The woman golfer of the 1880s and 1890s – in Britain and the United States – came to the course wearing a long, flowing skirt that brushed the ground, under which were multiple petticoats. These had to be controlled while swinging by an elastic band known as a 'Miss Higgins', after the American golfer who invented it. A woman's waist, expected to be wasplike, was corseted and secured by a stiff belt. Her blouse, topped by a rigid collar that chafed the neck, had sleeves so voluminous that they, too, had to be battened down with a strap around the left arm so a woman could see her ball while swinging at it. Finally, the fashionable woman required a proper hat – initially a sailor hat or motor cap that had to be kept from falling off by hat pins or tied round the neck with a veil. 'How on Earth any of us ever managed to hit a ball, or get along at all in the outrageous garments which fashion decreed we were to cover ourselves is one of the great mysteries of that or any other age,' Stringer mused.

UNSHACKLED

Ladies may have accepted the dictates of fashion, but in every other way, the years before and after the turn of the century were a time in which women threw off the shackles placed upon them by a patriarchal world. With the British Empire approaching its peak and America thriving in its Gilded Age, many women were no longer willing to be housewives and mothers whose sole entertainments were reading, music and making crafts to sell at the local bazaar. Sport was among the earliest examples of women defying convention to create new lives for themselves. Even as Pearson and Stringer met at Littlestone, The London Library issued a telling volume known as *The Gentlewoman's Book of Sports*. Edited by Lady Violet Greville, author of a column in a popular periodical known as the *Graphic*, it made the case that women were every bit as capable as men of enjoying the sporting life – one of boating and fishing, fencing and archery, cricket and golf. Chapters on each of these pursuits were written by high-society women, nearly all of them titled, featuring vivid tales like the story of a woman who tumbled into a stream, bloodying her knee in the process, in her zeal to land two giant trout.

Even before Lady Greville's book was published, women had a shining example of the heights they might reach in tennis phenomenon Lottie Dod – the famed 'Little Wonder' – who went on to become a multi-sport star long before anyone had heard the name Babe Didrikson. In 1887, aged 15, Dod won the first of her five tennis titles at Wimbledon, including three straight from 1891 through 1893. She went on to win the British Ladies' Golf Championship in 1904; to earn a gold medal in archery at the 1908 Olympics; to play for the English national field hockey team; to pass the famously difficult figure-skating tests for both men and women at St Moritz, and to set the women's speed record for toboggan on the dangerous Cresta Run at that same Swiss resort. Perhaps most symbolically of all, in 1896, Dod literally showed women there was no mountain they could not climb by joining her brother in scaling two of the highest peaks in Switzerland, both in excess of 4,000 metres, and then repeating the feat the following year in Norway.

Still, the progress women made in sports paled by comparison to the resolute manner in which they began to demand their rights in the political arena, not simply in America and Britain, but around the globe. As early as 1832 in Britain and 1878 in America, bills were submitted in Parliament and the US Congress which required women to be granted equal voting rights with men. Those legislative efforts marked the beginning of the long – and at its peak shockingly violent – suffrage movement, which would unfold in lockstep with the emergence of women's golf on both continents. In the United States, it would be largely a political debate. The most outrageous acts there included Susan B. Anthony's arrest for voting in 1878 and the burning of President Woodrow Wilson in effigy in front of the White House in 1920. That could not be said of Britain, unquestioned leader of the worldwide suffrage movement. In 1903, as the Ladies' Golf Union celebrated its 10th anniversary, British women fed up with Parliamentary foot-dragging formed the Women's Political and Social Union under Emmeline Pankhurst and launched a campaign of militancy.

In the years that followed, women took such bold steps as invading Parliament en masse, leading to hand-to-hand fighting with police, and padlocking themselves to the prime minister's residence at 10 Downing Street. The resulting arrests led to hunger strikes and the ugly spectacle of women being force-fed in prison, shocking the nation. By 1913, just as the Ladies' Golf Union was coming of age, Pankhurst and her followers declared war, launching a campaign that included bombings, arson and window smashing. 'The object was to create an absolutely impossible condition of affairs in the country,' wrote Lilian Lenton, a professional dancer and militant suffragette, 'to prove that it was impossible to govern without the consent of the governed.'

Golf, ever the bastion of wealthy and powerful men, became a particular target of suffragettes. Herbert Asquith, prime minister from 1908 to 1916 and a staunch foe of giving women the vote, was attacked no fewer than four times on golf courses. Greens at numerous links were damaged with acid, and the pavilion at Manchester Golf Club was set aflame, as was one at Roehampton.

Those were among more than 50 attacks on sporting facilities throughout Britain. Insurers estimated that damage had exceeded £270,000 – the equivalent today of nearly 10 times that amount. The horrifying height of the militancy came at the 1913 Epsom Derby, when Emily Wilding Davison ran on to the track mid-race, grabbed the King's horse by its bridle and was trampled to death in the process. Tens of thousands attended her funeral.

Whether or not Issette Pearson believed women should have the vote, she was not about to let suffragettes disrupt one of her tournaments. When Princess Victoria attended the 1913 Championship, the Czar hired Boy Scouts to police the grounds and prevent any unseemly disturbance. Nevertheless, there can be no doubt that the Ladies' Golf Union included many who sympathised with the cause – chief among them the voice of golf, Auntie Mabel. Twice in her memoir, Stringer shares anecdotes that make no secret of her belief in the cause of women's rights. The most telling is Stringer's response to a player pulling her drive so far left that it hit a baby carriage with two infant boys inside, both unharmed: 'There spoke the true suffragette!' she quipped.

PREMATURE PREDICTION

Despite their remarkable progress on so many fronts, Alexander Doleman's prediction in *The Golfing Annual* that women might one day play well enough to enter the Amateur or Open must have seemed premature during that first decade of women's golf. In truth, when he wrote those words, the only serious threat was Lady Margaret Scott, who swept the first three championships with consummate ease. At Cheltenham Club, she held the women's course record with a score of 80, just three strokes higher than the men's mark. But few other British women were nearly as skilled. Among the lowest scores posted over a full-length course in those years was an 89 by Scotland's Sybil Wigham at Royal

Portrush in 1895. Scores tended to be at least half a dozen strokes higher. In 1898, for instance, former ladies' champion Amy Pascoe set the women's course record over the 5,565 yards at Woking with a score of 98. Driving distance was the major issue. Most women did not hit the ball far enough to score low. At Littlestone in 1894, the long-drive contest was won by a shot that carried 133 yards. Six years later at Royal North Devon, Wigham drove a few beyond 200 yards – almost as far as a typical man might drive – but shots of that length were rare.

While comparisons can be difficult, given that nearly all women's golf was match play and courses varied wildly, women in America seemed to lag behind their sisters across the Atlantic. Like Lady Margaret, Hoyt easily won three consecutive US Amateurs, her first in 1896 at the age of 16. Yet her scores in the qualifying rounds suggest she was no match for her English counterpart. Hoyt claimed the qualifying medal in all three of her championships, with scores of 95, 108 in foul weather and 92. Even accounting for differences in the courses, the gap between Lady Margaret's scores in the mid-80s and Hoyt's of 92 or higher is a substantial one. One thing is certain. On both sides of the Atlantic, women's skills were a far cry from those of men. From 1896 through 1898, qualifying scores posted by men in the US Amateur ranged from 82 to 87, fully 10 strokes better than Hoyt's over a longer course. British amateur men were even farther along. They regularly turned in scores in the mid-to-high 70s, and often posed a threat to win the Open Championship, as John Ball Jr. did in 1890 and Harold Hilton in 1892 and 1897.

The first big boost for the women's game came at the turn of the century, with the introduction of a rubber-cored ball. It was far easier to get airborne and flew farther than its predecessor, the gutty. Women benefited enormously from the new ball, even more than men. Otherwise the progress women made in that age, in Britain and America, came the way it always had in men's golf – from new champions who arose to raise the level of the game.

Ireland produced the two brightest stars of that first decade of women's golf in Britain, May Hezlet and Rhona Adair. In 1899, a week after having claimed her first Irish Amateur at the age of 17, Hezlet dazzled the crowd in Northern Ireland by winning the British Ladies' Championship at Newcastle, County Down, which would go on to receive royal designation in 1908. Hezlet would win two more British Ladies' Championships, in 1902 at Deal and again at County Down in 1907, along with four other Irish Amateurs, a run of three in a row from 1904 through 1906 and her last in 1908. Brilliant as she was, Hezlet had no hesitation in proclaiming her compatriot, Rhona Adair, as the greatest woman golfer of that first decade after the founding of the Ladies' Golf Union. 'Miss Adair is far and away the most consistent lady golfer in the world,' Hezlet wrote.

In 1900, aged 19, Adair repeated Hezlet's feat of sweeping both the Irish Amateur and the British Ladies' Championship, held that year over the windswept links of Westward Ho!, Adair would go on to win her nation's championship the next three years running and to take a second British Ladies' at Royal Portrush in 1903. Her true claim to fame, however, was going toe-to-toe with leading men, most famously golf's Grand Old Man, Tom Morris of St Andrews. They played a 36-hole match in 1900 and another over 18 holes the following year, both with no handicap strokes involved. Morris won the first match 1 up on the 36th, while Adair took the second by the same score. By 1901, of course, Morris was 80 years old. What is most notable, then, is not that Adair was able to get the better of him the second time, without the strokes a man would ordinarily give a woman, but that a golfer so advanced in age could still play so well.

By 1903, Adair's fame had reached such a peak that she was invited to tour the United States, where golf was still very much in its infancy and Henry Ford was just opening his new car company. Three years earlier, British legend Harry Vardon had given the American game a jump-start by playing 98 exhibition matches across the length and breadth of the nation. Adair's visit had much the same effect, inspiring a new generation of American women to take up the game. During her tour, the Irish star competed in an invitational tournament at Merion in Philadelphia, beating a field that included America's best, Genevieve Hecker and Margaret Curtis. Hecker had won the US Amateur the previous two years running, and Curtis would win that championship three times, in 1907, 1911 and 1912. After her trip, Adair wrote an article for *Illustrated Sporting News* and a chapter for Hecker's book *Golf for Women* in which she concluded, as scores suggested, that women in the US were not up to the standard of the British and would be soundly defeated in an international match.

Adair's remarks laid down a challenge. Two years later, in 1905, the first contingent from the States crossed the Atlantic to compete in the British Ladies' Championship, a quest that would continue between and beyond the two world wars. Conducted at Cromer, the 1905 Ladies' Championship was preceded by a friendly match pitting America vs England, an idea that captured the imagination of the two Curtis sisters. From that day forward, Margaret and Harriot would work tirelessly to establish a formal match and, in time, donate the trophy that gave the competition its name, the Curtis Cup. When comparing golfers of the two nations, Adair gave British women the edge in every respect except driving. Margaret Curtis regularly drove the ball more than 200 yards – a distance even the best British women, like Sybil Wigham, were hard-pressed to match. 'American women really drive quite as well, if not better, than do English women,' Adair wrote, 'and, for this reason, I am convinced that the time is not far distant when the standard of skill will be as high on this side of the ocean as it is on the other.' Still, Adair wrote, it was the obsession with long driving that she believed held American women back as they did not spend nearly enough time practising the rest of the game, especially their irons. Here Adair put her finger on the principal issue confronting the women's game – iron play. Hemmed in by their garments and social conventions, women in Britain and America, even the hard-hitting Adair, cultivated long, slow, sweeping swings. They did not attack the ball anywhere near fiercely enough to be effective with irons.

It would be five years after Adair returned home to Ireland that the game would see the first player who truly lashed at the ball, ushering in a new era of women's golf. Fittingly, she would make her debut the first time the British Ladies' Championship was conducted at St Andrews, and would be nurtured by the very woman who had started it all – Issette Pearson.

Four

SHE IS FIERCE

———••●●●••———

FOR the women who had worked so tirelessly to elbow their way into golf, being invited to host the Ladies' Championship over the Old Course – to see the flag of their Union flying proudly above the Royal and Ancient Golf Club – was akin to visiting Mecca. 'I suppose the St Andrews Championship in 1908 will always be regarded as the most epoch-making event in the history of the Union,' wrote Mabel Stringer, 'for not only did our presence there indicate that any prejudices against women's intrusion on men's *rights* had been overcome, but the subsequent happenings of the week clearly justified our *rights* to play over the ground.' Not only were women allowed use of the links, they were also invited into the R&A's clubhouse to see the game's most sought-after trophies and to hear tales of golfing lore in St Andrews, an invitation Stringer considered especially gracious.

Old Tom Morris, the man who had built women the first course of their own, spent the week standing sentry outside his shop along the 18th hole or beside the starter's box, 'with a cheery greeting for all the strange golfers, to whom he was no stranger,' Stringer wrote. Like everyone else in town, Auntie Mabel made a point of stopping to chat with the Grand Old Man. 'He took the greatest interest in the play all that week,' she noted. 'He said that he had always hoped to live to see a Ladies' Championship at St Andrews.'

The tournament came down to a battle royal between Maud Titterton and Old Tom's favourite, Scotland's Dorothy Campbell. Three down with five to play, Campbell fought back bravely to square the match at 18, only to be finished off by Titterton's daring approach to the first extra hole, a brassie hit bravely over the Swilcan Burn. 'It was,' Stringer declared, 'the greatest final it has ever been my lot to witness.' But neither that scintillating final match, nor the presence of Old Tom, nor the Union flag flying above the Royal and Ancient was the reason the first Ladies' Championship at St Andrews would be remembered forever. It would be remembered for the astonishing debut of 'the Silloth flapper', 17-year-old Cecil Leitch. Her swing was a revelation. It was nothing like the long, slow, sweeping move then in vogue. Leitch took a shorter, more furious lash at the ball – 'a perfect ferocity of hitting' as it was described by Eleanor Helme, a spirited woman who had joined Stringer as a golf correspondent, competitor of consequence and tireless worker for the Ladies' Golf Union.

Leitch 'showed the world of ladies' golf that with the iron clubs they *must* hit, and hit hard, and hit only,' Helme added. 'Henceforth, if we were to have any pretensions to first-class form, we were to stand up to our work like a man, and hit the ball with the irons.' The teenager from Silloth came to St Andrews dressed for that job. Her hair was tied up in a black bow, her skirt reached no lower than mid-calf, and her white blouse was accented by a black tie pinned smartly to her chest. The contrast she made with Titterton and Campbell could not have been starker. Their waists were tightly cinched, their long, flowing skirts barely cleared their ankles, and their wide-brimmed bonnets were securely fastened beneath their chins with yards of sheer chiffon. They looked as if they might be attending a lawn party, not teeing off in a championship. Leitch proved to be a trendsetter, starting the transition to more sensible clothing for women golfers fully a quarter of a century before Gloria Minoprio shocked the world by showing up at the 1933 championship in trousers.

Unknown before the tournament began, Leitch's triumphant procession into the semi-final left no doubt that her slashing style was the way of the future in women's golf. Having drawn a bye in the first round, she came up in the second against poor Marjorie Phelps, a member of the American contingent that came to compete that year. Phelps managed to halve only one of the first 10 holes and was swept aside 9 and 8. Leitch faced two close encounters en route to the semi-finals, both times prevailing on the final green, but in her other two matches she was as merciless as she had been against Phelps, never needing more than 14 holes to finish off her foe.

Leitch's extraordinary run looked for all the world as if it might continue in the semi-final against the veteran Titterton. 'The Silloth flapper' strode confidently into the lead, taking four of the first seven holes. Even before they reached the seventh, however, Leitch's troubles had begun. On the fifth, she broke her favourite brassie – the old traditional name for a No 2 wood – the source of the length that terrified her opponents. Without that weapon her confidence waned and holes began to melt away. Titterton took her first lead at the 12th, and when they reached the famed Road Hole she was two holes up with just two left to play. The enormous crowd following the match – even at that age Leitch exuded the charisma that would make her a fan favourite all her life – was left to hope a miracle would save young Cecil. They very nearly witnessed one. Leitch stumbled on the 17th, requiring four shots to reach that narrow, dangerous green. To take the match to the final hole, Leitch needed to sink a putt of some 36 feet, and hope Titterton would miss hers from six. Leitch bravely holed that putt, and 'the huge crowd so completely lost control over its feelings that a burst of applause and continuous cheering broke from it,' Stringer recalled. 'This ill-timed spontaneous applause frightened a young horse in a two-wheeled cart standing in the road, and he bolted amongst the crowd, causing a regular stampede.' Titterton was so rattled that she missed her putt to win, but as fate would have it she was immediately saved by a miracle of her own. Titterton topped her tee shot at the last, but somehow it bounded over the Swilcan Bridge into the fairway, enabling her to halve the 18th and win the match.

To a 17-year-old Leitch, the week had seemed surreal – from falling in love with St Andrews and its ancient golf links to spending her own few moments in the presence of Old Tom Morris. 'It was like a dream, one of those delightful and romantic dreams from which one awakes to dull and unromantic fact,' Leitch wrote in her 1921 book *Golf*, part memoir and part instructional manual. 'On May 15, I regarded myself as more or less a beginner, a week later I was playing in the semi-final of the Ladies' Open Championship before thousands of spectators on the most famous course in the world.'

Leitch returned home to Silloth with a bronze medal, 'so small in size, but so big in what it meant to me and my career . . . I now knew that I could make a showing in good company, and I was just tingling with ambition and determination.' Two days later came the tragic news that Old Tom Morris had died, weeks shy of his 87th birthday. He had not simply got his wish to see a Ladies' Championship conducted at St Andrews. He had also lived to witness a turning point in the women's game – the dawn of an age when ladies would, indeed, live up to Alexander Doleman's bold prophecy.

ON SOLWAY FIRTH

The virago who ushered in this new era – Charlotte Cecilia Pitcairn Leitch – was born on 13 April 1891 in Silloth, a remote village in north-west England, just across Solway Firth from Scotland. Cecil, as she came to be known, was one of seven children born to Dr John Leitch, a Scotsman from Fife, and his wife, Catherine, an Englishwoman whose father was the local rector. Dr Leitch was the pioneer of golf along Solway Firth. Even before the Silloth on Solway Golf Club was founded in 1892, he had laid out a nine-hole links on the common and begun playing with his sister. 'The natives of the place regarded them as a pair of lunatics,' Cecil wrote. Nevertheless, Leitch and her siblings would all fall under golf's spell – she, Edith and May becoming so proficient at the game that they would one day play for England in international matches. 'There were hereditary reasons why I should not only play golf but become "mad" on the game,' Leitch acknowledged. 'And I may say here that never once since I first took a club in hand has there been any doubt about my love for golf.'

Using an old-fashioned cleek and a gutty ball, Leitch played her first golf at the age of nine on 'The Banks', a stretch of land 200 yards wide and a quarter-mile long that was later subsumed by Solway Firth. 'Our fairways were the paths made by pedestrians,' she recalled fondly, 'our putting greens the good patches on these paths, our holes cut by ourselves and lined with treacle tins, and our "trouble" the bents, sand holes and wire grass common to seaside links.' The most famous story about Leitch involves a club member named James Graham arriving at the 14th at Silloth – the Heather Hole – to find a curly-haired young girl in a white sailor's coat, a blue serge skirt and black patent-leather shoes hacking away in the heather, as her sister looked on. 'I can't get it out,' young Cecil lamented. 'No, it needs strength and you lack it,' her elder sister, May, responded matter-of-factly. The irony is that no woman would ever develop a more forceful swing than Cecil Leitch, who at five feet nine inches tall was capable of producing considerable power.

Like her sisters, Leitch was a self-taught golfer. While she never took formal lessons, she did pick up tips from professionals she met during her career. The first among them was Silloth's Tommy Renouf, a Channel Islander. Her only genuine instruction came from a weighty tome written by her golfing hero, James Braid. Leitch read his *Advanced Golf* so religiously that it had to be confiscated by the teacher at Carlisle High School, where she and her sisters were educated. Leitch gripped the club in the palm of her hands, taking a flattish swing that featured a full body turn and a slight duck of the right knee on the follow-through. It was not a pretty move, but an enormously powerful one that produced a long, low, piercing ball flight ideal for the windy conditions that prevailed at Silloth and elsewhere in Britain.

It was not simply her swing, but her flamboyant personality and fighting spirit that drew crowds to Leitch from the moment she debuted in St Andrews. 'Think of Madame Defarge leading the women of St Antoine against the Bastille, think of anything frightfully grand, and you have a picture of Miss Leitch,' as Bernard Darwin once put it, comparing her to the hero of Charles Dickens's *A Tale of Two Cities*. Leitch and her sisters regularly took part in competitions at Silloth, one of them frequently heading the list, but they had no idea how they stacked up against other women golfers in Britain until the spring of 1907, when Eustace White paid a visit to Cumberland. White was the golf correspondent for *Ladies' Field* magazine, and thus a pipeline to Issette Pearson and her minions in women's golf. He let everyone know how deeply impressed he was by the Leitch sisters.

Later that year, Mrs Archibald Smith, a leader in Yorkshire golf, made the trek to Silloth in the hope of convincing Leitch and her sisters that they played as well as most women who would compete in the Ladies' Championship the following spring at St Andrews.

'We did not share this flattering opinion of our own play,' Leitch humbly recalled, 'and would certainly have gasped had anyone predicted that one of us would come within measurable distance of winning the open championship in less than a year.' Still, the seed had been planted, and it bore fruit because of Dr Leitch's ties to Fife. The Leitch sisters had a cousin, William Leitch Stuart, who studied at St Andrews University. That made the proposition impossible to resist, so Edith and Cecil entered for the championship. Ever vigilant for new talent that could move the women's game forward, Pearson kept a watchful eye on the Leitch sisters that week, even as she worked feverishly attending to the details of a tournament that represented her crowning achievement. 'Nothing could have exceeded her kindness to me and all the young players, for whom she always kept a very warm corner in her heart,' Leitch remembered. 'Although so busy, she found time to look after us and give us a word here and there of encouragement and advice.'

Leitch's sparkling debut drew worldwide attention. Stringer's coverage of golf's latest prodigy – whom she dubbed the 'girlchild from Cumberland' – appeared in newspapers as far away as the United States and New Zealand. Ever after, Leitch would be, as Joyce Wethered described her, 'the big noise in women's golf'. Pearson, along with nearly everyone else, was convinced that Leitch was destined for greatness – that she was the long-sought player fierce enough to carry the women's game into a new age. Leitch left St Andrews with 'a burning fever' for success, but she was, after all, still a teenager. There would be many lean years before her breakthrough – a fate not unlike that of another prodigy who arose a generation later, Atlanta's Bobby Jones.

MEN VS WOMEN

The trouble with bringing along a potential star like Cecil Leitch was that she lived in a remote corner of England, where the competition she so desperately needed to sharpen her game was simply not available. There was no county golf in Silloth to provide the steady diet of match play that helped other up-and-coming women learn the art of winning with everything on the line. Leitch's only option was to attend Open Meetings, as she did in the summer of 1908 at Walton Heath, where she showed a regrettable tendency to snatch at the ball and top it, one of many issues holding the young star back. Issette Pearson worked tirelessly to clear Leitch's path to success, suggesting in those early years that she test her game against the toughest opponents available to her – men. Pearson had no trouble arranging such matches. In 1909, she dispatched Leitch to West Lancashire Golf Club to establish its par for the Ladies' Golf Union, and to play an 18-hole match from the men's tees against the club's professional, Tom Ball.

From the outset, Leitch thrived in matches against men. They stoked her fire in a way few other competitions did. She went around West Lancashire in 82 to Ball's 75, and having received the standard handicap of nine strokes, defeated him on the final green 1 up. By then, Leitch explained in her memoir, the question of how to handicap matches between men and women had become known as golf's 'eternal problem'. It was understood that women could, potentially, develop as much skill as men at the short game and putting.

But if women and men played from the same tees – as they usually did in that age, and often over the game's most difficult courses – how many strokes were required to compensate for the reality that men were stronger and could hit the ball further? The standard had largely been set by the sharpest golfing mind of the age – two-time Amateur and Open champion Harold Hilton, then the editor of *Golf Monthly*. He had written that any first-class man could spot the best of women nine strokes and still win. Hilton based his conclusion on a series of matches he played in 1903 against Rhona Adair – the same woman who had caused such a sensation by competing against Old Tom Morris on level terms. Hilton gave Adair nine strokes in each of those encounters, and won most of them. Once again Eustace White, the *Ladies' Field* correspondent who discovered the Leitch sisters, saw an opportunity and seized it, with the full support of Pearson and the Ladies' Golf Union.

The magazine took Hilton up on his boast and challenged him to a 72-hole match against Leitch, which unfolded in the autumn of 1910, with 36 holes each at Walton Heath and Sunningdale. Whether or not Pearson and the *Ladies' Field* intended it, this much-hyped contest against Hilton thrust Leitch and women's golf into the national debate about suffrage, even as Emmeline Pankhurst waged her campaign of militancy. That much was evident the moment Leitch stepped on to the first tee. 'I shall never forget my surprise when I arrived at the clubhouse at Walton Heath to find a crowd of about 3,000 spectators, one of the biggest crowds ever seen on a southern course,' she recalled.

Until that match, Leitch had never seen Hilton play, though she was well aware of his accomplishments – having won the Open in 1892 and 1897 and the Amateur in 1900 and 1901. In a practice round at Walton Heath, where her idol James Braid was the professional, Leitch went around in 80 to Hilton's 74. Braid encouraged her not to be intimidated by Hilton's record, 'just to play my own game and I would come through.' In truth, Leitch was catching Hilton at a low ebb. It had been nine years since his last victory of consequence. Both he and Leitch played scratchy golf at Walton Heath, despite ideal weather. Leitch did not win a hole outright until the 457-yard 17th, where she banged a brassie up to the flag and made a tidy four. Hilton finished the day 1 up, and it might have been all square had Leitch not missed a four-footer on the final green.

The weather took a turn for the worse two days later at Sunningdale, where Leitch and Hilton played in a gale of wind and drenching rain. By the lunch break, Leitch was four down. She bounced back to win the first hole in the afternoon, but when Hilton took the next two, despair set in. 'I felt that any chance of success I had ever possessed had now finally vanished,' Leitch remembered. 'Five down with 15 to play with eight strokes to come! The only thing that now interested me was to make my defeat as light as possible.' And then, on the fourth green, Hilton missed an easy putt to hand Leitch a hole, and, suddenly, Madame Defarge turned up. From then on, Darwin wrote, 'Miss Leitch was undismayed and played with unruffled confidence. Amid a great scene of enthusiasm, she took the lead at the 11th, and playing with all the coolness and determination of a veteran, won the match on the 17th green.' She had gone around in 76, just a stroke higher than Hilton's 75.

Leitch's 2 and 1 victory took on a powerful symbolism in that age of suffragettes. She became the idol of women everywhere – the 19-year-old flapper from Silloth who had vanquished a legend of men's golf, competing on his own terms. One newspaper cartoonist summed up the sentiments that match inspired by drawing a man wearing a placard reading: 'GREAT GOLF TEST. Man, twice Open and twice Amateur champion, DEFEATED by a mere girl. How about votes for women NOW?' Leitch's victory dramatically increased interest in the women's game, ensuring that the 'eternal problem' of men vs women remained centre stage into the age of Joyce Wethered and Glenna Collett, when the question would come to be viewed in an entirely new light. That match against Hilton was also the inspiration for an annual event pitting men against women at Stoke Poges in London, where Leitch herself thrived but men nearly always prevailed. While she endured her share of losses, the scalps Leitch took at Stoke Poges and elsewhere, always with the aid of strokes, included some of the most famous names in golf, Cyril Tolley and John Henry Taylor among them. Still, Leitch could not muster the same poise and fire in championship matches against other women, and the ambitions she and Pearson harboured remained far off.

LEAN YEARS

Given the sensation created by her comeback victory over Hilton, and the way she had mauled opponents at St Andrews, Leitch became a perennial favourite to win the Ladies' Championship. Year after year she fell short, a failure that seemed utterly inexplicable. Playing alone, with a card and pencil in hand, Leitch had demonstrated that she could produce extraordinary golf. Twice during her lean years, in 1909 and 1911, she won the medal-play event that preceded the Championship, at Birkdale with a solid 83 and at Portrush with a brilliant 74. In 1909, she went around Silloth from the back tee in 72 strokes, two better than the men's record. That score was so outlandish that it drew worldwide news coverage, even if it did not constitute a new record because it had not been made in competition.

Nevertheless, when it came time to face another woman with the title on the line, Leitch simply could not deliver her best. During three lean years, she was out of the tournament early, swept aside twice in the first round and once in the second. Only once did she make it as far as she had in her debut. The way she lost in 1910 at Royal North Devon was emblematic of the ragged golf that repeatedly afflicted Leitch in the Ladies' Championship. That year, she came to the 16th, a 140-yard par three, leading by two holes with just three to play. She promptly topped her tee shot into the Cape bunker, lost her confidence, and with it the match. 'Another championship gone for me,' Leitch lamented, 'knocked out too in the first round, so that it seemed regression rather than progression, and the realisation of my ambition further off than ever.'

One reason success eluded Leitch early on was that she came of age at a time when women's golf had already made considerable strides, producing legendary champions Dorothy Campbell and Gladys Ravenscroft, who knocked Leitch out of the Open in both 1911 and 1912. Together, those two women accounted for half the championships during Leitch's lean years. They would also be the first to complete the double – winning both the US and British amateur championships. Campbell swept the titles in the same season, 1909, two years before Harold Hilton repeated that feat. Ravenscroft took the British Ladies' in 1912, and the US Championship the following year. In more than a century since, only nine other women have completed the double.

Formidable as those two were, they were not the only reason for Leitch's drought. In addition to her tendency to snatch at the ball, and her bouts of sloppy golf, Leitch was an unreliable putter and too often showed how young she was by making poor decisions. Pearson concluded that Leitch simply lacked seasoning, the experience of competing regularly against other women in matches that truly mattered. In 1910, Pearson changed eligibility rules for the International Match, clearing the way for 19-year-old Leitch to join the English side. Leitch quickly demonstrated that competing for a team stoked her fire just as much as playing against men did. She won eight of her first nine matches, nearly all of them convincingly, her only loss coming when she overslept and almost missed her tee time. Leitch came to conclude that she had a split personality as a golfer. 'In medal rounds, for a team, or against men I was one player,' she lamented, 'against female opponents in a championship [match] with only myself to think about, I was quite another.' Pearson saw it differently. Competing in the International Match helped, but it clearly wasn't enough. She began hatching plans to make Leitch eligible to play County Golf, which Pearson was convinced would provide the final piece of the puzzle.

Living in remote Silloth, Leitch had never been eligible for the week-in, week-out grind that helped sharpen the game of virtually every other competitor in the championship. Pearson took the first step towards solving that problem in 1912, the same year the world was shocked by the unfathomable sinking of the *Titanic*. She persuaded Leitch, now of age at 21, to move to London and join Bushey Hall Golf Club in Hertfordshire. By 1914, Pearson had again changed eligibility rules to pave Leitch's way, in this case allowing women whose county had no team to play for another after two years of membership at a local club. Leitch joined the side for Herts, as it was popularly known.

The move to London proved to be a turning point. In 1912, Leitch began a three-year run of victories in two prestigious tournaments, the Kit-Cat Medal and *Golf Illustrated* Gold Vase. That same year she also won her first important match-play title, avenging her losses to Ravenscroft in the Ladies' Championship by beating her 6 and 5 in the French Open at Le Touquet. Leitch would stumble only once more, an embarrassing first-round loss to Scotland's Frances Teacher in 1913 at St Annes, before realising her ambition the following year at Hunstanton. Leitch signalled that great moments were in the offing by starting the 1914 season in a blaze of glory. She won her third consecutive Kit-Cat medal with a record score of 67, brilliant even over the short links at Ranelagh. A week later, she made the *Golf Illustrated* Gold Vase her own by winning it for the third time in succession. Knowing Hunstanton would host the Championship, Leitch had travelled to Norfolk the previous autumn, and taken a fancy to that seaside links where a stiff breeze was always blowing over the natural sandhills. It felt almost like being home at Silloth. 'I have a vivid recollection of finding the game very easy,' Leitch wrote of that championship. No wonder. She drove the opening hole, 270 yards away, and finished off her first opponent 9 and 8. Leitch remained utterly merciless until the semi-final, dispatching every one of her foes before the 13th.

In the late stages of her semi-final against the formidable Elsie Grant Suttie, however, Leitch and her legion of fans must have felt a sense of foreboding. Leitch walked off the 14th green 3 up with four to play; then the old demons resurfaced, and ragged golf allowed the entire lead to slip away. The match came down to a single putt, an eight-footer Leitch faced to win on the 18th. As it trembled on the lip of the hole, seemingly for an eternity, her mind raced. 'Would it never go in? Was I really in the final? Or would I have to play the 19th, and could I win it? It did go in.

The next day, in the final, Leitch again faced her nemesis, Ravenscroft, who had returned to Britain bearing the title of US Amateur Champion. This time they competed over 36 holes, a change adopted the previous season as the Ladies' Golf Union celebrated its coming of age. 'My chief recollection of the final,' Leitch wrote, 'was of very bad putting and approaching.' In the morning round, she reached nearly every green in fewer shots than Ravenscroft, but simply could not find the hole. At lunch, the match was all square. Leitch settled into her game in the afternoon. She was 2 up by the time they turned for home, and despite a few missteps on the final nine, was still leading by a hole as they played the 17th. Both played good drives and sound seconds, leaving difficult pitches over rough, sandy ground. Leitch played the better shot, leaving hers two feet from the cup. When Ravenscroft missed her putt for four, she 'sportingly' knocked Leitch's ball away and shook her hand as the new champion. 'At last, after seven years of striving, I had realised my ambition,' Leitch wrote, the sigh of relief almost audible in those words, 'and my feelings can be better imagined than described.'

That victory at Hunstanton proved the charm. The following week, over the Old Course at Walton Heath, Leitch won her first English Amateur Championship, surviving two 19-hole matches, before defeating Gladys Bastin on the 35th hole of the final. A few days later, at La Boulie, Leitch won her second French Ladies' Championship – her third title in two months – again by defeating Bastin on the 35th hole of the final. The streak came to an end the following week as Leitch fell to Ravenscroft in the semi-final of *The Ladies' Pictorial* at Stoke Poges, her only loss of the year. Even there she created a sensation by posting a record score of 79 in the qualifying round.

Fate is kinder to some golfers than others, and it was exceedingly unkind to Cecil Leitch. On 4 August 1914, at the very moment when she had reached the peak of her powers and stood ready to conquer all before her, Britain was swept into the Great War, and no one knew how many years would pass before there was another championship to win. The United States would not join the fight against Germany until the spring of 1917, but even amid the distractions of wartime, Leitch surely took note of the stir created overseas that autumn by the emergence of another bright, young star in women's golf.

Five

AMERICA'S ANSWER

IN SEPTEMBER 1914, a freckle-faced, teenaged redhead from Atlanta named Alexa Stirling made her first appearance in the US Women's Amateur Championship at Nassau Country Club in Glen Cove, New York. She did not arrive unknown, as Cecil Leitch had at St Andrews. Three years earlier, aged 13, Stirling foretold her arrival by winning the qualifying medal at the first Southern Amateur Championship with a score of 95. Still, at Nassau the young prodigy would experience nothing like Leitch's miraculous run to the semi-final. Stirling fell in her first match, losing to former champion Georgianna Bishop on the 17th hole. Even in defeat, however, the way Stirling lashed at the ball caught the eye of John Anderson, correspondent for *Golf Illustrated*. 'Her style is crisp and the ball leaves her club with no unsteadiness,' he wrote. 'She is but 16 years old and gives promise of developing into a crack golfer.'

Anderson would prove a prophet. Just as Leitch had done in Britain, Stirling would go on to inspire a new generation of American women golfers, chief among them Glenna Collett. Born on 5 September 1897 in Atlanta, the first star of American women's golf was the daughter of Dr Alexander William Stirling, an eye, ear, nose and throat specialist from Peebles, Scotland, and his wife, Nora, an opera singer from Yorkshire, England. In 1893, the couple emigrated to America, where Dr Stirling spent his first two years lecturing at the New York Post Graduate College, with plans to settle in Chicago. A New Year's Day visit to Atlanta, where moderate weather prevails even in winter, changed his mind. He decided to make his family's home in the new capital of the American South. Dr Stirling established his medical practice in downtown Atlanta, where he also served as British Consul. Two years later, when Alexa was born, the family faced a new challenge. She was a small, sickly child, homeschooled to avoid the infections prevalent in any public classroom.

By 1908, when Alexa was 11 years old, the family had concluded that moving to the country would be best for her health. They moved into a new home beside a golf course the Atlanta Athletic Club was building at East Lake. The Stirlings were not intending to raise a golf champion when they relocated to East Lake, but the truth is Alexa's interests had always been different from those of a typical young girl. 'Even when I was a tiny tot,' Stirling told Canadian golf writer James Barclay, 'I did not play with dolls as most girls do. I played instead with hammer and nails, and I still have scars on my hands where the hammer hit me instead of the nail. I like to do carpentry and plumbing jobs around the house,' added Stirling, who learned the art of making tongue-and-groove furniture. 'I do it because I get a lot of fun out of it. I cut the lawn, tinker around with my automobile, and do a lot of things that men usually do.' As a young girl, Stirling also developed a passion for the violin. From a cigar box, a stick and some string, she built herself a makeshift instrument. It didn't produce sound, but it did persuade her parents to buy her a second-hand violin for $7. Stirling became a gifted musician, performing at a young age with the Atlanta Symphony Orchestra. Ever after, she valued music every bit as much as golf.

It was golf, however, that introduced Stirling to the world, and she could not have learned the game at a better place than East Lake, where her childhood companion was a boy who would grow up to be America's sporting idol, Bobby Jones. Like Stirling, Jones was a sickly child whose parents schooled him at home and moved to the country to get away from the pollution of Atlanta, where the air was fouled by coal-fired furnaces and wood-burning stoves. Both of them would fall under the influence of Stewart Maiden, a taciturn Scotsman from Carnoustie who became the professional at East Lake in 1908, replacing his brother Jimmy. Jones, who was four and a half years younger than Stirling, never took formal lessons. He simply followed Maiden around the course, mimicking his every move. Stirling, however, became the Scotsman's star pupil, developing a swing so identical to Maiden's that she could be recognised from a distance anywhere on the golf course. Maiden was convinced that if Stirling devoted herself to golf, and stopped spending so much time on music, she could become a superstar. 'If she'd only leave the damned fiddle bide awhile,' the Scotsman once remarked, 'she'd be a braw player.'

Stirling and Jones played their first competition together during the summer of 1908 at East Lake, along with two other pals, Perry Adair and Frank Meador, whose parents operated a boarding house where the Jones family lived during their first years at the golf club. Organised by Mrs Meador, as part of a house party she was throwing, the tournament consisted of six holes of stroke play. A three-inch-tall silver cup she had purchased was offered as the prize for the lowest score. When the round was completed, a complication arose. At least that was how Frank Meador saw it, and as the oldest of the children he was charged with tallying the scores. Stirling had posted the lowest score, but Meador was not about to let a girl win, and rejigged things to make it appear that Jones had emerged as the victor. Young as he was, just age six then, Jones still sensed what had happened. 'I'll always believe Alexa won that cup,' he wrote in his memoir, *Down the Fairway*.

Still, he cherished that little silver trophy so much that he took it to bed with him that night. 'I've a hundred and twenty cups and vases now, and thirty medals,' Jones added, 'but there's one little cup that never fails of being kept well polished. And I never slept with another one.'

In his prime, Jones would earn a reputation as the finest gentleman in the game, but he would readily admit that his first lessons in deportment came from playing with Stirling. When she began to take the game seriously, her father gave her a code to live by: 'Play to win. But even more important than winning is your conduct on the course. Do not lose your temper at a poor shot. Do not sulk in defeat. Be gracious in victory.' The person who most needed to hear that lecture was Stirling's playmate. Even as a child, Jones's swing showed that he was destined for greatness, but he did have one obvious flaw – his volatile temper. 'Let him make a poor shot and he'd turn livid with rage, throw his club after the ball or break it over his knee, or kick at the ground and let out a stream of very adult oaths,' Stirling wrote. 'As I grew into my teens, Bob's temper tantrums began to embarrass me.'

The breaking point came during the war years, when Stirling, Jones, Adair and Elaine Rosenthal played a series of exhibition matches to raise money for the Red Cross. During one match, at Brae Burn Country Club in hide-bound Boston, Jones missed an easy shot. 'I saw the blood climb his neck and flood his face,' Stirling wrote. 'Then he picked up his ball, took a full pitcher's wind-up and threw the ball into the woods. A gasp of surprise and shock went through the large crowd watching us. I only wished the ground beneath me would open and let me sink from sight.' Stirling berated Jones mercilessly for that outburst – a lesson that would take seven long, lean years to sink in before Jones finally mastered himself 'and was ready', as Stirling put it, 'to become the greatest champion in the history of the game.'

BOOM YEARS

For American golf, the years when Alexa Stirling was growing up in Atlanta were, in many ways, like the golf boom Britain had experienced a generation earlier during the 1890s. In 1901, just three years after the founding of America's first permanent golf club, *Harper's Weekly* estimated that 150,000 Americans had taken up the game. By 1915, spurred on by the tours of Harry Vardon and Rhona Adair, the *New York Times* reported that the number had swelled to more than 2.5 million. Part of the reason golf grew so rapidly was that those early years of the 20th century, following a pattern established in Britain, were halcyon days for American amateur golfers. That was critically important because, as had been true across the Atlantic, the upper classes were the first to embrace golf in the States, and nothing spurred their interest like seeing amateurs defeat professionals. The moment that assured the future of golf in America unfolded at the very place where Frances Boit's long-ago visit to Boston inspired the creation of a golf course, The Country Club at Brookline.

There, in the autumn of 1913, a 20-year-old amateur named Francis Ouimet pulled off the most shocking upset in golf history, defeating visiting British legends Harry Vardon and Ted Ray in the US Open. It did not hurt that two other amateurs – Jerome Travers in 1915 and Chick Evans in 1916 – followed Ouimet with Open victories, a run reminiscent of the one John Ball Jr. and Harold Hilton pulled off in the 1890s to fuel the Great English Golf Boom. Stirling would stoke that fire by becoming the first breakout star in women's amateur golf, a fame redoubled by her association with the golden boy, Bobby Jones. During her childhood, however, the American South lagged behind the Northeast and Midwest in developing competitions for up-and-coming women players.

Perhaps not surprisingly, it was Chicago, home of C.B. Macdonald, a driving force behind the founding of the USGA, that hosted the first amateur championship for women, staging the Western Amateur in 1901 at the Onwentsia Club in Lake Forest, Illinois. The North and South Amateur, played at the popular East Coast resort in Pinehurst, North Carolina, followed in 1904 and two years later came the inaugural Women's Eastern Amateur. By the summer of 1910, Mrs George Harrington of East Lake and Mrs Willard Parker of Birmingham decided the time had come for southerners to have a championship of their own, and together they established the Women's Southern Golf Association. They had hoped to stage the inaugural Women's Southern Amateur that autumn at East Lake but could not find a spot open on the club's calendar until May 1911. That first tournament became a memorable one when Stirling claimed the qualifying medal as a mere child.

It would take just four seasons for the young star from Atlanta to come into her own. She claimed her first Southern Amateur in 1915, and rode the momentum of that victory into her second Women's Amateur Championship that September at the Onwentsia Club in Chicago. From the outset, Stirling demonstrated she was a force to be reckoned with, sticking doggedly to Mrs A.G. Hammond before dispatching the former Western Amateur champion on the 19th hole. Stirling also swept aside her next two opponents, closing out both matches early, and breezed into the semi-final against reigning Eastern Amateur Champion, Florence Vanderbeck. Their match was covered for *Golf Illustrated* by former champion Dorothy Campbell, who by then had married steel magnate Jack Hurd and lived in Pittsburgh. Even as she continued to compete, Campbell joined Mabel Stringer and Eleanor Helme in the long line of distinguished women's golf correspondents, writing under the byline Dorothy Campbell Hurd.

Hurd declared the battle between Stirling and Vanderbeck – the eventual winner of that Amateur Championship – 'the best match of the whole tournament. Both played par golf practically all the way, and it was only by two small mistakes which showed the Southern player's inexperience that Mrs Vanderbeck was 2 up at the fourteenth hole.' Stirling may have been down, but she was not out. At the long 15th, she cut Vanderbeck's lead to one hole with a brilliant four. The two halves that followed, however, left Stirling on the brink of defeat as the competitors teed off on the 18th. With everything on the line, Stirling pulled her drive left into the rough, finding a terrible lie under a tree. Vanderbeck knocked one straight down the middle and placed her second on the green. 'It looked as though the match was finished then and there,' wrote Hurd, 'but Miss Stirling made a most wonderful recovery and, after a deliberate survey of her five-yard putt, actually won the hole in 3 to 4.' That miraculous turn of events squared the match and sent every fan on the golf course scrambling to the first tee to watch Stirling and Vanderbeck fight it out in extra holes. Three nail-biting halves followed, before Stirling 'at last showed some sign of weakness'. At the fourth, she was nearest to the green in two, and appeared poised to win, but took four more to get down and lost that thrilling match on the final putt. 'It was certainly a wonderful game to watch,' Hurd concluded, 'and the crowd who followed was unanimous in saying that Miss Stirling's day for winning the championship was not far off.' High praise indeed for a golfer who had celebrated her 18th birthday the morning before the tournament began.

SEMINAL CHANGE

The golf cognoscenti in both Britain and America were well aware that a seminal change was unfolding in the women's game. In April 1915, a month before Stirling won her first Southern Amateur, *Golf Illustrated* ran a full-page spread showing motion pictures of Cecil Leitch playing a full shot with a cleek, equivalent to a 1 or 2-iron. The editors marvelled at how she was 'possessed of a most impressive and powerful style'. The magazine also reported rumours that she would follow in the footsteps of Gladys

Ravenscroft and Dorothy Campbell Hurd by crossing the ocean to play for America's title. That turned out to be wishful thinking, a dream to be realised only after the war. Even early on, it was obvious that Stirling was demonstrating to American women what Leitch had shown their sisters in Britain – how to attack the ball. Stirling attributed the power she put into her shots, especially irons, to the strength she had developed in her wrists by pursuing her passions for carpentry, plumbing, automobiles and the violin. 'My wrists are more like a man's than any other woman golfer I know,' Stirling said. 'The iron shots of women are not compact. They are weak. Women do not put what you call "stuff" into their shots.'

By the spring of 1916, when Stirling showed up in Montgomery, Alabama to defend her Southern Amateur title, she was putting so much 'stuff' into her shots that most of the 87 other competitors considered the outcome a foregone conclusion. In his *Golf Illustrated* column, John Anderson reported overhearing the following conversation among women gathered around the first tee at Riverview Golf Club, where the championship was conducted. 'Why of course she will win it. Who is there to stop her? She can outdrive everybody, she plays her irons better than anybody here, and she is a good putter. What can we do?' Those words turned out to be prophetic. Stirling took the qualifying medal with an 88, the only score below 90. She also won contests for long driving, approaching and putting – and the championship itself – without ever being seriously tested. She never once played more than 13 holes, winning the final by 6 and 5. 'That she will be a formidable contender for the national title this year goes almost without saying,' Anderson wrote.

The Women's Amateur returned to Boston that autumn, conducted in the first week of October over the testing 6,250-yard course Donald Ross had designed for Belmont Springs Country Club. A month earlier, Stirling's childhood playmate, Bobby Jones, had made Atlanta the centre of the golfing universe with his debut in the men's Amateur at Merion Cricket Club, near Philadelphia. Just 14 years old then, Jones stunned the crowd at Merion by defeating his first two opponents, Eben Byers and Frank Dyer, before being knocked out in the quarter-final by defending champion, Robert A. Gardner.

When 63 competitors gathered at Belmont for the Women's Amateur Championship, it is safe to say that no one was rooting harder for Stirling than Jones and the golfers of Atlanta. That morning, before Stirling stepped up to the first tee, a telegram arrived from her home town. It read: 'You have done it before; do it again. Cut loose and go for it; we are pulling hard and so proud we are about to bust.' – The Jones Family. The field was far smaller than usual, down from 119 the previous season at Onwentsia, and among those missing were the defending champion, Florence Vanderbeck, and the two Curtis sisters, Margaret and Harriot, who had sailed for France.

The course showed its teeth starting with the qualifying round, where only one score below 90 was posted, by the redoubtable Hurd, with an 86. Stirling placed sixth, with a 91, hardly her best, but it nevertheless earned her a berth in match play. From the outset, it was obvious that Stirling would not enjoy the kind of triumphal procession she had experienced earlier that season in winning her second Southern Amateur. Her first match against Mrs E.H. Baker Jr., a member at Belmont, was a ding-dong battle in which Stirling only prevailed on the 17th hole, winning by 2 and 1.

She found the going easier in the second round, winning 5 and 4, but in the third she came up against one of the favourites, Chicago's Elaine Rosenthal, with whom Stirling would soon find herself touring the country. Rosenthal impressed the crowd by driving the ball farther than ever, well beyond 200 yards, but the rest of her game was shaky. She and Stirling were all square at the turn, but Rosenthal frittered away her chances by missing putt after putt, and 'Queen Alexa', as southerners had taken to calling her, survived again with a 2 and 1 victory on the 17th.

Stirling came out firing in her semi-final match against Mrs Charles C. Auchincloss, bombing drives into a stiff breeze and sinking one putt after another to reach the turn in the astonishingly low score of 39. Anderson described it as 'an exhibition of golf which I am not afraid to say would have beaten not a few of the golfers who qualified in the National Championship at Merion'. Auchincloss was 4 down by then, but far from ready to concede defeat. She righted the ship on the homeward nine, narrowing Stirling's lead to a single hole by the time they reached the 17th green. There Auchincloss faced a must-make putt of just six feet. 'All was silence as the putt which would have squared the match was played,' Anderson wrote, 'but the ball just looked lazily in and lay provokingly on the edge of the cup.' A tidy four on the 18th sent Stirling into her first championship final against Mildred Caverly.

Stirling and Caverly did not exactly approach that round as cut-throat competitors. They spent the afternoon before the final taking a leisurely ride together in an automobile – after which Stirling spent some time giving Caverly tips on playing her mashie, the equivalent of a 5-iron. That display of sportsmanship earned high praise from Anderson. 'There was none of the competitive spirit which goes too much with our Amateur Championship,' he wrote. 'That feature more than any other, perhaps, impressed me and set a standard which the men might do well to follow.' From the moment Stirling and Caverly teed off in the 18-hole final – the Women's Amateur would not move to 36 holes until after the war – the match was distinguished by outstanding golf. The lead changed hands five times on the opening nine, with neither player ever more than a hole ahead. Stirling reached the turn in 41, Caverly in 43. Both had shaved multiple strokes off their qualifying score and were on pace to match, or better, the 86 that won the medal.

For the first few holes of the homeward nine, Stirling appeared ready to draw away from Caverly. She won both the 10th and 11th, and when she escaped with a lucky half on 12, her lead of 3 up with six holes left to play seemed an imposing one. Undaunted, Caverly fought back. She won the 14th when Stirling drove into a bunker, a first for either player that afternoon, and had a chance to cut the lead to a single hole at the next, but her five-foot putt would not drop. On the 16th, a 114-yard par three, Stirling gave Caverly another opening by leaving her tee shot short and chipping to within a foot of the cup. Caverly faced a 30-foot putt she desperately needed to hole. 'Too bad there were no motion pictures of that putt, which went straight as a die and into the very heart of the hole for a wondrous 2,' Anderson wrote. 'No wonder there were murmurs that after all the supposed favoured one for the title would lose.'

With all to play for, both golfers stumbled at the treacherous 17th, a hole in which the second shot had to clear a creek on its way to the green. Stirling hit a solid drive, then drew her brassie from the bag in hopes of carrying the hazard and leaving an easy third. Uncharacteristically, she hit the ball so poorly that it did not even have enough 'stuff' on it to reach the water. Caverly was not so lucky. Her lie from the tee was a poor one, but under the circumstances she had no choice but to risk the carry. A half top sent her ball bouncing into the creek, landing just on the other side of the brook. Once Stirling had chipped to within six feet, Caverly bravely waded into the water to play her shot. It landed on the green, but not close, and when her putt did not fall, Stirling resolutely rolled hers in to claim the championship. 'There was admiration for the other's game manifest in the eyes of the two golfers as they shook hands,' Anderson wrote.

When Stirling drained that final putt, Anderson noted, she had taken just 76 shots, leaving her with a four on the last for a brilliant 80. 'I feel correct in saying that never has the standard of play been so high in the final round as it was in this one,' he said. He was not alone in being impressed. 'Other golfers will come and go, but Miss Stirling will be in the championship ranks for many years,' predicted the *Boston Herald*. Stirling's game showed 'a boldness new to women's golf in this country,' added *The American Golfer*. 'Miss Stirling will undoubtedly begin to post scores in the 70s and other women golfers will follow her.'

Those scores, tragically, would have to wait. By April 1917, the US had entered 'the war to end all wars', American soldiers were en route to Europe, and patriotic US citizens were singing along to the words of George M. Cohan: 'We'll be over. We're coming over, and we won't come back till it's over over there!' As Leitch had been before her, Stirling was sidelined just as she came into her own.

WOMEN IN WARTIME

During the war years, on both sides of the Atlantic, the role women played in society underwent profound and lasting change. With every hand needed to carry on the fight, a woman's place was decidedly outside the home – volunteering for the cause or filling jobs soldiers had left behind. Leitch had been swept up in this massive change for two years before it subsumed Stirling. Throughout 1915 and 1916, as Leitch cared for her widowed mother in Silloth, she used her considerable fame to raise money for the war effort. She joined Mabel Stringer's appeal to buy toys for the children of soldiers, and she hosted a 'pound day' at Silloth encouraging golfers to donate a £1 bag of groceries as provisions for the Belgian Army. Leitch was most devoted, however, to raising money for the Scottish Women's Hospital in Serbia, where her fellow golfer, Margaret Neill Fraser, had died while serving as a nurse during a typhoid outbreak. In April 1916, Leitch joined Issette Pearson and others in asking every golf club in the kingdom to help raise £5,000 to fit out 200 beds at the hospital, as a memorial to Fraser.

Charity golf would also be part of her work for the cause. In July 1915, for example, Leitch and her sister May teamed up in an England vs Scotland match at Ranelagh to raise money for the Red Cross, defeating Eva Anderson and Elsie Grant Suttie 1 up. It wasn't until the autumn of 1916, however, that Leitch got a chance to do what thousands of other women had already done – take a job ordinarily occupied by a man to free up another soldier for the front. She became a clerk in the town office at Carlisle, learning secretarial skills through a correspondence course and commuting 30 miles daily by train, as she had during her school days. Two years later, she moved to London with her sister, Edith, and took a second post as a clerk. Interestingly, in September 1918, newspapers announced that Leitch had become engaged to 2nd Lt. Henry Willock-Pollen of the Coldstream Guards. By the following spring, those same papers reported that the marriage had been called off. No explanation was given.

Alexa Stirling's experiences in wartime were similar to Leitch's. Her skills as a driver and auto mechanic allowed her to free up a man to join the fighting by becoming an ambulance driver on the home front. She joined the Army Medical Corps and achieved the rank of 2nd Lieutenant. Among the tragedies Stirling responded to was the Great Atlanta Fire, which broke out on 21 May 1917, just a month after war had been declared, and burned for 10 horrifying hours, consuming 300 acres, destroying 1,900 structures and displacing 10,000 people, but miraculously resulting in only a single death. Not since General William Tecumseh Sherman laid Atlanta to waste on his march through Georgia during the Civil War had the city experienced such destruction. All day, Stirling drove in and out of the charred ruins, transporting the wounded to hospitals.

Exhibition golf played a far larger, and more memorable, role in Stirling's wartime life than it did for Leitch. Stirling spent much of 1917 and 1918 touring the East Coast with Bobby Jones, Perry Adair and Elaine Rosenthal to raise money for the American Red Cross – matches that earned the so-called 'Dixie Whiz Kids' considerable fame. Arranged by sporting goods manufacturer Wright & Ditson, the tour featured daily matches between the four players – Jones and Stirling teaming up one day, Adair and Stirling the next. Together they raised $150,000 for the cause, an amount equivalent to some $4 million today.

The lives women led during that war accomplished something that had eluded suffragists in Britain and America, both the reasoned voices like Millicent Fawcett and Carrie Catt and the firebrands like Emmeline Pankhurst and Alice Paul. The reality that women sustained the war machine by working in place of men created unstoppable momentum for giving them the right to vote. All suffragettes in British prisons were freed as soon as war broke out, and the vast majority of them, as well as their compatriots in the cause, went to work on behalf of the empire. By January 1918, Parliament had passed legislation granting the vote to British women over the age of 30, enfranchising some 8.4 million. It was hardly the total victory suffragettes demanded, and the fight would go on, but it was a significant step forward. It would not be until 1928 that British leaders stepped into the modern age by allowing women to vote on equal terms with men, granting that right to every woman at the age of 21.

Across the Atlantic, Congress passed the 19th Amendment to the US Constitution in June 1919, just six months after the war ended. It granted all women over the age of 21 the right to vote. The measure was sent to the 48 states for ratification, which was finally achieved on 18 August 1920. On that day, by the narrowest of margins, Tennessee became the 36th state to approve the so-called Susan B. Anthony Amendment, making it the law of the land.

The war that produced this profound change came to its bloody end on 11 November 1918, marking the dawn of a new post-war age in America and Britain. The decades ahead would be a time of firsts for women, and not simply the first time a majority of them had a say in how their country was run. In Britain, Nancy Astor would become the first woman in Parliament, and Oxford would admit the first 100 women to study for degrees. In America, novelist Edith Wharton would become the first woman to win a Pulitzer Prize for her novel *The Age of Innocence*, and Amelia Earhart became the first woman to cross the Atlantic in an aeroplane.

Since the dawn of the suffrage movement, golf had been a vivid example of the way women were asserting themselves in a man's world. In the spring of 1919, as championships resumed on both sides of the pond, Leitch and Stirling returned to showing women their proper place in the greatest of games, even as a new generation was poised to come to the fore.

Six

CORONATION AT PRINCE'S

—— • ◦ ● ◦ • ——

CECIL Leitch was 23 years old when Britain declared war on Germany in August 1914. Before she had a chance to compete for another title, she had celebrated her 28th birthday. Had fate not intervened, the golfing world agreed, Leitch surely would have won more championships during those war years, as so few were able then to stand against her. 'She was on the crest of a wave, and seemed likely to go on winning,' *Times* correspondent Bernard Darwin wrote after watching Leitch's breakthrough victory at Hunstanton months before hostilities began. The pride of Silloth's luck did not improve after the war. By May 1919, when tournament golf resumed in Britain, the powerhouse Surrey team had already taken on the 18-year-old who would dethrone Leitch as the greatest of women golfers. It would be another year, however, before Joyce Wethered announced her presence in shocking fashion at Sheringham.

The first championship since summer of 1914 – the English Amateur – was played in the spring of 1919 over the Old Links at St Annes. It drew a mere 40 players, the smallest field in ages, mostly because winding down a war machine is a slow process.

'Many of the English golfers were not yet "demobbed", so that the field could scarcely be called quite representative,' explained Mabel Stringer, who nevertheless described the event as 'a delightful reunion'. From the qualifying round on, it was obvious that most of the golfers were rusty – everyone, that is, except the indomitable Leitch. On a morning buffeted by brisk winds blowing off the Irish Sea, Leitch posted an 84 to win the medal, the only score below 90 and 24 strokes lower than the player who finished last at 108. 'Perhaps it would have been a little disgraceful if anybody had played too well,' Eleanor Helme observed dryly. 'Somebody might have been tempted to ask, "And what did you do during the Great War?"'

The match-play rounds of the championship were no different from the qualifying. With an enormous crowd in tow, Leitch bowled over one opponent after another like so many ninepins. During the entirety of the championship, she lost only two holes. Having all but strolled into the final, Leitch found herself facing her most formidable pre-war rival, Gladys Ravenscroft. In August 1915, Ravenscroft had married Temple Dobell, a timber broker from Lancashire, and, according to Stringer, had played very little golf during the intervening years. That much was obvious from the moment she and Leitch started out in the 36-hole final. The problem was not Ravenscroft's ball-striking. It was on the greens that she failed miserably. Missing one tiny putt after another, Ravenscroft managed to halve only a single hole. 'Unfortunately,' wrote Leitch, 'my opponent's putting was pathetic, and largely on account of her weakness in this department, I was allowed to retain my title by a margin of 10 and 8.'

Even if a full field had assembled for that first post-war tournament, Stringer is convinced the outcome would have been the same. 'I do not think anyone would have been able to stand against Cecil Leitch, whose play was far and above that of any other entrant.' Before that season began, the Ladies' Golf Union had decided that it was too difficult to stage a British Ladies'

Championship so soon after the cessation of hostilities. Instead of its usual spot in spring, the tournament was scheduled for the autumn of 1919.

Rebounding after a war was not the only challenge involved in staging that tournament. It was also the first not run by Issette Pearson. In 1911, she married the widowed Thomas Miller, an early supporter of women's golf. Three years later, she relinquished her post as Honorary Secretary of the Ladies' Golf Union, after 21 years at the helm. The scheduling of that first post-war Ladies' Championship turned out to be another tragedy for Leitch. By October, when the tournament was to be played at Burnham, Britain was crippled by a rail strike and the championship was cancelled, depriving Leitch of a fifth straight opportunity to add to her laurels.

The Ladies' Championship did not resume until May 1920 at Royal County Down, a long, testing links in a nation struggling with a conflict of its own. The Irish War of Independence was still raging in the south, a reality that limited the field to just 57 entries. Among those who did make the journey, however, were several prominent golfers from across the Atlantic, the first sign of what would develop into a great post-war invasion, one that would have devastating consequences for Britain in both the men's and women's games. The American contingent included former Amateur champion Florence Vanderbeck, runner-up Mildred Caverly, Rosamond Sherwood and Marion Hollins, who would go on to become a larger-than-life figure in the world of women's golf. Canada sent its champion, Ada Mackenzie, along with rising star Florence Harvey.

When the competitors had assembled at Royal County Down in the second week of May, the weather refused to cooperate. The competition was delayed two days by howling wind and slashing rain, which eventually diminished but remained an issue all week. Leitch had long wanted to play County Down because it presented such a formidable test for women. Even a long hitter like her acknowledged that 'there is only one green on this long links which can ordinarily be reached by a lady player with anything less than a wooden club.' Between the weather, the course and a draw that pitted them against one another, the North American contingent found the going tough. Hollins survived the longest, lasting until the fourth round. There she fell to eventual semi-finalist Molly Griffiths, a newcomer from Surrey.

Leitch remained in overpowering form, brushing off both Ravenscroft and Doris Fraser en route to the final. The only opponent who gave her any trouble was pre-war rival Gladys Bastin, whose run of threes and a two did nothing more than stave off the inevitable defeat. From the outset, Griffiths had been singled out as the player most likely to conquer Leitch. Small and shy by nature, Griffiths had worked during the war as a greenkeeper at Sunningdale, and was known for her brisk pace of play and quicksilver swing. Like Leitch, Griffiths sailed through her half of the draw, being pressed seriously only by Cecil's sister, Edith, who took the Surrey player to the 19th hole before succumbing. In the end, even Griffiths could not give the defending champion a fight. 'I experienced one of those pleasant days when the hole appeared to be of twice its usual dimension,' Leitch explained. Rolling in putt after putt, she built a six-hole lead by the time they broke for lunch. The afternoon round was no different, with Leitch continuing to putt like a woman possessed and cruising to victory by 7 and 6. Walking with the crowd, Mabel Stringer heard one Irishman sum up Leitch's victory brilliantly: 'Begorra! She's never been stretched!' Even in her moment of glory, however, Leitch had become aware of the new challenge looming on the horizon. Earlier that spring, she had begun receiving 'glowing accounts' of the new player on Surrey's team, a tall, willowy woman with an absolutely gorgeous swing.

WHAT TRAIN?

The mystery player on the Surrey side was better known in those days as Roger Wethered's sister. Roger was captain of the golf team at Oxford, and that made him and his sister, Joyce, golf royalty. It was a time of intellectual ferment in the game, as golf's brightest minds applied themselves to subjects ranging from architecture and agronomy to the science of the swing, and the Oxford and Cambridge Golf Society was at the centre of it all. The two universities were home to the best amateur golfers in the land, and had produced such leading thinkers as John Low, the man who inspired the Golden Age of Golf Course Architecture, and Bernard Darwin, golf correspondent of *The Times*.

Joyce and Roger grew up in this heady atmosphere and travelled almost exclusively in an elite circle of amateur golfers, as the children of an exceptional Oxford man, Herbert Newton Wethered, and his wife, Marion. Wethered's grandfather had earned generational wealth in coal mining, and he married into a fortune made in manufacturing yarn. That enabled Newton, as Joyce knew him, to lead the leisurely life of an English gentleman. He achieved the classical ideal of being an all-rounder – a painter and writer who also excelled at cricket and golf. During his life, Newton would write nearly a dozen books on topics ranging from gardening and medieval craftsmanship to the art of Thackeray and golf course design. *The Architectural Side of Golf,* which he wrote with Tom Simpson in 1929, is revered as a classic even today.

Joyce was born on 17 November 1901, nearly three years after her brother. Her father apparently had definitive ideas about what subjects his children needed to learn, as he had both of them schooled by private tutors at their home, Tigbourne Court, in Godalming, Surrey. Golf was always a family affair for the Wethereds, who were members at West Surrey and Puttenham golf clubs. Newton played to a single digit handicap, although

Marion never broke the ranks of bogey golfers. Joyce's earliest golfing memory was of playing on holiday as a child in Cornwall. Her real education in the game, however, began as a teenager, when her family started spending summers at Dornoch, in northern Scotland.

Wethered fell deeply in love with Scottish golf – her name is on Dornoch's honour board five times – and that affection would, one day, tempt her into the crowning moment of her career. 'Could anyone help it playing in such heavenly surroundings?' she wondered. At Dornoch, Wethered fell under the influence of her brother, Roger, whom she described 'as an autocrat where the seriousness of golf was concerned'. Roger insisted that they track their progress by keeping a chart of their scores. They kept that chart religiously, watching their scores creep lower and lower, until he enrolled at Oxford in 1917.

Ever after, the influence of her brother and his university friends shaped the way Wethered approached the game. That was especially significant given that no less than Bernard Darwin had ranked Roger and his classmate, Cyril Tolley, as the two greatest British amateurs of that age. Oxford regularly played matches against the leading London clubs, and those became family outings for the Wethereds. They afforded Joyce the chance to study the styles of Britain's best players – as well as to play plenty of golf with them. 'Playing with men stronger and better than oneself is the quickest and most certain way of improvement for a girl,' wrote Wethered, echoing the advice Issette Pearson had given to Cecil Leitch. 'It meant that when I played in ladies' matches, the difference from being continuously outdriven and outplayed made the game seem much easier and gave one additional confidence.'

It was far more than that. Roger's Oxford crowd was obsessed with the mechanics of hitting a golf ball, constantly discussing the finer points in minute detail. Joyce absorbed it all, finding herself inexorably drawn to the elusive pursuit of the perfect swing.

Listening to Roger and his friends persuaded Wethered that she needed to make her swing less flat and more upright, with the wide arc and full extension typical of a woman who stood five feet ten inches tall. Ever after she worked tirelessly to perfect that move, to improve her rhythm, transfer her weight more freely and gain all-important distance.

It was through Roger, in fact, that she met Bobby Jones, the player who became her idol, and whose swing she imitated so precisely that hers became a mirror image of his. Wethered was also among the first women to stop holding the club in the palm of her hands and adopt the overlapping grip popularised by Harry Vardon. Perfecting the full swing was not Wethered's only challenge in those early years. She also struggled with putting and approaching, especially learning to hit mashie shots crisp enough to impart the backspin that would make them stop close to the cup. 'I can even recollect particularly agonising moments when I saw the ball almost through a mist of tears when practising with this exasperating club,' she wrote.

By 1919, as she approached her 18th birthday, Wethered's game had progressed sufficiently that she was invited to play for the Surrey women's team, holding a position near the bottom of the line-up. The following spring she entered the county championship, and made it as far as the semi-final before being knocked out. The winner of that event was her dear friend, Molly Griffiths, who would be among the favourites in the English Amateur to be played that June at Sheringham, a picturesque Norfolk fishing village along the North Sea. Wethered went to Sheringham more as Griffiths' companion than as a competitor, although she clearly planned to enter the tournament. Before leaving, she took a putting lesson from Albert Howlett, the pro at West Surrey, that 'miraculously' resolved a weakness in her game.

That season the English Amateur added a qualifying round for the 64 spots in match play. Wethered's 94 got her into the championship, but was such a mediocre effort that no one paid much attention to her. That changed the moment match play began. Shockingly, Griffiths was knocked out in the first round. Even more surprisingly, Wethered began a steady march to the final, going from strength to strength with each round. 'One by one her opponents through the week came in and said they didn't mind being beaten, it was such a glorious young player who had done it,' wrote Eleanor Helme. 'Surrey began to forget their disappointment over Miss Griffiths' first-round defeat and to take interest instead in her pale-faced pal.'

In the other half of the bracket, the reigning champion, Leitch, was hanging on for dear life. 'With the tired golf I was playing, I never deserved to get through the first round let alone the last,' as she put it. Leitch's one moment of glory came on the 17th hole of her third round when she was 1 down and facing elimination. Her drive left her a long carry over a cross bunker guarding the green, a brassie shot given the stiff breeze blowing in her face. 'All of us held our breath as she took her stance, put on her "Roman Emperor" face, played a magnificent shot clearing everything, and won the hole,' marvelled Mabel Stringer. That brilliant shot saved the match, allowing Leitch to pull it out of the fire on the 19th.

Throughout her career, Leitch showed a capacity to toss off scratchy golf and summon her best when it counted. She did just that in the morning round of the 36-hole final against Wethered, heading into lunch with a 4-up lead over the newcomer from Surrey. In the afternoon, Wethered fell 6 down by botching the first two holes, and had won only two of those back by the time they turned for home. Then a miracle began to unfold. Wethered seemed to retreat into a cocoon, shutting out everything except the next shot, and began to play with extraordinary brilliance, winning five consecutive holes to take a 1-up lead at 14. Leitch squared the match again at 15, but even that gave her 'no feeling of "confidence", as Miss Wethered was playing with the utmost calmness and seemed oblivious that she was fighting out the final of the first championship in which she had ever taken part'.

The proof of Leitch's intuition came at the 17th, alongside a railway line that ran into Sheringham. Just as Wethered was about to putt for the title, a train rattled noisily past. Paying no heed, she rolled the ball into the cup. 'Didn't the train put you off?' a reporter asked afterwards. 'What train?' Wethered replied, creating in her first championship a legend that would follow her all her life. 'What concentration!' marvelled Leitch, and indeed even Wethered herself later acknowledged that 'it was largely due to a faculty for shutting my eye to all but the immediate shots before me that made me successful.'

Wethered had played the final eight holes of that championship in 33 shots – one over the ideal of level fours – an achievement the *Times* correspondent described as 'simply astounding'. Even more astounding was that she had done it while seriously ill. All week, Wethered had been fighting a rising temperature. Afterwards, she was diagnosed with whooping cough. It kept her out of action for the next three months, as Leitch crossed the English Channel and bounced back with another dominant victory in the French Open.

SHE'S COMING OVER

In any other year, women's golf would have been obsessed with the prospect of a rematch between Wethered and Leitch. That wasn't the case in 1921. That year, all the talk was about the news from America: Alexa Stirling was coming to compete in the British Ladies' Championship. Her arrival was part of the greatest US invasion ever, in both men's and women's golf. Stirling was joined on the trip by 10 other women, among them Marion Hollins. Eleven American men also came to challenge the British in the Open Championship later that summer at St Andrews, their costs covered by a fundraiser launched the previous autumn by *Golf Illustrated*. They included Walter Hagen, Jim Barnes and

Jock Hutchison. Big names from the States entered that year's Amateur at Hoylake, too, stars like Frances Ouimet, Chick Evans, Jesse Guilford and Bobby Jones, who extended his stay to compete in the Open as well.

In the face of such an invasion, Brits put aside thoughts of anything beyond keeping their cherished trophies from crossing the Atlantic. That was no sure thing at Turnberry given the way Stirling had swept all before her in North America over the past two seasons, adding the 1920 Canadian Open to her laurels as well. During the 1919 Women's Amateur at Shawnee on Delaware, in eastern Pennsylvania, Stirling impressed reporters and fans alike by hitting the ball even farther than she had before the war, especially with her irons. 'The crispness and firmness with which she hit her shots up to hole side would have done credit to the best professionals in the country,' declared *The American Annual.*

It wasn't just Stirling. Every woman seemed to have taken a cue from her and Leitch in developing shorter, firmer, more vigorous swings. 'The outstanding feature of the tournament,' the *Annual* noted, 'was the great length from the tee that many of the players were getting.' Stirling entered the tournament in peak form, having posted a 79 at the narrow and difficult Druid Hills course in Atlanta that year, as well as an 83 at East Lake, a score equal to what men shot in that season's Southern Amateur. Her form showed no sign of slacking at Shawnee on Delaware as she took the qualifying medal with an 87 before winning four matches to reach the Amateur final, among them victories over Hollins and former champion Florence Vanderbeck. 'Stirling was reeling off par figures with the monotony of a Walter Hagen,' the *Annual* marvelled, and she kept right on doing that in the championship match against Margaret Gavin, rolling over her by 6 and 5.

The 1920 Women's Amateur at Mayfield Country Club in Cleveland was a similarly triumphant procession. Again, Stirling breezed through her early matches, defeating both Elaine Rosenthal and Edith Cummings before posting a record score of 80 to knock out Vanderbeck again in the semi-final. Dorothy Campbell Hurd proved no trouble for Stirling in the championship match. Alexa went around the opening nine in 40, established a 5-up lead, and finished off the two-time champion by 4 and 3.

Stirling had now won three consecutive Women's Amateurs – a feat that had earned golfers immortality since the days when Young Tom Morris reeled off three Opens in a row to claim The Challenge Belt. Americans were convinced 'that there is no woman player in this country who can give Miss Stirling a match,' wrote the *Annual*. The question on the table was whether any woman in Britain could. Naturally, the nation's hopes rested with Leitch. 'There was much speculation as to what would happen in a match between Miss Alexa Stirling and myself,' Cecil recalled. 'Fate was apparently determined that nothing should prevent our meeting, as the draw brought our names "out of the hat" together in the first round of the championship.'

The scene at Turnberry that spring was a stark reminder of post-war reality in Britain. Since the outbreak of hostilities, the course had been used as an airfield. Many of its majestic dunes had been flattened for runways, and a few Air Force buildings were still visible alongside the course. A month before the tournament came the great coal strike of 1921, and the hardships it caused miners were made painfully evident 'by the appearance of sad, hungry-looking women down by the links, who rattled collecting boxes under our noses and asked in hoarse tones for food for the wee bairns,' as Mabel Stringer put it. When the day for the Leitch–Stirling match arrived, the weather could not have been more grim. 'It was the West Coast at its worst – lashing rain, tearing wind, cold – altogether an abomination of desolation,' wrote Eleanor Helme. That did nothing to deter some 4,000 fans from gathering to watch the showdown between America and Britain, many of them striking miners rooting for their hero, Leitch. Nasty weather was nothing new for Leitch, having grown up in windswept Silloth, and she seemed to revel in her defiance of the tempest. Stirling faced it bravely, especially for a woman who was never in robust health. She stuck close to the reigning champion all the way around, finally succumbing on the 16th green by 3 and 2. 'The American girl fought magnificently against the heavy odds and won all our hearts by her pluck and true sportsmanship,' Stringer concluded.

Britain would not be so lucky in the Open Championship. For the first time, the Claret Jug was carried off to America by the St Andrews native turned US citizen, Jock Hutchison, the beginning of what would turn out to be a long, dark night for the United Kingdom. With all eyes focused on the Leitch–Stirling match, Joyce Wethered had been all but forgotten in the other half of the bracket, and she was not playing anything like the golfer who had sprung a surprise at Sheringham. In the International Match that preceded the championship, Wethered lost in singles to Scotland's Jean McCulloch, and in the first round she only squeaked by Gladys Bastin on the 19th hole. 'I was none too happy about the way I was playing,' recalled Wethered, who fought a slice all week. 'By the time the last day arrived, the error had begun to creep into almost every full shot.'

Wethered did make her way to the final, but she had no answer for the brand of golf Leitch was playing. Twice in the same round she saw Leitch hit two mighty wooden shots on to the green at the long fifth – 'a feat quite beyond the capacity of any other lady in the field'. On the morning of their 36-hole final, Wethered played especially poorly, falling 7 down by the time they broke for lunch. 'In the afternoon, she came back to the attack like a lion,' wrote Helme, but it was no use. Leitch dispatched her 4 and 3. Now Leitch, too, had reached that sacred number of three successive championships, and the victory celebration continued in the French Open at Le Fontainebleau, south of Paris.

There Stirling took centre stage to start. She won the qualifying medal with a sparkling 79, and made it to the semi-finals before losing to Wethered by 5 and 4. Despite the lopsided victory, Wethered was 'struck by her beautiful style of play'. She sensed, however, that Stirling was more interested in the attractions of Paris than in playing golf. The final of that championship again came down to Wethered and Leitch, and again it was no match. By lunchtime, just as she had at Turnberry, Wethered had fallen 7 down. This time, however, there was no rally, and on the 31st hole in the afternoon she succumbed by 6 and 5. The victory gave Leitch another triple – her third consecutive French Open and fourth since 1912 – and she was duly honoured with life membership in Le Fontainebleau Golf Club.

PRINCE'S, SANDWICH

Joyce Wethered walked away from the 1921 season with a clear understanding of where the bar was set in golf. 'Cecil that year was unquestionably a far better player than I was in every department of the game,' she acknowledged. 'I had still to prove that Sheringham was something more than a flash in the pan.' Wethered was nothing if not single-minded, and she focused tirelessly on closing the gap between her game and Leitch's, an assignment that could not have been better timed. At that moment, Wethered and her brother were working on an instructional book titled *Golf from Both Sides,* published in 1922. The original idea was for Joyce to write a book for girls, but when Roger volunteered to add ideas for boys, a new concept was born. Joyce's contributions to the book – chapters on women's golf, putting and the bulk of what was written about driving – demonstrate one truth unequivocally. Even at the age of 20, Wethered had developed a deep understanding of the theory of the golf swing. 'She was not a natural golfer or a child prodigy,' wrote her biographer, Basil Ashton Tinkler. 'She had worked hard, with both muscle and brain, over a number of years to accomplish her skills.

The reward was that, when she hit a good shot, she knew exactly why she had done so, and when things went awry, again she knew the reason.'

By the autumn of 1921, when the English Amateur was contested at Lytham and St Annes, it was clear that Wethered's game had made considerable strides since Turnberry. Only once in the six matches leading up to the final did Wethered have to play the last two holes. The vast majority of her matches ended by the 14th as she demonstrated a supremacy over the field rarely seen in golf, men's or women's. In the final she faced poor Mrs Mudford, who was summarily dismissed by 12 and 11. Indeed, the only news of note from that championship was the debut of a new Surrey golfer, Molly Gourlay, who like Marion Hollins would go on to be a singularly important figure in the women's game.

While Wethered had never been more dominant than she was at Lytham and St Annes, the one caveat was that she did not get a chance to measure her progress against Leitch. After her victory at Turnberry, Leitch and her sister, Edith, decided to spend the rest of that season touring the United States and Canada and competing in the national open of both countries. Leitch remembered the trip fondly. 'I was left with wonderful impressions, delightful memories,' she wrote. 'Nothing could have exceeded the kindness and hospitality that were extended to us by the American and Canadian peoples.'

Truth was, however, that Leitch encountered more than her share of trouble on that journey. She arrived in Canada that August, only to be sidelined by a bout of laryngitis, and she returned to Britain in early November with her right arm in a sling. Leitch did manage to capture the Canadian Open at the Rivermead Golf Club in Ottawa, where she met reigning champion Stirling in the semi-final. Their match was a near replay of Turnberry, a see-saw battle that ended with Leitch winning 3 and 1. 'It was a great match, and the enormous gallery appeared to enjoy it as much as the players,' Leitch recalled. In the final against an inexperienced and overwhelmed Molly McBride, Leitch set a record unlikely to be broken, crushing her opponent by the unheard of score of 17 and 15.

Leitch found the going tougher when she set out to achieve her principal goal, carrying home the Robert Cox Trophy awarded to the winner of the US Women's Amateur. The tournament was contested that year over the Hollywood Golf Club in Deal, New Jersey, which at 6,700 yards Leitch declared to be 'the most difficult I have yet seen, and one of the longest I have ever played over'. The 18-year-old who tied for first in the Amateur's qualifying round – Glenna Collett, with an 85 – made a lasting impression on Leitch. 'Good though she now is, this young player will be a still more dangerous opponent in the near future when she steadies down,' Cecil warned.

Shockingly, Leitch herself was knocked out in the second round, losing 1 up to F.C. Letts by three-putting the 18th hole. Marion Hollins went on to dethrone three-time winner Alexa Stirling by 5 and 4, her first and only victory in that championship. Failing in the Amateur gave Leitch a fresh perspective on the challenges faced by Americans like Stirling and Hollins, who crossed the Atlantic in quest of the British Ladies' Championship. 'Not as an excuse at all, but as a matter of interest I may perhaps be allowed to say that during the first three weeks of our visit to the United States we found the game an effort and could sympathise with American visitors to Great Britain, who fail to do themselves justice until they become acclimatised,' Leitch wrote.

If losing in the Amateur was a blow, it was nothing compared to what happened during the final round of that trip as Leitch and Hollins played a friendly foursome at the National Golf Links of America against golf architects Devereux Emmet and W.H. Follett. 'While attempting with customary force to dig their ball from an awkward fairway lie, Cecil severely damaged muscles and associated nerves in her right arm,' wrote historian John Pearson. Leitch played on, and she and Hollins won 2 up, but afterwards, doctors put Cecil's arm in a sling and told her she needed an extended break from golf. The injury occurred on 31 October, just as Cecil and Edith were preparing to set sail for home.

It would not be until the following spring, in May 1922, that Wethered got another chance to test herself against Leitch in the British Ladies' Championship at Prince's, a classic links spread out along the shores of Pegwell Bay near the quaint village of Sandwich. Nothing stirred Wethered like the chance to play such a famous course. 'There is something . . . particularly inspiring in the atmosphere, a kind of faint intoxication that brings out one's best efforts,' she wrote. Long and narrow, with punishing bunkers seemingly lurking everywhere, Prince's was ideally suited to Wethered's game. Even she acknowledged, however, that when the wind was up, as it so often is at Sandwich, 'it can be heartbreaking enough to all but the strongest and most philosophical.'

The draw for the tournament delivered what every fan craved – Leitch and Wethered in opposite halves of the bracket – and they obliged the crowd by making their way into the final. On the morning of their 36-hole championship match, a gale blew in off the bay. 'The sand was being driven in every direction,' Wethered remembered, 'and all through the day we had to walk with our eyes half shut.' Often a slow starter, Wethered wanted, above all, to avoid a repeat of what had happened at Turnberry and in France, where she had fallen so far behind in the morning round that her situation was irretrievable. She did just that, blazing through the first five holes in 19 strokes – one under level fours – and found herself sitting on a 2-up lead. 'I realised it was going to be a match after all, and that was all I really cared about at the time,' Wethered wrote. Leitch battled back fiercely, seizing a 1-up lead at 13, but Wethered soon poked her nose in front again and would have gone to lunch 2 up had Cecil not bravely holed a six-footer on the last.

By the end of that round, one thing had become clear, R.E. Howard wrote for *Golf Illustrated*. Wethered was now the longer player, either by virtue of her own improvement or because Leitch was hampered by the lingering effects of her arm injury. 'It was an entirely new experience for the player who had dominated ladies' golf since 1914,' Howard wrote of Leitch. 'It worried her that she was outdriven at every hole . . . and had to take wooden clubs to reach the green while her opponent was getting there with irons.' At times, Howard said, he found it 'almost painful to watch'.

In the afternoon, Wethered again came out firing, this time playing the first four holes in 20 strokes, winning four of them, and taking a commanding 5-up lead with 14 to play. True to form, Leitch played the sixth brilliantly, making two perfect shots, a tidy chip and a six-foot putt for her first win of the round. That cut the lead to 4 up and gave her a realistic chance. Curiously, it was at the very next hole that Leitch cracked, although Howard reported that she had seemed on edge all day, distracted by noisy fans in the gallery and especially by the clicking of camera shutters. 'Just when everybody was saying that she had struck the right note at last, and would be off in pursuit of Miss Wethered, she played just about the worst hole of which I have ever seen her guilty,' Howard wrote. 'She topped her drive 100 yards; chipped her third shot into a bunker under her nose; went from there to another bunker 20 yards ahead, and altogether would have done well to hole out in eight – if she had not given up the hole.' Leitch had nothing left and the match ended at the 11th, Wethered prevailing by the astonishing margin of 9 and 7.

Even Leitch's most fervent fans – and perhaps Cecil herself – had come to Prince's worried that she might finally meet her match, Howard wrote, and that had proved to be the case. When Wethered 'applied the pressure with one of the most brilliant displays of golf ever seen in the Ladies' Championship,' he concluded, 'the title-holder was utterly powerless to resist it.' Wethered was over the moon about her victory, aware now that she was unquestionably the better player in every department of the game. 'Perhaps the happiest moment of one's golfing career is the winning of an open championship for the first time,' she wrote. Still, it must have been an odd experience for her to see how stricken everyone else was about Leitch's demise. When it became obvious that Cecil was beaten, an admirer who had been assigned as referee for the match could take no more and retired from the field in tears. Even two years later, when she composed her memoir, Stringer struggled with her emotions. 'The memory of the final is still too fresh to write about without a pang,' she admitted, 'not because Joyce Wethered did not thoroughly deserve her victory, but because no one could witness the debacle of Cecil Leitch without very intense sympathy.' Stringer and Helme both believed Leitch's arm injury flared up again that afternoon – Cecil would not play again for two years – but even they understood that at Prince's they had witnessed the crowning of a new champion, a woman capable of almost inhumanly perfect golf.

The question now was whether any woman in golf was capable of giving Wethered a match. History has a way of repeating itself, and again the challenge would come from America. There, just months after Wethered's breakthrough, the young star who had so impressed Cecil Leitch in the 1921 US Women's Amateur would make her ascent to the top.

Seven

THE GREAT GLENNA

———•◦●◦•———

GREATNESS was expected of Glenna Collett from the moment she first stepped on to a golf course. Quite literally. In the summer of 1917, when she was 14 years old, Collett's father George took her along one afternoon as he was playing golf with friends at the Metacomet Club near their home in Providence, Rhode Island. Collett was watching from the clubhouse veranda, perched on a hill high above the links, as her father, a talented athlete himself, smashed a drive far down the fairway. The sight of the ball soaring in the air stirred something in young Glenna and she scrambled out to the course to ask her father if she could take a turn hitting the ball. Collett was but a slip of a girl then – in her prime she would stand five feet six inches tall and weigh 128 pounds – but when she stood up to the ball and took a swipe, it sailed straight down the fairway, carrying some 100 yards. 'The coming champion!' shouted one of her father's amazed friends, who insisted that Glenna play along with them. 'His comments were followed by others of lavish praise and warm encouragement as I moved from hole to hole,' Collett recalled. 'I had a natural golf swing. With proper training and instruction, said my enthusiastic supporters, I could hit a golf ball as far as any of the women players, if not farther.' Listening to all of this, Collett remembered, 'my head was bursting with soaring dreams that only the very young and ambitious live and know. As I came off the course after the first game, my destiny was settled. I would become a golfer.'

Truth is, George Collett probably expected his daughter to do something remarkable that afternoon at Metacomet. Glenna was a natural athlete, as she had shown all of her young life. Born in New Haven, Connecticut on 20 June 1903, Collett was six years old when her family moved to Rhode Island. They bought a Victorian home on a leafy green street in fashionable East Providence and young Glenna attended the Lincoln School for girls, graduating in 1921.

Early on, Collett demonstrated her preternatural athletic skills. By age nine, she excelled at swimming and diving. At 10, she learned to drive a car, and all her life she would have a reputation as a woman who was a bit wild behind the wheel, with a taste for speed. It was at baseball, however, that Collett truly stood out. Her older brother, Ned, and his friends played sandlot ball near their home, and truth be told Glenna had one of the best arms on the team. Those skills were in the blood for Collett. Her father, who worked in the insurance business, had been a national bicycling champion and a gifted bowler, having once rolled a perfect game of 300 in New Haven. Her mother, Ada, also wanted Glenna to be involved in athletics – that was the very ideal of the so-called New American Woman – but she preferred a game considered more ladylike than baseball. Initially, she steered her daughter towards tennis, another sport popular with women, and it was likely with Ada's encouragement that George brought his daughter with him to the golf club that afternoon.

Given the promise she had shown during that first round, George Collett taught his daughter all he knew about golf and arranged for her to have lessons from the professional at his club,

John Anderson. Her progress was painfully slow. Collett remembers her next round of 18 holes as a dreadful ordeal. 'Struggling along, missing more shots than I made, getting into all sorts of hazards, and finishing with the embarrassing score of 150, I was ready to give up the game,' she wrote. Young Glenna needed inspiration, and it arrived right on time in the form of an appearance at Providence's Wannamoisett Golf Club of the 'Dixie Whiz Kids', who were then making their wartime tour to raise money for the American Red Cross. Collett's father took her to see the famous foursome of Bobby Jones, Perry Adair, Elaine Rosenthal and Alexa Stirling, who had won the first of her US Women's Amateur Championships the previous autumn, before the nation entered the Great War. 'Naturally, I was curious to see these famous players,' Collett recalled, 'and awaited their arrival impatiently. My interest in the game soared when I saw how young they were – just one or two years older than I. Accordingly, my eagerness to see them in action increased twofold and I fluttered about the club in a high pitch of excitement.'

Nearly everyone was focused on Jones, the 15-year-old who had made such a sensational debut in the 1916 Amateur, handsomely attired in a flaming red beret. Collett, however, had eyes only for Stirling and Rosenthal. 'The first thing about Alexa that attracted my admiration was her wonderful poise, especially under fire,' Collett remembered. 'She was never flustered, never hurried. I believed that she possessed the perfect temperament for a golfer.' Rosenthal was equally impressive. 'She was not so contained or business-like as Alexa, but I remember her golf,' Collett wrote. 'She went around Wannamoisett in 80, the last word in women's golf at that time.' That afternoon in 1917 spent following two of the game's greatest women golfers, studying every shot they made, provided just the tonic a young Collett needed. 'I picked up enough during the exhibition matches to go out the next day, and for the nine holes had a 49!' she remembered. 'That was by far the best score I had ever made and I was pleased beyond measure. The second nine was not so good, but what of it? I had broken 50 and felt as though I had conquered the game of golf. I was eager to play and determined to practise constantly in order that I might one day compete with such players as Alexa Stirling and Elaine Rosenthal.'

For the rest of that season and the next, Collett worked diligently on her game under Anderson's watchful eye. She entered the 1918 Rhode Island Championship, finishing last with a disappointing score of 132, as well as a number of local match-play events, in which she was usually knocked out by the second round. 'I was consistently long off the tee,' she recalled, 'but my work with the brassie and the putter was pitifully weak, and I never seemed to have the well-balanced game that would carry me to the top.' The avenue to change all that opened up the following spring, when Collett met the man who vowed to make a champion of her.

THE CARNOUSTIE EFFECT

The first time Collett played in a big championship – the 1919 Eastern Amateur at Apawamis in Rye, New York – she caught the attention of sportswriter H.B. Martin, and not because she was dressed for the occasion in a wide-brimmed red picture hat. Martin had made his fame as a cartoonist, creating the Weatherbird character in the *St Louis Post Dispatch* before going on to edit golf magazines, help found the Professional Golfers' Association and write 15 books on the game, including the first serious history of golf in America. When Martin saw the 16-year-old Collett take a swing, he was just as mesmerised as her father's friends at Metacomet had been two years earlier on the afternoon of her debut. 'She hit as beautiful a drive down the fairway as ever came from the club of a champion,' he marvelled. A man who recognised talent – Martin had also had spent time managing superstar

Walter Hagen – the sportswriter made a point of tracking Collett down to talk to her about her game. 'Glenna admitted that she could hit a few good tee shots, but that was about all,' he recalled. 'I remember distinctly inviting her to come to Shennecossett in Connecticut and take a few lessons from Alex Smith.'

The Colletts were clearly anxious to take Martin up on his offer because that very weekend they showed up in New London to meet Smith, a two-time winner of the US Open and a teacher famous for having coached Jerome Travers to four US Amateur titles. Smith was sceptical about taking on a 16-year-old, but given his relationship with Martin, he agreed to take a look at Collett's swing. 'I'll give her a few lessons and report to you in a week,' said the dour Scot. It took only one lesson before an excited Smith returned to Martin with his verdict. 'I won't have to wait a week to pass an opinion on that lassie,' he reported. 'The kid is good, and if I can't make a champion out of her, I'm a disgrace to the Smith family.'

The story of how Smith shaped the career of Glenna Collett is a microcosm of the larger tale of how a great Scottish diaspora helped to spread golf around the globe just before and after the turn of the century. In 1898, when the great American golf boom was just picking up steam, Alex Smith and his brother, Willie, were among the first Scots to move to the United States and take jobs as professionals at the rapidly growing number of clubs. A great wave would follow, some 250 from Smith's home town of Carnoustie alone, among them Stewart and Jimmy Maiden, the Scots who had such influence over the development of Atlanta superstars Alexa Stirling and Bobby Jones. During the formative years of American golf, these immigrants taught an eager nation how to play the Scottish game, just as their brethren were doing in England, Australia, South America, Africa and every other nation where golf was taking root. Immigrant Scots and Englishmen were so dominant in early American golf that they claimed the first 16 US Open Championships, including two won by Alex Smith and one by his brother, Willie. The first American win did not come until 1911, when Philadelphia's Johnny McDermott finally took the trophy for the United States.

Over the next five years, starting with that first visit to Shennecossett in 1919, Collett took lessons twice a week from Smith. She remembered him as a 'whimsical character' who taught her not only how to play the game, but helped her develop an attitude towards golf that would serve her well all her life. From the moment they began working together, it was obvious to Collett that Smith had 'a natural impatience with lady-like hitters of the golf ball'. Just as his fellow Scot Stewart Maiden did, Smith wanted his students to hit the hell out of it. He taught Collett a powerful, modern swing along the same classic lines as Stirling's, featuring a full body turn, distinctive footwork as she shifted her weight on the backswing, and a full follow-through that saw Glenna up on both toes at impact, putting every ounce she had into the shot. Under Smith's tutelage, Collett became one of the strongest drivers of her day. When she was just 18 years old, she hit the longest shot yet recorded by a woman, measured at an extraordinary 307 yards. Smith also taught Collett to hit crisp irons by shortening her backswing and making a decisive move through the ball. That gave it enough backspin to stop near the hole, enabling Glenna to aim not at the middle of the green but directly at the flag. The least reliable part of Collett's game, as is often true of pre-eminent ball strikers, was putting. Smith showed her how to be more consistent by making a compact stroke and by being more decisive about the line and speed required to find the hole. 'Miss 'em quick,' he would say, employing the sly humour common to Scottish professionals.

It all added up to a distinctive style that impressed everyone who saw Collett play, notably Herbert Newton Wethered, Joyce's father. 'She has evidently spared no effort to perfect her game technically,' he wrote. 'The speed of the footwork, the quick, decisive swing of the club, the fullness of the body motion and crispness of touch all point to an intelligent appreciation of the approved methods of her country.' Still, the most important lesson Smith taught Collett had nothing to do with how to drive, hit irons or putt. It was how to accept the inevitable rubs of the green that can make golf such a maddening game. 'He was, and is, a fatalist in golf,' Collett wrote of her teacher. 'When the ball rolled against him – as the ball will do at times – instead of railing at the breaks or furiously setting himself to overcome his luck, he would just say: "Aweel, it's not my day."' Collett adopted that same attitude, perhaps because there was nothing she loved more than being in the arena, win or lose. Even in the most agonising moments of defeat, Glenna never failed to demonstrate perfect sportsmanship, a trait that made her one of the most beloved golfers of her age.

TRIAL BY FIRE

The appearance in the Eastern Amateur that brought Collett to the attention of H.B. Martin was the beginning of a season that amounted to something of a trial by fire for 16-year-old Glenna. From June to October, Collett entered 10 tournaments, beginning with Apawamis. Her championship debut did not end well. In both rounds, she went around in 107, finishing a full 37 strokes behind the winner, veteran Nonna Barlow.

Not long afterwards, Collett got the kind of emotional boost she sorely needed at the Griscom Cup, an annual competition between golfers from Boston, New York and Philadelphia. The Boston team found itself one player shy of a side, and given that Collett was from nearby Providence, she was invited to fill the spot. It turned out to be a wise choice as she was the only Boston player to win a match against the powerful squad from Philadelphia. Collett continued to make modest progress in the Massachusetts Women's Amateur that year, qualifying for the match-play rounds with a score of 103. She marched out to a 5-up lead against the first player she faced, only to wilt afterwards and be knocked out by 4 and 3. That hurt, but it was nothing compared to the beating that followed in the Griswold Cup, an annual event held at Shennecossett. Matched against Barlow, the Eastern Amateur champion, Collett halved only one hole, and that by laying a dead stymie. She was humiliated 9 and 8. 'I felt pretty rotten about it and remember walking back to the clubhouse from the tenth green fighting back the tears,' Collett wrote. 'My aspirations to become a real golfer were certainly blasted that day.'

By the autumn of 1919, when Collett was preparing to try her hand in the upper level of women's golf dominated by the likes of Alexa Stirling, Cecil Leitch and Joyce Wethered, the lessons Glenna had been taking with Alex Smith were just beginning to bear fruit. In the qualifying round of the US Women's Amateur, conducted at Shawnee on Delaware in Pennsylvania, Collett posted a 93, her best score ever. That placed her eighth among the 76 entrants, six strokes behind the two players who tied for the medal, Margaret Gavin and Alexa Stirling, who would go on to win the second of her three successive national championships that year. Collett did not last long in the championship itself, falling in the second round, but she had played well enough for *The American Annual* to single her out, along with Chicago socialite Edith Cummings, as one of the rising stars who made their Amateur debut that year.

The following summer, in 1920, Collett would at last deliver on the promise she had shown since she walloped that first drive down the fairway at Metacomet. In her second Griswold Cup at Shennecossett, she made an 86 in qualifying to share the medal with Nonna Barlow, then fought her way into the final match against Elaine Rosenthal. Facing one of the stars of the wartime exhibitions that had inspired her to pursue golf, Collett harboured no illusions about winning that match, and that may have made the difference. 'I went out with everything to gain and nothing to lose, played my best game, and came home a winner by 1 up,' she remembered. 'Victory was sweet indeed.'

Her confidence boosted, Collett travelled that autumn to Mayfield Club in Cleveland, Ohio, for her second appearance in the US Amateur. Again she made 93 in qualifying, but with women's golf progressing so rapidly it was only good enough for 18th this time. The winner, with a record-setting 82, was Marion Hollins. In the first round of that championship, as luck would have it, Collett was drawn against the same woman she had faced at Shennecossett, Rosenthal. 'By way of proving that my earlier victory had been but a flash in the pan I was beaten this time by 2 and 1,' Collett mused. What Collett remembered most from that tournament was not her loss to Rosenthal, but a tip she received one morning from Stirling, who established her supremacy in American golf that year by winning her third consecutive Amateur title. 'She said that at the top of my swing with the driver, and I presume with all the clubs, the face of my club was pointing upward instead of being perpendicular to the ground,' Collett recalled. 'This had caused most of the unsteadiness and bad direction in my driving and I immediately corrected this fault by keeping my left wrist under the shaft at the top of my swing.'

That was not the only important development that year in Collett's training as a golfer. It was also in 1920 that Alex Smith was hired by Belleair Golf Club in Tampa to serve as its professional during the winter months, when Shennecossett was snowed under. He would remain in that post until 1924. Soon after he was hired, Glenna and her family began spending the first three months of each year at the Belleview Inn, the luxurious 600-room 'White Queen of the Gulf' along the shores of Clearwater Bay. That enabled Collett to continue her training with Smith on the two courses laid out at Belleair by famed architect Donald Ross. Nearly every northern golfer of consequence headed south for the winter, most often to Florida, where tournaments in Tampa, Palm

Beach and Miami helped prepare them for the season's main events, especially the North and South Amateur at Pinehurst.

By 1921, between her lessons from Smith and the experience she had gained in competition, Collett's game was rounding into the kind of form expected of her since she'd been declared 'the coming champion'. That season she won the Rhode Island and Massachusetts amateurs, made it to the semi-final of the Griswold Cup after taking the medal with an 87, and very nearly claimed her first Eastern Amateur, losing to veteran Florence Vanderbeck by a single stroke. That autumn she entered her third Women's Amateur at Hollywood Golf Club in Deal, New Jersey, coming into the event with high hopes despite the reality that Cecil Leitch had come from Britain to compete alongside Alexa Stirling and the ultimate winner, Marion Hollins. Collett started brilliantly, winning the qualifying medal with an excellent score of 85, but her hopes were dashed in the first round by Leitch's sister, Edith, who knocked Glenna out by 3 and 2.

Collett did not have to wait long to redeem herself. The very next week, in the Berthellyn Cup at Philadelphia's Huntingdon Valley Country Club, she found herself matched in the opening round against Cecil Leitch herself. Taking the same approach she had the first time she faced Rosenthal, Collett went into that match with a single goal – to halve as many holes as possible and make Leitch fight for her victory. Leitch won the first hole and Collett was nearly undone emotionally, but having bounced right back with a win at the second, she began to play as if she were in a trance. At 16, she holed a 'treacherous' putt to take a 1-up lead, and on the 18th green Collett found herself staring down a 10-footer to defeat the reigning British champion. 'Taking my stance, measuring the lie, I gently tapped the blade against the ball,' she recalled. 'It moved slowly over the green. Like a creeping terror. The acute agony of that second! Straight and true to the mark, the ball flirted with the lip of the cup and dropped in, giving me the match.' Her spirits soaring after having proved herself against the best the game had to offer, Collett went on to the final of that event, where she defeated Margaret Gavin to claim the title. 'I had gained much needed confidence,' Collett wrote. 'My nerves were steadier, my shots bolder – no opponent held any terror for me now.'

AN AWFUL BURDEN

Defeating the brilliant Cecil Leitch at the peak of her powers may have given Collett all the confidence in the world, but it did nothing to lift the awful burden of expectation. For nearly four years, reporters and friends had hailed her as a national champion in the making, and she entered the 1922 golf season believing that 'if I ever intended to win the title, I had to do it that year.' Collett wrote: 'My newspaper reputation had outdistanced my natural development until the disparity between the two disturbed my peace of mind.' Besides that, there was her father, 'secretly hiding his disappointment in my failure to win the year before at Deal'.

More motivated than ever, Collett played like a woman possessed from the moment she set foot in her winter haven at Belleair Golf Club. In March, playing for the Augusta Trophy, she torched the Tampa club's No. 2 course with scores of 82 and 76 and won going away. That 76 caught the eye of Grantland Rice, the nation's most famous sportswriter, moving him to note in *The American Golfer* that with this new crop of women players, scores in middle-to-low 70s were no longer simply the province of men – not when he watched Collett reach par fours longer than 400 yards with a drive and an iron.

If there was any doubt that Collett was a woman on a mission, it was dispelled in April at Pinehurst, where she warmed up for the North and South Amateur by going around the resort's No. 3 course, then considered its toughest, in a record score of 80. She kept right on playing sensational golf in the match-play rounds, sending her first opponent packing after 13 holes and coming in with an 81, before defeating the formidable Nonna Barlow in the semi-final by 3 and 2. The final pitted Collett against Mary Fownes, daughter of the famed Oakmont founder H.C. Fownes. She had no answer for the kind of golf Collett was playing, falling four down after the first seven holes and succumbing on the 16th green 4 and 2. Dorothy Campbell Hurd, correspondent for *Golf Illustrated*, described Collett's performance as 'some of the best women's golf ever played at Pinehurst', which in those days still had sand greens. The Collett juggernaut continued in June at the Westchester-Biltmore in Rye, New York, where she ran away from the field in the Eastern Amateur by posting scores of 81, 80 and 85 for a record total of 246 and the easiest of victories over Edith Cummings.

By September, when the US Women's Amateur was to be played at The Greenbrier in White Sulphur Springs, West Virginia, Collett had emerged as the heavy favourite to claim her first national championship. Players loved competing at The Greenbrier – and not simply because they merely had to stroll to the first tee from the comfort of the luxurious resort hotel beside the links. Set in a valley of the Allegheny Mountains, the picturesque course of 6,200 yards presented a sound test of golf, with the principal hazard represented by a stream that meanders through the property and must be crossed at half a dozen holes along the way. The course was made all the more difficult that year because West Virginia was experiencing a severe drought, making it devilishly difficult to stop approach shots on greens baked dry by the sun.

While Collett could not have been in sharper form, she was nevertheless intimidated as she surveyed the field – defending champion Marion Hollins; three-time winner Alexa Stirling; Chicago star Edith Cummings; the redoubtable Margaret Gavin, and 'giant killer' F.C. Letts, who had knocked out Cecil Leitch in 1921. 'How could I play through this worthy group of golfers and win?' she wondered. 'It was going to be mighty hard work.'

Collett's anxieties were put to rest two days before the tournament began when she went around The Greenbrier with a spectacular score of 75, the lowest she had ever made. The night before she put up that score, Collett had dined on lamb chops, creamed potatoes and string beans. Being as superstitious as any golfer, she decided to eat that same meal every night of the event and to wear the same outfit she'd had on for that magical round.

For the qualifying round, she was paired with Hollins, whose powerful swing had been an inspiration to Collett. The two of them put on a brilliant display for the fans, Glenna coming in with 81 to claim the medal and Marion following close behind at 83. From there, it was nothing but a victory march for Collett. On her way to the final, she easily swept aside three of her four opponents and was pushed to her limit only by the fierce golf of Cummings, over whom Glenna prevailed 2 up on the 17th green. Dorothy Campbell Hurd expected the 36-hole final against Gavin to be a battle royal, but when the reigning Canadian champion came out for the morning round it was evident to all that she was a tired golfer. Collett went to lunch sitting on a 6-up lead, and Gavin did herself proud to extend the match to 32 holes before succumbing by 5 and 4. 'Of the new champion's game, much has been said in praise during the last year,' Hurd wrote, 'and her game at White Sulphur Springs showed that all the eulogies on her prowess have been thoroughly deserved. She typifies the new hard-hitting school of golf which is so much more inspiring to watch than the kind of player who swept the ball away in a more or less half-hearted manner.'

Collett herself was overwhelmed, not quite ready to believe she had finally achieved her ambition and fulfilled Alex Smith's prophecy that he would make her a champion. For the first time that week, she took her eye off the ball and soaked in the beauty of her surroundings. 'Flushed with the realisation of victory, I took in the magnificent panorama of wooded hills and trees tinted with the flaming colours of dying summer,' she wrote. 'My first national championship! The beauty of White Sulphur Springs on that . . . afternoon is printed indelibly on my memory. It meant something to win that title.'

Collett's ascent to the top of American golf, coming just months after Joyce Wethered's coronation at Prince's, assured that 1922 would be remembered as an epochal year in the women's game. Both Britain and the United States had seen the emergence of stars whose brilliance eclipsed even the trailblazing golf of Cecil Leitch and Alexa Stirling, the two players who had forged a new pathway for women's golf in the years before the Great War. Wethered, Collett and this new generation of women were hitting the ball farther and farther and posting scores that crept ever closer to those made by the best of men, a trend that would continue over the next few seasons. The women's game had never been more popular, a reality preserved for all time in F. Scott Fitzgerald's *The Great Gatsby*, which is set in the year Collett won her first Amateur. A searing examination of life in America's Roaring Twenties, the novel's principal characters include a top-flight amateur golfer named Jordan Baker. Fitzgerald modelled that character, at least physically, after Collett's great rival Edith Cummings, the dazzling Chicago socialite who in August 1924 would become the first woman athlete featured on the cover of *Time* magazine.

Fitzgerald had come to know Cummings while growing up in Chicago. In 1914, she joined Ginevra King, Courtney Letts and Margaret Carry in declaring themselves the Big Four, the richest and most beautiful debutantes coming out that season in the Midwest. Cummings and Fitzgerald met because the novelist had fallen in love with her friend, King, who also served as the model for a character in his book. She was the inspiration for Daisy Buchanan, the woman with whom Jay Gatsby was so utterly obsessed.

Even Issette Pearson would never have dreamed that less than three decades after she founded the Ladies' Golf Union, the women's game could have become so deeply ingrained in a culture still mostly dominated by men. The best, however, was yet to come. Over the next two years, as Collett and Wethered proved themselves to be the greatest women golfers the game had ever known, the sporting world would become as obsessed by the prospect of a clash between them as Gatsby was with the green light flashing from the end of Daisy's dock.

Eight

INHUMANLY GOOD

EVEN before she dethroned Cecil Leitch at Sandwich, Joyce Wethered was aware that there was a big difference between gunning for the reigning champion and defending the title. 'I had not yet experienced the rather precarious position of standing up to be shot at,' she mused. 'I was still in the position of doing the shooting, and of the two alternatives it is the better fun, I think.' Wethered's first opportunity to stand up and take fire arrived in the spring of 1923 at Burnham in Somerset, where she entered the British Ladies' Championship for the first time as its defending champion. 'That Miss Wethered would inevitably win was the natural expectation,' wrote Eleanor Helme. 'Though we rather feared some of the visitors from overseas, particularly Miss Edith Cummings of the U.S.A., Miss Wethered at least was supposedly immune from all attacks.'

Cummings, it turned out, was not immune, falling early to the reigning British Girls' Champion. Wethered, however, did exactly what was expected of her, methodically brushing aside one opponent after another. She never fell behind in a match and only once had to play beyond the 13th hole to send her opponent packing.

The first sign of trouble for Wethered came in her semi-final match against Muriel Dodd, who had claimed both the British and Canadian amateurs in 1913. During the war, she had married Lt Allan Macbeth, but was still known by friends simply as 'Doddie'. Wethered badly botched the opening hole against Dodd, 'losing in the sort of figure that you only mention to your neighbour in strict private' as Helme put it. After that, Joyce was not her usual invincible self. When the two players arrived at Burnham's 17th, a blind par three played over a massive dune, Dodd was 1 up with just two holes left. Everyone present expected her to wilt, but she took her spoon and hit a brilliant shot that stopped a yard from the cup. Wethered's answer went long, rolling just off the back of the green. Wethered calmly made her par, but when Dodd drained that putt for 2, the unconquerable champion had, indeed, been shot down. Dodd's caddy knew it was a moment to be savoured. 'There was something very triumphant in the way he clanged the bell which told the couple behind that the green was clear,' Helme wrote.

Exhausted by that match, Dodd went on the next morning to lose the 36-hole final to another star of pre-war days, Doris Chambers, who had played in her first Ladies' Championship at Burnham in 1906. It was fitting that a star from yesteryear would win that championship, given that it was the last ever covered by Mabel Stringer. At the end of that season, aged 55, she retired from her job as a women's golf correspondent and beloved 'Auntie' to scores of promising young players.

Disappointed as Wethered must have been by her defeat, she at least had the consolation of being free to witness her brother's finest hour – his only victory in the Amateur Championship. Although she and her parents were on the other side of the country, they decided without hesitation to do whatever it took to get to Deal by morning for the championship final. 'After dinner we set off in the car,' Wethered remembered. 'It was a glorious moonlit night and we wasted little time in covering the two hundred odd miles to London. In the intervals of dozing and falling asleep after a week of strenuous golf it all seemed tremendously exciting, speeding through the night . . . with little time to spare and many thrilling events awaiting us.' The Wethereds reached their London hotel at 5 a.m., snatched two hours of sleep, caught the 8 a.m. train to Dover, hired a car and motored to Deal, arriving just as Roger was hitting his approach to the 13th green in the morning round of his 36-hole final. 'Standing near the green we saw the crowd surging towards us and a shot out of the blue fell with a thump at our feet, fortunately missing us by a matter of inches,' Joyce recalled. 'Roger's rather unexpected form of greeting.'

Roger rewarded his family's dedication by going on to win that Amateur over Robert Harris, with a score of 7 and 6, made 'under conditions of sleet, hail, wind and rain storms that beggared description – probably the finest exhibition of golf he has ever given,' as his sister remembered it. Glorious as that accomplishment was, it would soon be Roger's turn to be known as Joyce's brother, so overpowering was the golf she played over the rest of that season and the next. The run began with the English Amateur that autumn at Ganton in Scarborough.

Wethered had a special place in her heart for the English championship. It had 'proved a staunch ally of mine in moments when the prospects may have looked a little gloomy,' she wrote. After Leitch humbled her at Turnberry in 1921, Wethered had come back to win her second consecutive English title at Royal Lytham and St Annes, annihilating her opponent in the final by 13 and 11. The following year at Hunstanton, Wethered made it three victories in succession – that sacred number – although not without surviving a nail-biter in the semi-final against Molly Gourlay. She took Wethered to the 19th hole before yielding.

There would be far less stress at Ganton. Wethered's first two matches that week would extend to the 17th, but after that she never had to play more than 14 holes on her way to the final. That match ended early, too, as a merciless Wethered won by 8 and 7.

With that victory, Wethered reached a milestone. Only one player in history had ever won a championship four times in succession, and that was the immortal Young Tom Morris, who had four Open Championships to his credit by the time he came of age.

The extent to which Wethered had separated herself from every other woman would become vividly clear in the 1924 British Ladies' Championship at Portrush, where Cecil Leitch would return after a two-year absence to allow her injured arm to heal. Leitch had begun her comeback earlier that season in county matches, losing to Wethered in one of them, but despite that defeat, 'Controversy raged perpetually round the question of which of these two was the more inhumanly good player,' wrote Eleanor Helme. That debate was settled at Portrush, a stern test of golf that Wethered thought the Ladies' Golf Union had neutered in its zeal to set tees as far back as possible. Even long hitters like her could not reach par fours in two, leaving far too many holes to be halved in ho-hum fives.

Wethered and Leitch met there in a quarter-final match, a tense affair in which no blood was drawn for the first seven holes. Twice during that stretch, however, Leitch missed easy putts to win, and Wethered considered herself lucky not to be 2 down. 'The strain became more and more intense,' Wethered remembered. 'By the time we reached the eighth hole I fancy we both had the feeling that whoever took the lead for the first time would prove to be the winner in the end.' That, in fact, is what happened. 'I won the eighth and ninth,' Wethered wrote, 'and then Cecil's game went to pieces and the match finished 6 and 4.' Leitch did not win a single hole. Amid all that excitement, Helme was enjoying one of the finest moments of her golf career. She earned her first and only bronze medal by making it into the semi-final against her friend and Surrey teammate, Wethered. Helme was, of course, no match for Joyce, going down meekly by 4 and 3. 'To be the opponent of the great one on these occasions may make you feel that you are merely a doormat on which she is giving a feet-wiping exhibition,' she mused, 'but the main thing is to enjoy being a doormat, and the crowd is always very kind to the underdog.'

Having dispatched her 'great friend', Wethered went on to another take-no-prisoners performance in the final, winning by 7 and 6 on an afternoon of torrential rain. The English Amateur that October at Cooden Beach offered Leitch another chance to prove she was still a match for Wethered. In a practice round, Cecil demonstrated how sharp she was by going around the rain-soaked, 6,300-yard course in the astonishingly low score of 71. Writing for *Golf Illustrated*, Dorothy Campbell Hurd noted that Leitch's swing was more rhythmic than it had been when she toured the US in 1921, and that she had eliminated the awkward duck of the right knee that had always been characteristic of her follow-through.

The two champions met in the quarter-final, playing before a crowd so massive that 'it seemed as if all of Sussex had turned out to see the battle between Miss Wethered and her greatest golfing rival.' As the match unfolded, Hurd noticed two things. Leitch's tee shots 'gave the impression that she was hitting tremendously hard, and in the match she outdrove Miss Wethered over and over,' Hurd wrote. 'To the onlooker, however, Leitch gave the idea that she was conscious all the time of the disheartening reality that she had lost to Miss Wethered in their . . . previous matches.' By the time they reached the turn, Leitch was 1 down, and the match ended on 15, with Wethered prevailing 4 and 3, again largely because Leitch missed so many putts she might have holed. Wethered went on to the easiest of victories in that English Amateur Championship, strolling home in the final by 8 and 7. In seven matches, only Leitch had taken her beyond the 13th, a dominance rarely seen in golf, men's or women's. In that moment at Cooden Beach, Wethered stood alone in the long history of the game as the only player ever to have won a championship five consecutive times. 'This is a record unapproachable in either men's or ladies' golf and may very well stand for all time,' Hurd wrote. 'Miss Wethered has stamped herself as the world's greatest lady golfer of this or any age.'

AMERICAN IDOL

Glenna's Collett's first experience as America's reigning champion would be eerily similar to Wethered's. In October 1923, she arrived at the Westchester-Biltmore Country Club in Rye, New York, as the heavy favourite to repeat as winner of the US Women's Amateur Championship. That was hardly surprising, given the impressive victories she had racked up during the season. Collett started the year in ragged form, losing two of the three tournaments she played on the Florida circuit, but she utterly dominated the heart of the season – winning three of the four major events, each time putting on a dazzling show for the fans. In the North and South Amateur at Pinehurst, Collett concluded the winter season with a commanding victory over one of her generation's finest, Marion Hollins, by 5 and 4. In the Eastern at Whitemarsh, she ran away from Alexa Stirling by six strokes, having defied predictions that no woman could possibly break 80 on that beastly Philadelphia course by opening with a 78. In the Canadian Amateur at Mount Bruno, she won the qualifying medal with an 80 and again defeated Stirling on her way to a 2 and 1 victory in the final over defending champion Margaret Gavin.

Collett's only significant defeat that year came at Buffalo Country Club, whose invitational tournament was considered second only to the Amateur itself. Collett made her way to the final there, too, only to succumb to her Chicago rival, Edith Cummings, on the 17th green. *Golf Illustrated* correspondent Dorothy Campbell Hurd had seen enough to be convinced. Collett was so sharp, she wrote, that it appeared 'nothing could prevent her from adding the National Championship to the long list of victories she has gained this year.' Glenna herself was not so certain. Surveying the field arrayed against her, doughty veterans and rising stars, she compared herself to 'a fox thinking up new methods of outwitting the hounds as she scurries over the field with the snarling pack in pursuit'.

It turned out, just as it had for Wethered, that a wise old fox would be Collett's undoing. In the third round at Westchester, Collett was pitted against veteran Florence Vanderbeck, who had won the Amateur in 1915, before the US was dragged into the war and Stirling had begun her run of three consecutive national titles. Perhaps a bit fatigued from the long season, Collett simply could not find her form that morning, completing the opening nine in a disastrous 47. Vanderbeck, meanwhile, played what Hurd described as a 'series of delightfully finished golf shots', dashing the reigning champion's hopes of repeating on the 17th green, by 2 and 1. With Collett out of the picture, Cummings went on to win her first and only Women's Amateur that year, defeating Stirling in the final by the comfortable margin of 3 and 2.

The title of champion had never rested lightly on the shoulders of 20-year-old Glenna Collett. She felt pressure to play the brilliant golf expected of her – to live up to 'Old Man Reputation,' as she put it – and, being shy by nature, she struggled with the demands of celebrity. 'You are compelled to do many things you don't give two hoots about,' Collett complained, 'to go to parties when you just long to be in bed, to be nice to all sorts of people who ask all sorts of favours.' It was typical of Collett that losing her crown did nothing to dampen her confidence or to diminish her enthusiasm for climbing back into the arena and trying to regain it.

When the season began again in 1924, a reinvigorated Collett would play a brand of golf unlike anything ever seen in the United States, separating herself from the snarling pack in the same way that Joyce Wethered was doing across the Atlantic. From the moment Collett arrived at the Belleview Hotel in January until the US Women's Amateur was conducted in September at Rhode Island Country Club, she did not lose a single match. During the southern season, she won Florida's east coast championship at Palm Beach, a tournament at Mountain Lake and two events at Belleair, among them its west coast championship. In the process, she set a new women's record for the No. 2 course with a 75. Writing for *Golf Illustrated*, Hurd noted that Collett had ditched her old aluminium putter for a new model and was playing with renewed confidence on the greens. Her chipping had also improved so dramatically that it now reminded Hurd of Bobby Jones.

Collett had always been one of the game's most powerful ball strikers, but as the new season began, Hurd said, the Providence star was playing better than ever from tee to green. 'The length of her drives and brassie shots is absolutely phenomenal,' Hurd marvelled, 'with the result that the majority of men with whom she plays are left far in the rear.' Power and finesse is a tough combination to beat, and no one could keep pace with Collett in either the North and South at Pinehurst in April or the Eastern Amateur two months later in Boston. She won both for the third consecutive season, reaching golf's long-standing threshold of greatness twice in a span of months. That included firing a scorching 76 in her first round of the Eastern at notoriously difficult Brae Burn Country Club, only four strokes higher than the men's course record. 'Her game was a beautiful exhibition of almost mechanical accuracy that owed nothing to luck, for the longest putt she holed was not over eight feet,' wrote Hurd, noting that Collett went on to outdistance the field in Boston by a whopping 14 strokes.

The victory train rolled on through the Buffalo Invitational in July, where Collett won the qualifying medal with a sparkling 80, cruised into the final, and absolutely destroyed the formidable Cummings, sweeping the Chicago socialite aside by 6 and 5. By

September, when she arrived at Rhode Island Country Club for the Women's Amateur, everyone in golf considered it a foregone conclusion that Collett would regain the title of champion. She only redoubled those expectations by winning the medal with a 79, becoming the first woman ever to break 80 in a qualifying round.

What followed may be the most freakish upset in the history of golf. Having made her way into the semi-final, Collett found herself pitted against a childhood idol, tennis star Mary K. Browne. 'When I aspired to be a tennis player, Mary K. Browne meant as much to me as Babe Ruth to the kids on the lots, Bobby Jones to young golfers,' she wrote. 'The California girl, by her superb work on the tennis courts, inspired in me almost fanatical admiration.' Browne was not nearly as gifted at golf, and there was no earthly reason for Collett to fear her. Nevertheless, Glenna remained star-struck. 'Psychologists might describe my nervous apprehension as an inferiority complex,' she joked. 'And they might be right!'

When they arrived at the 18th tee of that semi-final, Collett was 1 up and ought to have put the match away right there. She had driven straight down the fairway and found the green with an iron, as Browne sliced her approach into the rough behind an apple tree. 'Mary was in a trying situation,' Collett wrote. 'After putting up a spirited fight, the California girl was in the tightest hole of the match. She faced a situation that would have tried the soul of a Bobby Jones or Walter Hagen with the same indomitable spirit and courage that marked her tennis game.' Taking a brassie, Browne slashed a shot out of the hay that hit a branch of the tree and bounced on to the green. Collett was so rattled that she failed to get the half and gave the tennis star another chance to win on the 19th. Feeling the pressure of that moment, both players dumped their approach shots into a greenside bunker. Collett played out first, going just over the back of the green, while Browne's escape stopped on the putting surface some seven yards short of the hole. Collett's putt for a four stopped three inches shy of the cup, and then came the moment of truth. Browne stood over her ball, showing no sign of nervousness, and sent it rolling towards the hole. 'On came her ball,' Collett remembered. 'It was going over – wide of the mark – then hit my ball, caromed off the side, and very slowly dropped into the cup! Mary K. Browne won the match.'

Reporters were shell-shocked. 'Never has the game of golf known a more sensational end to a match,' declared the Associated Press. If fate was unkind to Collett, it handed a gift to that most deserving of golfers, Dorothy Campbell Hurd, who went on to defeat Browne in the final by 3 and 2 and win her first national title in 14 years at the age of 41. She remains, even today, the oldest woman to have won the title.

Collett salved her wounds the following month by winning the Canadian Amateur, her second in succession, and finished the 1924 season with a record that will likely never be approached – 59-1. 'When my drives are no longer straight down the fairway, and I am repeatedly shunted to the gallery by flaming spirits on their way to the heights, I can recall the stirring events that enlivened the year of 1924 – and grin,' wrote a delighted Collett.

BEATING THE DRUM

For several years, as Collett and Wethered played what Eleanor Helme was fond of describing as golf beyond mere mortals, the press had been beating the drum for a match between them. Immediately after Wethered won her second consecutive English Amateur in 1921, *Golf Illustrated* published a prominent feature on her, just as it had on Cecil Leitch when she first claimed the British title. The full-page photo spread featured half a dozen images highlighting the way Wethered played her shots – drives, irons and approaches with the mashie. The caption read, simply,

'The style of Miss Joyce Wethered is considered by many critics to be perfect.' It was as if the magazine was letting its readers, and champions like Collett, know that here was the mark for American women to surpass. *Golf Illustrated* also abounded with rumours that Joyce and Glenna were about to come face to face.

At various points in 1923, the magazine reported that Wethered would come to compete in the 1924 US Women's Amateur, and that Collett would play in the British Ladies' that year at Portrush. It also primed the pump with that famous, full-page *Empresses of Golf* spread – the one featuring glamour shots of Wethered and Collett and a caption touting the delicious prospect of a meeting between the two overpowering stars of women's golf. Even before that was published in August 1924, when it had become obvious that Wethered would be staying in Surrey and Collett in Providence, Hurd bemoaned what she saw as a missed opportunity for the women's game. 'More than ever does it seem a pity that the Providence player and Miss Joyce Wethered will not have an opportunity of meeting this season,' the veteran columnist wrote. 'There is no doubt that a contest between these two leviathan hitters would arouse a hundred times more interest than any previous match between women players.'

Nine

LEVIATHANS AT TROON

IT WAS in the natural order of things that American golfers, from Glenna Collett to Walter Hagen, were fixated on dethroning the nation that had introduced them to the game. That had been true for the English before them. From the moment in 1890 when John Ball Jr. became the first Englishman to win the Open Championship, golfers south of the Scottish border became obsessed with vanquishing their northern neighbours. The years leading up to the Great War developed into a running battle between the English and the Scots for supremacy at golf. Now, in those early post-war years, America sought to stake its claim as the greatest of golfing nations.

The men, at least, were off to a rousing start. Jock Hutchison, a newly minted US citizen, had carried the Claret Jug home in 1921, a win coloured by the reality that he had been born on North Street in St Andrews and won over a course he'd played all his life. Hagen, however, delivered an unqualified American victory the following year at Royal St George's, nearly repeated in 1923 at Troon, and won again at Hoylake in 1924. America's women had yet to taste success, despite having sent overseas such luminaries as Margaret Curtis, Alexa Stirling and Marion Hollins, all winners of the US Women's Amateur. That did nothing to diminish *Golf Illustrated*'s appetite for a clash with Britain's best, especially now that Collett had risen into the stratosphere to stand alone beside Wethered.

In the early months of 1925, Collett gave the magazine and American golf fans their wish. She cut short her annual visit to Belleair to prepare for her first attempt at the British Ladies' Championship, which would be contested that May at Troon, in western Scotland. *Golf Illustrated* celebrated the news by offering fervent prayers that the luck of the draw would bring Wethered and Collett together – never a certainty – and by speculating on how that match of all matches might unfold. 'If anything, Miss Collett is a trifle longer with the wooden clubs, Miss Wethered a trifle more the master of her irons, and a little more invincibly steady,' wrote Hurd. The British press, ever fearful of the 'American Menace', considered Collett the biggest threat their women had yet faced, more frightening even than Stirling, a three-time Women's Amateur champion. Collett had, after all, beaten the great Cecil Leitch during her 1921 North American tour, when she was at the height of her powers.

As it happened, the luck of the draw did bring Wethered and Collett together, but not in the way the golf world would have preferred, in opposite halves of the bracket, with a championship riding on the outcome. Instead they met in the third round, only the second match for Collett. She received a bye in the first and soundly defeated the Welsh champion in her opening match. Wethered had played in both rounds, winning easily, including a 6 and 5 thrashing of her one-time conqueror, Muriel Dodd.

The course over which Collett and Wethered competed certainly provided a test fit for leviathan hitters. It had recently been toughened by James Braid, who added dozens of bunkers and redesigned the eighth hole to create the devilish par three known as the Postage Stamp. From the back tee used for the championship, Troon stretched to 6,415 yards. That is nearly as long as Lancaster Country Club played for the 2024 US Women's Open, a century later. Troon featured five holes longer than 400 yards, among them two that were nearly 600. Beyond that, it was subject to fierce winds off the Firth of Clyde. Par for women was set at 79. 'There was the usual gossip about the difficulties of the course,' noted golf correspondent Eleanor Helme, an echo of what she'd heard the previous season at Portrush. 'Nobody was going to get fours: the steady player who went out for nothing and was content with fives would win.'

The morning of Collett and Wethered's match dawned calm and grey, the storms that lashed players the previous afternoon having passed. As they faced the starter at 10.20 a.m., Wethered standing a head taller than Collett, the two women appeared relaxed and comfortable in one another's presence. It was not the first time they had met. Taking a cue from Stirling, Collett arrived early so she could acclimatise to British weather, which included buying the colourful Fair Isle sweater she was now wearing, as well as with a pair of sturdy boots that stood up better to the testing conditions. Before arriving at Troon, she and Wethered had competed together as partners in a foursome at Stoke Poges. Naturally shy people who played golf with dignity and reserve, they formed an immediate bond. It was no wonder. They were from the same social class, had chosen the same path in life and had succeeded at a level that separated them from their peers. What's more, both were passionately devoted to the amateur ideal popular in their age – that golf was a game, played for love and not for money, and that as important as sport was in the life of a well-rounded person, it should always be kept in its proper place. Time and personal choices would demonstrate how different they actually were, but Collett and Wethered would remain friends and correspondents for the rest of their lives. It would never become a relationship of intimate closeness, but it was always one of enduring respect.

From the moment the starter gave the signal to play away, it became obvious that their mutual admiration – combined, perhaps, with a healthy dose of fear – inspired the two of them to play as scintillating a brand of golf as any woman had ever produced. Both Wethered and Collett finished the first nine holes under par – an extraordinarily rare feat in women's championship golf, especially on such a difficult course. Collett drew first blood at the 450-yard third, reaching the green in two and rolling in a long putt for three to go 1 up. Wethered rebounded at the 580-yard sixth with a brilliant five, as Collett's first real mistake of the match, a topped drive, left her fighting for a six. Two holes later, at the famed Postage Stamp, Collett poked her nose in front again with a par, as Wethered missed that tiny green and made her first and only bogey of the day. The ninth hole proved to be the turning point. No doubt feeling the pressure of Wethered's flawless display, Glenna topped another drive, making a five to Joyce's four and handing the lead right back to her.

As they made the turn, Wethered stood two under par, Collett just a stroke higher – scores as close to perfection as anything the Ladies' Championship had ever witnessed. Still, Collett knew a player of Wethered's calibre would punish mistakes like the one she had made on nine, and that is precisely what unfolded. Wethered went on one of her patented tears, making birdies on the next three holes to go 3 up with six left to play. Collett would not recover from that assault. When Wethered stuck grimly to par over the next three holes – one fewer than Collett – it was over. Joyce prevailed by 4 and 3. 'After fifteen holes of the best golf I have ever played – I was just one stroke over par at this stage – I was out of the tournament,' exclaimed a stunned and awed Collett. Helme was full of praise for the golf the American played that afternoon. 'Miss Collett stood up very bravely to an absolute hurricane of an attack,' she wrote. *Golf Illustrated* added that Glenna had also 'won the goodwill of all who witnessed her play or had the pleasure of conversation with her.'

Collett had simply come up against an unstoppable force. Wethered played those 15 holes in level fours. Had she finished with three pars, her score for the round would have been 73, six under the women's par. That would have been competitive in the Open Championship played at Troon two years earlier, from the same tees. The winner, Arthur Havers, posted 73 in three of his four rounds, coming in with a 76 on his final trip around the course to nip Hagen by a stroke. 'Who cared a hoot for all that rubbish about fives being good enough,' wrote Helme. 'Fours were hardly good enough.'

Collett was ready to declare Wethered the greatest woman golfer the game had ever known, writing: 'As a stylist, she is as fine as Bobby Jones. She has the unruffled calm of Walter Hagen, the confidence of Gene Sarazen, and the fighting spirit of Jess Sweetser.' Wethered was equally impressed by Collett. 'Glenna presents the most detached of attitudes in playing a match,' she wrote. 'She intrudes her presence to the smallest degree upon her opponents. I would even say that she appears to withdraw herself almost entirely from everything except the game, and her shots alone remind one of the brilliant adversary one is up against.' Neither woman would ever forget that afternoon at Troon. Both wrote extensively about it in their books – Collett's published in 1928, Wethered's in 1934 – describing it as the closest they had ever come to playing perfect golf, or perhaps ever would. The new-found friends could not have known it then – although they surely must have hoped it would be true – but four years later they would meet again for an even more magnificent match, this time at the home of golf.

LEITCH'S LAST STAND

Wethered may have dispensed with the 'American Menace', allowing British golf to breathe a massive sigh of relief, but she still had work to do if she wanted to retain her title. Having faced former champions in two of her first three rounds, she had two others standing between her and another chance to play in the final of the British Ladies' – Doris Chambers and Gladys Ravenscroft. She destroyed both, defeating Chambers by 5 and 3 and Ravenscroft by 6 and 5, going out in 33 strokes against poor Gladys, a mind-boggling six under par in just nine holes. Wethered won her matches with such ease that she made it all the way to the final without ever having to play the last three holes at Troon. With all eyes focused on Collett and Wethered, Cecil Leitch's progress had gone all but unnoticed. She wasn't playing her best golf, narrowly escaping defeat in two matches, but she nevertheless made her way to another championship final against her long-standing rival.

By 1925, Wethered had established such dominance over Leitch, and everyone else, that there was not nearly the excitement about another meeting between them as there had been in previous years. *The Glasgow Herald* described it as 'an oft-fought fight that had become just a little stale'. Wethered was not looking forward to it, either. Truth is, Leitch had never been Wethered's cup of tea, a reality that is evident in reading her memoir and an interview she gave during her golden years. 'To watch any match in which she was engaged was to be conscious of a presence dominating the situation to the exclusion of any other person or consideration,' Wethered wrote of Leitch. 'That is a remarkable feature in anyone, especially when it is combined with the fighting qualities that distinguished her career.'

The boisterous scene that surrounded Leitch and her loyal band of followers was simply too much for Wethered. She much preferred the calm reserve of a golfer like Collett. Wethered did, however, develop a tactic for playing her best amidst all that commotion. 'The reason why I was successful against her was due to the one rule I followed, and without which I should have continually failed, the necessity of realising that any disturbing personality must be shut out of my consciousness and that the game must be played against no particular opponent, but with the sole idea of producing the right figures,' she wrote. Wethered was even more bluntly honest when, aged 83, she gave a rare interview to golf correspondent Lewine Mair. 'People either adored Cecil, or they didn't,' Wethered said, and the inescapable inference is that she fell into the latter category.

By the time they met in the 36-hole final at Troon, Wethered had faced Leitch seven times, winning five of those matches. Their last three encounters in a championship had not been close, with Wethered romping 9 and 7 at Prince's, 6 and 4 at Portrush and 4 and 3 at Cooden Beach. The Cecil Leitch who turned up at Troon, however, was not the same player who had faltered in those three matches. It was the woman who once had *Times* correspondent Bernard Darwin comparing her to Madame Defarge storming the Bastille. Always one to rise to a big moment, Leitch was no doubt inspired by the enormous crowds that swarmed the course for the final, some 10,000 or more, as schools, shipyards and shops closed for the day. 'After every shot it was a struggle to keep one's feet in the rush that followed,' Wethered wrote. 'We never saw a sight of our shots from the moment that the ball left the club. As soon as the click of the shot was heard, the gallery poured forward from every side and the ball had scarcely reached the ground before it was surrounded again.'

From the opening hole, Leitch made it clear that this would be a blood match. She chipped in for a three to win and seize the lead – an ominous sign given how often the first player to land a blow had gone on to win matches between those two. Wethered did not falter, draining a long putt at the fifth to square the match, but Leitch came roaring right back. By the time they reached the turn – Cecil in 38, Joyce in 40 – Leitch had pocketed two more holes. When she added the 10th to go 3 up, Wethered's fans had to be alarmed. The 12th, playing a stout 385 yards, saw Wethered claim her second hole of the morning with another remarkable three, leaving Helme in awe of the scoring she was witnessing. 'Fives good enough forsooth! Fours good enough! In this match, it had to be threes,' she exclaimed. The 14th hole may well have been the turning point of the match. There Wethered drained a 10-footer for a half, an absolutely critical putt at that moment. 'It showed that, down though she was, there was nothing beaten about her,' Helme wrote. By 16, Wethered had squared the match again, and despite Leitch rallying to win the 17th, it remained knotted going to lunch after Joyce holed a long putt from across the green on the morning's final hole.

Leitch came out for the afternoon round intent on proving there was nothing beaten about her, either, and reclaimed the lead at the second hole. Wethered pulled her back with a birdie at the fifth, only to fall behind again with a mistake at the eighth. There, Joyce accidentally stymied herself and lost a hole that ought to have been halved. In that age, in match play, golfers were not allowed to mark their ball on the putting green. If an opponent's ball lay between theirs and the hole – as Cecil's did when Joyce's putt fell short – players were simply stymied. They had to putt around their opponent's ball or loft a shot over it using a niblick, the equivalent of a modern sand wedge. Losing that hole may have forced Wethered's hand at the ninth, where a similar turn of events produced one of the most dramatic moments of the match. Joyce was on the green, with two putts for the half, when Cecil laid her a stymie. Now Joyce faced a choice, play safe for the half or boldly go for the win by lofting her ball over Cecil's and into the cup. 'It was growing late in the day to rest content with the position of 1 down when there was any chance of a win,' Helme observed. 'The risk must be taken. The crowd knew it, yet they held their breath when the niblick came out, and only dared breathe again as the ball dropped.'

Buoyed by that brilliant shot, Wethered took her first lead of the day at the 10th, added the 12th for good measure, and had a chance to put the match away at the 16th, a 560-yard behemoth of a hole. Leitch had already sprayed her third shot into the rough right of the green when Wethered took her iron in hand for the approach, a shot she would execute to perfection nine times out of ten. 'No doubt, I realised the position of the match too acutely, hurried my shot in the anxiety to see the ball on to the green and pulled it into a bunker,' Wethered lamented. 'The hole ended in a half where it might so easily have seen the end of a gruelling contest.' Emboldened, Leitch won the next two holes, taking the 17th with a perfect three and the 18th with a four, after Wethered hit another 'truly deplorable' approach into the deep rough. That brought the match back to all square, stirring the massive crowd to a fever pitch and forcing the two players to return to the first tee for extra holes. 'All that day's hard work, and all those miles we had run, and all those thousands we had pushed had left matters precisely where they had been seven hours earlier,' marvelled Helme.

At the 37th, both players bombed magnificent tee shots straight down the fairway. Leitch played first for the green, an uninspired effort that landed short and left. Wethered then faced a shot nearly identical to the two she had bungled to allow Leitch back into the match.

'I remember how depressed and downhearted I felt when I was faced again at the 37th with the same length iron shot as the two last I had played so disastrously,' Wethered wrote. 'How I loathed the sight of the club! But I could see no alternative.' The champion that she was, Wethered stood tall in that moment and placed her shot just on the front of the green. When Leitch failed to get down in two, leaving her chip seven yards short and missing the putt, Wethered calmly holed out for a 4 and won the championship. She had gone around that afternoon in a pair of 75s, by far the most brilliant performance the Ladies' Championship had ever seen. Leitch may have lost again, but those who watched her play at Troon – and Cecil herself – agreed that it had been her finest hour. 'Everyone felt that it was a great pity that the

Championship could not be halved and the throne shared for the ensuing year,' as Darwin put it.

STEPPING AWAY

Wethered had come to Troon with her mind made up. Win or lose, this would be her last championship. The golfing world was crushed to hear the news, but not surprised. The previous year, Dorothy Campbell Hurd reported in *Golf Illustrated* that Wethered had considered stepping away in May 1924, after winning her second British Ladies' at Portrush. Having already defended her English Amateur title four times, Hurd wrote, Wethered was of a mind to let others take up the battle when the championship was played again that autumn at Cooden Beach. In the end, she was persuaded to compete, and when her fifth victory in succession established a record unlikely to be broken, Wethered was more than ever resolved to step away from the rigours of championship golf. Troon, she decided, would be her final appearance. After all those summers in Dornoch, Wethered never could resist the temptation of competing over a classic Scottish links, a reality that would surface again in just four years.

Walking off the 37th green after that heroic final battle with Leitch, Wethered could not have been happier with her decision. Championship golf took a lot out of her, never more so than that afternoon. 'I can truthfully say that I have never been more exhausted after any game in my life,' Wethered wrote. Even Collett could see the toll tournaments took on her new friend. 'To the onlooker she is phlegmatic, cold – no nerves,' she wrote. 'Yet after a strenuous week of championship golf she is forced to rest and leave golf alone for a fortnight or more. The strain tells on her.' There was more to it than that. For Wethered, golf had always been more about the pursuit of the perfect swing than the thrill of competing. She had never loved being in the arena, and all the tumult that came with it. Championships were simply the venue for demonstrating how close she had come to that mythical ideal of the perfect golfer.

By 1925, Wethered justly felt she had proved to herself – and the golfing world – that she could play the most difficult of games as flawlessly as any player, man or woman, had ever done, and that was enough for her. Stepping aside at the peak of her powers set a precedent that would be followed five years later by another golfer who engaged in that same relentless pursuit of perfection and suffered just as mightily when he played tournament golf to prove it, American superstar Bobby Jones. 'I was only too glad to feel that the following year would not call for further efforts on my part,' wrote a clearly relieved Wethered. 'A less active role has always suited me perfectly.' Wethered's decision to leave the championship stage to others created an opportunity for Leitch to take what the golfing world would have agreed was one final, well-earned bow.

The 1926 British Ladies' Championship, which had to be postponed from May to June because of a rail strike, was conducted at Royal St David's in Wales, better known by its nickname, Harlech. Against a field greatly winnowed by the postponement – 55 of the original 124 starters dropped out – Leitch breezed into the 36-hole final and won it with a grand display of golf, prevailing by 8 and 7 over Marjorie Garon. That victory placed Leitch in a singular position in the history of women's golf as the only player ever to have won the British Ladies' Championship on four occasions. What's more, she had earned a title in each of the nations that comprise the United Kingdom – England in 1914, Ireland in 1920, Scotland in 1921 and now in Wales. With that, Leitch, too, decided that her championship days had come to an end at the age of 35. Fate kindly gave her a send-off befitting the first breakthrough player in women's golf. The final that afternoon coincided with a music festival being conducted at Harlech Castle overlooking the links, allowing Leitch to walk off to the glorious strains of George Frideric Handel.

CONTINENTAL ADVENTURES

Glenna Collett's trip overseas had always been about more than competing in the British Ladies' Championship, even if winning that event had been her driving ambition. Collett was not yet 22 years old, but she had already been at the year-long grind of amateur competition for seven years. She longed for a break, a chance to see more of the world, to take in its sights and its golf. 'I needed this form of diversion to refresh my enthusiasm for tournament golf,' Collett explained. In the run-up to Troon, she had played many of Britain's most famous courses, among them St George's, Lytham and St Annes and Gleneagles, her particular favourite. Collett's plans following the championship had always been to spend three weeks sightseeing on the continent before trying her hand in the French Open.

She and her small party of friends stopped first in Switzerland, where Collett enjoyed a round at Lucerne Golf Club, a nine-hole layout set amid snow-capped mountains. From there, they left their clubs behind and travelled through Italy and Paris on their way to the Amateur at La Boulie in Versailles. During her stay in Versailles, Collett met the young French prodigy, Simone de la Chaume. Just 16 years old, she was a student of the legendary Arnaud Massy, who shocked the world in 1907 by becoming the first golfer from outside Britain to win the Open Championship. The previous season, in 1924, de la Chaume had followed in her teacher's footsteps by becoming, aged 15, the first overseas player to win the British Girls' Championship. Her game made an immediate impression on Collett. 'Slight of build, she affects a rugged, full swing, which gives her remarkable distance off the tees,' Collett wrote. 'Her short game is equal to the best, and added to that she has a charming personality that endears her to any gallery.'

As fate would have it, Collett and de la Chaume met in the final of the 1925 French Open. 'It was a thrilling duel, with

Simone displaying a high degree of intrepidity and skill for the first 18 holes,' Collett wrote. 'We were even, but in the following round she failed to put forward the blazing exhibition of golf that marked her initial game and I won on the 35th green.' Even in defeat, de la Chaume proved, to Collett at least, that she had the game to win championships. That was borne out two years later at County Down, where she matched her teacher Massy's feat by becoming the first woman outside Britain to win the Ladies' Championship.

Before sailing home to America, Collett and her party returned to London, leaving time for a final round with Wethered over her home course at Worplesdon and one with Leitch at Chislehurst. Like everyone else in golf, Collett was disappointed that Wethered had decided to withdraw from championship golf. Glenna remained hopeful, however, that Joyce might be persuaded to tour America, as Rhona Adair had done all those years ago. It would take a decade, and a cataclysm, but Collett would eventually get her wish. Those weeks spent in Britain and on the continent would have a significant impact on Collett's career, and the way she was viewed by the golfing world. Coming home as the reigning champion of France – to go with the titles she had previously won in the US and Canada – cemented her place among the game's greats.

Playing against the world's best golfers also instilled in Collett a passion for international competition. She would never cease her quest to carry home the Ladies' Championship trophy, just as American men were doing with the Claret Jug. She would also become a driving force behind the creation and success of the Curtis Cup, the biannual amateur match between teams from the US and Great Britain and Ireland. Beyond that, the trip had accomplished exactly what Collett hoped it would. She returned to the United States rejuvenated and ready to deliver a brand of golf beyond anything yet witnessed in America. Dorothy Campbell Hurd, veteran correspondent of *Golf Illustrated*, was not sure what to expect when Collett defended her title that August in the Griswold Cup at Shennecossett Country Club. 'No player of championship rank has ever crossed the Atlantic without some change, muscular or mental, in their game,' Hurd noted. 'People are apt to say that Miss Alexa Stirling never quite recovered her nerve because she did not win a championship on the other side, and this fact shook some of the confidence that was an integral part of her splendid game.'

Collett's circumstances were different, of course, and she had every reason to be confident as she demonstrated by winning the Shennecossett tournament for the third year in succession. That earned her permanent possession of the Griswold Trophy, and it seemed fitting that she had done it at the very course where Alex Smith taught her the game. A month later, in the US Women's Amateur at St Louis Country Club, Collett, Stirling and the new generation of American women golfers would stage what *Golf Illustrated* reporter Lucille MacAllister described as 'the greatest championship ever played'.

Designed by Charles Blair Macdonald, the course at St Louis played 6,408 yards for the Women's Amateur, the first held west of the Mississippi River. That was just 100 yards shorter than it had played when the men's championship was conducted there two years earlier. The course included so many long holes that the par for women was set at 81. Beginning with the qualifying round, the scores posted at St Louis were astonishingly low. Stirling set the tone with a 77 to win the medal – the lowest score ever posted in a women's qualifying round – with Collett coming in a stroke behind her at 78. Collett and Stirling wound up in opposite halves of the match-play bracket, setting up the delicious possibility of a meeting between them in the final. Both had a tough road ahead, however. Collett would first have to defeat Canadian champion Ada Mackenzie, Fritzi Stifel and former US Amateur winner Edith Cummings. Stirling's line-up included the giant killer F.C. Letts, Mary K. Browne and Louise Fordyce. The two of them did make their way to the final, although both survived close shaves along the way. Collett barely defeated Mackenzie and Cummings – prevailing over both by a single hole – and Stirling had to go a full 19 holes before shaking off Fordyce. For the first time, the two greatest stars of American women's golf would face one another with the national championship on the line. On the only other occasion when Collett made it to the final, in 1922, Stirling had been knocked out early.

Much had happened in Stirling's life since the last time she wore the crown as America's champion. In 1921, she moved to New York and took a position with S.W. Straus & Co. of Chicago as a bond trader, becoming one of the first women to work on Wall Street. That same year, while competing in the Canadian Amateur at Rivermead Golf Club in Ottawa, Stirling attended a dinner at which she met Dr Wilbert G. Fraser, an ear, nose and throat specialist like her father. Four years later, in 1925, they were married at Stirling's home in East Lake, and took up residence in the Canadian capital.

One other change had also occurred, and it would play a substantial part in the outcome of the 1925 US Women's Amateur. The championship final was now contested over 36 holes, and that proved a challenge for Stirling. Sickly as a child and never a robust woman, she struggled to stay the distance, especially after the grind of a qualifying round and five preliminary matches.

From the moment the two women teed off for their first 18 holes, Collett could tell that Stirling was not herself – despite an extra day's rest provided when their match was postponed from Saturday to Sunday by torrential rain. 'Alexa was obviously tired, although she would not admit it,' Collett wrote, 'and for that reason I was able to win quite easily.' Collett finished the morning round 4 up, and never gave Stirling a chance in the afternoon, polishing her off 9 and 8, a victory as dominant as Wethered's had been at Prince's, with Stirling winning only three of the 28 holes played. 'It was too one-sided to be interesting, and all the attention fell to Miss Collett, who was playing in a fabulous and dazzling fashion,' MacAllister wrote for *Golf Illustrated*. 'She literally crushed her opponent.'

Collett's friends marked the occasion by gifting her a blue Mercer Raceabout, a popular sports car in that era, in which she went zipping around Providence, nearly always with a dog at her side. What most impressed MacAllister was not that Collett won – that much was expected – but the incredibly low scoring throughout the tournament. 'Four years ago, it was miraculous for a woman to score in the seventies,' she wrote. 'In this year's tournament it was an almost daily occurrence.' Collett, in fact, took pains to putt out on every hole and finish her rounds even when the match had concluded, and her two scores against Stirling were 77 and 75. Combined with what Wethered had done at Troon – going around in level fours against Collett and posting two rounds of 75 against Leitch – it was clear that MacAllister was on to something. Glenna Collett and Joyce Wethered had combined to raise the bar in women's golf to a previously unimagined level, and MacAllister was hardly alone in taking notice.

Ten

THE ETERNAL PROBLEM

———•◦●◦•———

THE question Alexander Doleman laid on the table all those years ago – would a woman ever be capable of competing in a men's championship? – became the topic of the moment after 1925, the year Joyce Wethered and Glenna Collett posted all those otherworldly scores. Golf's eternal problem was certainly on Collett's mind in 1927 when she was writing *Ladies in the Rough,* a book that is part autobiography and part instruction, as was the fashion in those days. Her opening chapter is devoted to the subject, and in it she makes a cogent observation: 'It is always the man who asks: "Will the best women players ever be able to compete with the best men?"' Collett herself had concluded that 'women lack the strength to play golf as well as men, and there the matter rests,' although she did allow for the possibility that one day a woman might come along who was strong enough to change that immutable equation.

Reading golf coverage during those post-war years, one cannot help but get the sense that men were nervously looking over their shoulders as women closed in on them. Back in 1922, when America's two most promising women golfers were tearing up

Belleair's courses with 76s and 77s, sportswriter Grantland Rice put it this way: 'The men's golf world was badly jolted early this spring by the scores posted in Florida where Miss Glenna Collett and Edith Cummings were busy giving par the battle of his young life.' Rice went on to add, 'With two or three more years' experience, there is no reason why Glenna Collett shouldn't occasionally wander down among the 72s and 73s. Not often, perhaps, but often enough to make more than a few ambitious males start gnashing their teeth.'

In 1928, writing for the Sunday magazine of the *New York Times*, William D. Richardson sounded a similar theme, predicting that men watching the Women's Amateur that September in Hot Springs, Virginia, would be dumbfounded by the golf they witnessed. What they would see, he said, was women knocking the ball more than 200 yards off the tee, slashing woods or irons on to greens 180 yards away, and casually dropping putts for pars and birdies – all evidence of their remarkable progress in golf. 'So marked has been this progress of late that the question is frequently debated: Will the time ever come when the stars of the two sexes will be on equal footing?' Richardson wrote. 'Perhaps not, but in making that declaration, I do so with reservations.'

Americans were not alone in noticing the gains made by women. Richardson mentions having discussed the issue with George Duncan, a Scotsman who won the 1920 Open Championship and was among Britain's leading thinkers on golf. He believed that if Wethered entered the men's British Amateur she would easily advance to the final 16. Duncan was hardly alone. At Troon in 1925, Eleanor Helme overheard a Scottish spectator arguing that Wethered was too good to compete against other women. 'It's the men's championship she should be playing in, not the women's at all,' he declared. It was not a hypothetical proposition that women were gaining on men. Qualifying scores for the Men's and Women's US Amateur Championships provide a window into what was unfolding. Results from 1895 through 1935 reveal that women's scores were decreasing much faster than men's were during those 40 years. From 1895 through 1904, for example, the average 18-hole qualifying score posted by men fell by slightly more than seven strokes. During those same years, the average score posted by women dropped by more than 16 strokes, meaning that women had gained a full nine strokes, albeit usually over a slightly shorter course than men played.

The pattern holds through each of those four decades. By 1935, women's scores were, on average, 20 strokes lower than they had been 40 years earlier, while scores posted by men had decreased by just 11 strokes. Women were, indeed, gaining on men, and quickly. Dorothy Campbell Hurd attributed women's improvement to four things: wearing clothing appropriate for golf, the fierce swing introduced by Cecil Leitch and Alexa Stirling, the easier-to-hit rubber-cored ball, and the advent of motion pictures that enabled players to analyse their own swings and the swings of their idols. 'Instead of blindly groping in the dark, we can release the reels of pictures of our own swing and check up on exactly how we made shots when we delighted ourselves by lowering our own record score by four strokes,' she wrote, anticipating the modern age of launch monitors.

It is no wonder that the question of how women would fare against men in a championship remained front and centre in those years between the two wars, given how regularly ladies and gentlemen competed with and against one another during that age. On both sides of the Atlantic, and especially in Britain, events pitting men against women were built into the golf schedule. It was a tradition that dated to the earliest days of women's golf. In her memoir, Mabel Stringer recalls the first men vs women match ever conducted, which took place at Claygate Club in 1898 between a team led by Issette Pearson and one of the men from the golf club. Even then, men worried about their fate. 'It is an open secret in Claygate that the gentlemen are in considerable trepidation as to the result, and we must say that they may be rightly so,' wrote Stringer.

The match was played on level terms because all the women on Pearson's side were first-class golfers, while the club's team included run-of-the-mill players. Men needn't have worried. They won easily, taking both the singles and foursomes sessions. Not long after Cecil Leitch defeated Harold Hilton in their famous 1910 match, an annual springtime event pitting men against women was begun at Stoke Poges, near London. Similar matches were held at places like Beaconsfield, Formby and elsewhere. It was Stoke Poges, however, that attracted the best of Britain, as well as American invaders like Stirling and Collett who were making their overseas debuts. While Stirling lost to cricket star Reymond de Montmorency at Stoke Poges, Collett distinguished herself by defeating former Amateur champion Cyril Tolley in singles and teaming up with Wethered to beat Tolley and S.F. Storey in a foursome.

It took longer for America to develop a similar competition, but from 1924 through 1929, women competed against men in the Gold Ball Tournament hosted by The Country Club of Fairfield in Connecticut. It was an intimate affair – some years featuring four men and women, others six – but it always attracted the cream of America's amateur crop. Men dominated both events, despite giving women strokes, a truth made painfully clear by Eleanor Helme when she reviewed the first dozen years of the Stoke Poges event in her memoir, *After the Ball*. 'This can only be a melancholy chapter,' she began. 'There have been three glorious years in the annual Ladies vs Men match at Stoke Poges when the feminine heart could rejoice over victory and once when honours were easy, but on the whole woman in that match is a failure.' Women received nine strokes at Stoke Poges, and while that usually meant victory for Wethered, even she had been beaten, losing in 1921 to Bernard Darwin. The annual match was not without bright spots, however, among them that women had become stronger over the years, halving in 1927 and winning in 1928 and 1929. Still, Helme was unequivocal: 'No, ladies are not successful against men.' Wethered was inclined to agree. 'However well we may play in championships,' she lamented, 'this one event in May reduces us to the dismal conclusion that as a side we compare more unfavourably than we ought with men.'

The situation was not much different in America's Gold Ball Tournament. Despite receiving strokes, women did not beat men in that event until 1928, when Collett's triumph over Sweetser sealed their first victory and inspired Richardson's article in the *New York Times*. During the 1920s, competitions between men and women were made considerably more engaging by the advent of a new method of handicapping them – the bisque, a way of assigning strokes that infused matches with strategy and excitement. In Britain, women traditionally received nine strokes from men, given at every other hole. The situation was similar in America, although there the gap was considered wider. Golf courses ordinarily set par for women 10 strokes higher than it was for men, a standard Collett believed was in serious need of being revised downward. Handicapping by holes necessarily meant that some strokes counted for nothing in the end, because they had been assigned to holes where the player did not need them to win or halve.

The bisque was deliciously different. It could be used at the conclusion of any hole during the match to change the outcome. A hole lost by a stroke could become a half, while a halved hole could become a victory. That flexibility meant fewer bisques could be given than strokes. Bisques were used at the Gold Ball Tournament, and over the years the number ranged from five to seven. In the 1928 Gold Ball Tournament, women received seven bisques – although Collett needed only five of hers to defeat Sweetser by 3 and 2, paving the way for that first-ever victory by women.

THE ETERNAL PROBLEM

MIXED FOURSOMES

Singles matches may have been the way that women's progress against men was measured, but by far the most popular – and important – format for bringing the sexes together was the mixed foursome. Men and women had been playing alongside one another since 1867, when Tom Morris built the Ladies' Putting Green at St Andrews, and mixed foursomes were perhaps the premier legacy of that tradition. They emerged early on as a staple of club life, a classic example being the mixed foursome Mabel Stringer competed in every Christmas during her days as captain of the Littlestone Ladies Club. On both sides of the Atlantic, exhibitions of mixed foursomes also became a popular way to mark any occasion, from the opening of a new golf course to the celebration of a club's centenary. The format received its highest expression in Britain during the years just after the Great War. In 1921, taking a cue from the mixed doubles at Wimbledon, Worplesdon Golf Club inaugurated a similar event for teams featuring one man and one woman.

The Worplesdon Mixed Foursomes, played every autumn, immediately became one of the signature events of the year, attracting virtually every leading amateur golfer in the kingdom. It became even more important after 1925, when Wethered announced her retirement from championship golf, as it became one of the rare occasions on which fans could see the greatest of women golfers compete. Wethered was in her element at Worplesdon, hobnobbing with amateur golf's social elite, both on and off the links. 'The foursomes have pleasant memories for us, as we lived not very far from the course and always collected amusing house parties for the week,' she wrote. 'I used to find that after the dramatic events of the year they came as a pleasant relief, and now that I have given up championships they have become the stirring events that take their place.'

Wethered's career at Worplesdon, whose tree-lined fairways and 10th hole water hazard made it ideal for foursomes, did not get off to the start she imagined. That first year, she and her brother, Roger, made it to the finals, only to be defeated by Tony Torrance and Eleanor Helme. Helme was scorching hot with the putter that afternoon, contributing mightily to 'the audacity of beating the brother and sister Wethered', as the veteran correspondent put it in recalling her finest hour in the game. The years after that initial defeat, however, would see Wethered assemble a record at Worplesdon that stands as one of the most remarkable accomplishments in the history of golf.

Between 1922 and 1936, Wethered won the event eight times, with seven different men as her partner – her brother Roger, Cyril Tolley (twice), John Morrison, Michael Scott, Raymond Oppenheimer, Bernard Darwin and Thomas Coke. Her performances over those 14 years belied the notion that no woman was strong enough to carry a man to victory. 'It would seem that whoever is destined to be her partner, she is able to steer the side through the shoals to ultimate safety,' wrote *Golf Illustrated*. Before the Second World War, only Molly Gourlay had a record to compare with Wethered's, having won three times at Worplesdon, twice with Major Charles Hezlet and once with Helme's original partner, Torrance.

Even though Wethered had won with her brother, Tolley and Scott – all British Amateur champions – her most talked-about partner, by far, was the golf correspondent of *The Times*. Darwin was a man of volatile temperament, whose tantrums on the course were the stuff of legend. He became a close friend of the Wethered family – they sometimes stayed with him at Aberdovey in Wales – but nevertheless Joyce found it trying to be his partner. 'The bravest thing I ever did was to partner him in the Mixed Foursomes at Worplesdon,' she recalled in an interview. 'When you played a shot, he would stand with his black cap pulled down and his hands half over his eyes. Then, if the shot was less than perfect, there was this dreadful muttering. You could never have put up with it if you hadn't known him well and been so fond of him.'

Mixed foursomes also contributed mightily to the lustre of Glenna Collett. They were a central feature of the annual Gold Ball Tournament in Connecticut, at which players competed for such prizes as a cigarette case or pitcher whose lid was adorned with a gold golf ball. Visiting players stayed in the homes of club members and were treated to lavish parties throughout the week, a combination that attracted the cream of American golf, from Francis Ouimet and Jess Sweetser to Marion Hollins and Edith Cummings. The early portion of the event was devoted to singles matches between men and women – Cummings dominated those with three consecutive wins over Amateur champion Max Marston – but on the final day, teams of one man and one woman competed for the mixed foursomes title.

Played over a testing 6,531-yard course designed by Seth Raynor, the Gold Ball was not conducted at alternate shot, as mixed foursomes were at Worplesdon. Americans preferred better ball, in which each side counted the lowest score of its two players. Collett dominated the event, although unlike Wethered she always played with the same partner, Sweetser. He won the US Amateur Championship in 1922, the same year she ascended to the top of American golf, and four years later secured his place in golf history by becoming the first US-born player to claim the British Amateur. Collett and Sweetser won the mixed foursomes in four of the six years the tournament was played, once posting a better-ball score of 70 on a course with the women's par set at 83.

Even still, Collett wasn't sure how valuable such competitions were when played over such a long and difficult course. 'If mixed matches are to have any real value, they should be played in conditions that recognise the fundamental fact that a woman cannot hit the ball as far as a man,' she said. The Gold Ball Tournament, however, was hardly the only place where Collett had an opportunity to shine in mixed foursomes. Whenever women and men gathered for a golf event, a match between them was likely to be part of the fare. That was the case in 1923, at the Westchester-Biltmore Country Club in Rye, New York, where a foursome match was arranged pitting America's best men and women against one another – Collett and Alexa Stirling vs Walter Hagen and Gene Sarazen. It was clearly a match that meant something to Collett as she devoted considerable space to it in *Ladies in the Rough,* taking pains to save the scorecard and analyse the results as the match was intended to be played. 'The men had agreed to play us a better-ball foursome and give us six bisques, and, I am confident, they expected to give us a beating,' Collett recalled. 'I am not sure just what came up to interfere with the program, but as the match was finally played, Sarazen and I played a foursome against Miss Stirling and Hagen.'

Collett never bothers with the result of that contest. Rather, she devotes all of her time to regaling readers with the tale of what would have unfolded had the match been conducted as the men vs women better-ball contest originally envisioned. The raw scores for the round were 88 for Stirling, 84 for Collett and 79 for both Hagen and Sarazen. Combining the figures, Collett shows that the women's better-ball score would have been 78, while the men's would have been 69 – a difference of nine strokes. In painstaking detail, she goes on to show, bisque by bisque, how she and Stirling would have won the match 2 and 1 on the 17th hole had they received the six bisques they were originally offered. There is something gleeful in the way Collett recounts the match. It is clear that she considers it the ideal test case – it is hard, in fact, to conceive of a better one – and that the result definitively answered the age-old question about the gap that separated men and women. How far were the best women golfers from the stars of the men's game? They were precisely six bisques away.

TRAILBLAZERS

Golf's ongoing conversation about men and women had never been solely about performance on the field. Since the days when Lottie Dod was winning tennis and golf championships and scaling the world's tallest mountains, sports had merely been another stage for demonstrating that there was no limit to what women might accomplish. That was never more evident than during those years between the wars, when two of the age's most prominent women golfers – Marion Hollins in the US and Molly Gourlay in Britain – broke through the glass ceiling in ways that would have been inconceivable in 1893 when Issette Pearson founded the Ladies' Golf Union.

Hollins may have won the US Women's Amateur, dethroning three-time champion Alexa Stirling in 1921, but it was her extraordinary accomplishments as a real-estate developer, oil prospector and golf architect that made her the most important figure in the women's game during the 1920s and 1930s, and perhaps of any other age. Born in December 1892, she was the daughter of Harry Hollins, a Wall Street broker to America's wealthiest men, among them robber barons like William K. Vanderbilt. She and her four brothers were raised on Meadow Farm, a lavish 600-acre estate in East Islip, Long Island. Marion grew up with horses, and at the age of nine famously drove a coach and four down the Champs-Élysées in Paris, a daring act that required strength beyond what most children could muster, as well as considerable dexterity in handling the horses. That was the way Hollins would lead her entire life – taking the reins and forging boldly ahead, shocking friends with her audacity but ultimately winning them over with her charm. Early on she demonstrated that she would be a star in many fields. Her exploits included appearing as one of the leads in a silent film titled *The Flame of Kapur*, riding in the National Horse Show at Madison Square Garden, becoming the first woman to drive in an automobile race, and earning a reputation as the best female polo player in America.

Golf was part of Hollins's life from an early age, too. Her father, Harry, was a member of several local clubs, among them St Andrews in Yonkers and Westbrook Golf Club, and at the age of five she began to take lessons from Arthur Griffiths, a pro her father had recruited to New York from Royal St George's on the south-east coast of England. Despite her many successes on the golf course, Hollins chafed at the way the game was dominated by men, especially the way all courses were built with only their game in mind, making it impossible for all but the strongest of women to play par golf.

In 1922, she set out to change that, organising a group of investors to form the Women's National Golf and Tennis Club, which would be built on Glen Head, Long Island, and run exclusively by and for women, with men allowed on the links only as accompanied guests. Hollins hired Devereux Emmet and Seth Raynor to design a course that would test the best of women, but not be impossibly difficult for more average players. Taking a page from architect Charles Blair Macdonald, she travelled to Europe to scout great holes that might be replicated during the construction of her new links. The club opened to great success and thrived until 1941, when the lingering effects of the Great Depression forced it to merge with the all-male Creek Club next door. Months afterwards, in an act of treachery, the Creek Club sold Hollins's course to pay off its debts.

It was in California, however, that Hollins made her most significant mark in golf and business. In 1922, having moved west to treat an illness, she was hired by S.F.B. Morse to sell real estate and serve as Athletic Director for his newly created Pebble Beach Golf Links. Hollins promoted the course by starting a golf tournament, which she would win herself eight times. In 1928, again working with Morse, Hollins was the driving force behind the creation of Cypress Point, the Sistine Chapel of American golf. She hired Alister MacKenzie to design the course, and worked beside him every step of the way, including making the fateful decision to build the iconic 16th hole as a par three across the Pacific Ocean.

That same year, a company Hollins formed to drill for oil in California's San Joaquin Valley struck one of America's richest deposits, netting her $2.5 million, a princely sum in that age. That put her in the position to add the final feather to her cap, the creation of Pasatiempo. Built on 570 acres in Santa Cruz, Pasatiempo was envisioned as the greatest sports and residential complex in America – featuring another golf course designed by MacKenzie, facilities for tennis, horse racing, polo and bathing, and a community that include homes, a hotel, schools and shopping. It opened to great fanfare in September 1929 as a crowd of 3,000 assembled to watch an exhibition match pitting Hollins and Bobby Jones against Collett and former British Amateur champion Cyril Tolley.

For years afterwards, Hollins used her oil largesse to entertain lavishly at Pasatiempo, seemingly able to bring the world to her door – Hollywood stars like Mary Pickford and Spencer Tracy, business tycoons like Harry Payne Whitney and Alfred Gwynne Vanderbilt, and sports stars like Babe Didrikson and Joyce Wethered. There was no livelier scene in American golf. In the first serious history of the game in the States, H.B. Martin summed up Hollins's brilliant career in a single sentence: 'No woman golfer has done more for the game of golf in America than Miss Marion Hollins.'

JOINING THE CLUB

Like Hollins, Molly Gourlay made her mark by penetrating that most exclusive of male clubs – the world of golf architecture, an art that even today, a century later, is practised almost solely by men. The decades after the turn of the century, a period now known as The Golden Age of Golf Course Architecture, were a time of fresh thinking about the way golf courses ought to be designed. In the game's formative years, the men who laid out golf courses focused on punishing the wayward, arranging hazards to snare shots that were sliced, pulled or topped. The result was often a dull brand of golf on courses that looked as if they had been imposed on the landscape.

The new generation of golf architects operated on two lessons evident to anyone who has thought deeply about the great links of Scotland, the Old Course at St Andrews in particular. Hazards should be placed not to punish, but to dictate the strategy for playing a hole, and a course ought to look entirely natural, as if it had existed since time immemorial. These ideas came to fascinate Gourlay, no doubt because she was such an accomplished golfer herself. Born in May 1898 in Hampshire, Mary Perceval 'Molly' Gourlay was the eldest daughter of the wealthy Dundee ship-builder Henry Gourlay and his wife, Mary Henrietta. While she was not destined to win the Blue Riband of women's golf – the British Ladies' Championship – Gourlay's pre-eminent ball striking would see her claim the French and Swedish amateurs three times each and the Belgian title twice.

She was also the quintessential Surrey golfer, winning the English Amateur on two occasions, the county championship seven times, and playing for England in the home international matches from 1923 through 1934. So much of her life was devoted to Surrey Golf – including succeeding Eleanor Helme as president of its Ladies' Golf Association – that an award for outstanding achievement is now given annually in her honour.

It was her fascination with the new ideas emerging in golf architecture, however, that would separate Gourlay from the crowd. By 1935, articles she had written on the topic caught the attention of one of the leading figures of that new age of design, Tom Simpson. Impressed by Gourlay's intelligence and her gifts for public speaking and writing – not to mention that she was an enthusiastic supporter of his ideas about design – Simpson took her on first as a pupil and then, in 1936, published an announcement that would have raised more than a few eyebrows in the patriarchal world of golf. Gourlay had been named a director of Simpson & Co., becoming Britain's first female golf architect, contributing her own ideas to projects and serving as a sounding board for Simpson's. The two of them celebrated the partnership that July by playing together in the Ashridge mixed foursomes.

Simpson was nearing 60 when he brought Gourlay into the firm, and during their years together, much of their work was done in Ireland. Images from the era show the two of them together at construction sites – Simpson wearing a suit and tie, Gourlay a cardigan, a skirt and a beret – deep in discussion about the shape of a green or placement of a hazard. Between 1936 and the outbreak of World War II, Gourlay and Simpson did design work or renovations at Ballybunion, Kilkenny and County Louth in Ireland, as well as at Golf du Sart Tilman in Belgium and the Schloss Mittersill sports and shooting club in Austria. Gourlay also wrote frequently on the emerging new theories of golf architecture – sometimes sketching holes to illustrate her point – including a series of articles on the design of one-, two- and three-shot holes that appeared in *Golf Illustrated* in 1938 and 1939.

In those pieces, she elucidated as well as anyone the key theories of that age – among them that a brilliantly designed golf course will challenge scratch players to the utmost, while not unduly torturing less skilled golfers, as old-style Victorian courses tended to do. Still, she lamented that so many golfers failed to take the safe pathway to the hole. 'I suppose it is all in the vanity of human nature that leads so many long-handicap players into needless trouble, simply in attempting heroics that are not meant for them,' Gourlay wrote. 'If they would content themselves with playing to their own standard, rather than slavishly following the plan of attack only intended for the scratch golfer, how much happier would they be, and how many fewer grumbles would we hear of courses being only fit for tigers.'

The outbreak of war in 1939 brought an end to Gourlay's work for Simpson & Co. – although she remained listed as a partner of the firm as late as 1958 – and led to perhaps the highest honour of her life. In addition to her other gifts, Gourlay possessed singular organisational skills, as she had shown during the Great War as a member of the Voluntary Aid Detachments that provided humanitarian aid to naval and military forces at home and abroad. When war came again, she enlisted in the Auxiliary Territorial Services, which provided a wide variety of logistical support. She was billeted to France and rose to the rank of lieutenant colonel. After the war, Gourlay was awarded the Order of the British Empire for her outstanding leadership of a group that came to be known as 'Molly's Mob'. Having such an organised mind likely motivated Gourlay to become one of the game's foremost experts on the rules of golf, making hers a familiar face as a referee at major championships.

With the rise of women like Hollins and Gourlay, the insanely low scores Wethered, Collett and others were posting, and the cultural embrace signified by Jordan Baker's appearance in *The Great Gatsby*, the two decades between the world wars would be remembered as the time when the women's game earned the respect of the wider golfing world. That much was guaranteed by a match that unfolded at the Old Course in St Andrews during the final year of the Roaring Twenties, providing a fitting coda to the age-old debate over how close women could come to playing golf as well as men.

Joyce Wethered (right) came to the 1920 English Amateur at Sheringham more as the companion of friend than as a competitor, but she shocked the golfing world by upsetting the reigning champion of the women's game – Cecil Leitch. (Reprinted by the kind permission of the Royal and Ancient Golf Club)

Between 1920 and 1929, Wethered amassed a record unrivalled in British women's golf – winning the English Amateur five consecutive times and taking the trophy for the British Ladies' on four occasions, her first at Prince's in 1922.
(Top: Courtesy of Hunstanton Golf Club.
Right: Courtesy of Princes Golf Club, Sandwich)

In the annual Worplesdon Mixed Foursomes, Wethered set a record unlikely to be broken, winning the event eight times with seven different men as her partner. including her brother, Roger (middle) and his Oxford teammate Cyril Tolley. (Both images Courtesy of Worplesdon Golf Club)

A natural athlete, the first time Glenna Collett ever swung a golf club, she belted a drive so far down the fairway that her father's friends declared her 'the coming champion!' And they were right.
(Courtesy of the United States Golf Association)

Collett was as dominant in the United States as Wethered was in Britain — winning the U.S. Amateur's Robert Cox Trophy six times, along with six victories in both the Eastern and North and South Amateurs.

(Top: Courtesy of Oakland Hills Golf Club. Left: Courtesy of the United States Golf Association)

Collett never realised her ambition to win the British Ladies' Championship, but her trips overseas instilled a life-long love of international competition against legends like Simone de la Chaume, whom she defeated at Hunstanton (shown here) and the French Open.

(Both images courtesy of Hunstanton Golf Club)

The first clash between Wethered and Collett – in 1925 at Troon – was wildly hyped, but lived up to its billing as the Englishwoman and the American put on the most brilliant display of scoring ever seen in a Ladies' Championship. (Reprinted by kind permission of the Royal and Ancient Golf Club)

Before a wild, scampering crowd at St Andrews in 1929, Wethered and Collett sealed their reputations as golfers for the ages during a pitched battle over the Old Course that is considered the greatest women's match ever played. (Both images reprinted by kind permission of the Royal and Ancient Golf Club)

Just before the Great War, Britain's Cecil Leitch (top) and America's Alexa Stirling ushered in a new future for the women's game by becoming the first players to truly lash at the ball – a 'perfect ferocity of hitting,' as Eleanor Helme described it.

Every woman golfer owes a debt of gratitude to those who founded and nurtured the Ladies' Golf Union. Above, founder Issette Pearson is seated between Gladys Ravencroft and Cecil Leitch (right). Below are correspondents Mabel Stringer (left) and Eleanor Helme.

(Top image reprinted by kind permission of the Royal and Ancient Golf Club)

Collett's great American rivals were the sweet-swinging Virginia Van Wie (top) and Edith Cummings. Van Wie won three consecutive Women's Amateurs beginning in 1932. Cummings was a dazzling Chicago socialite who served as the model for one of F. Scott Fitzgerald's characters in *The Great Gatsby*.
(Top: Courtesy of the United States Golf Association)

In that age of suffragettes, women were blazing new trails on and off the course. Marion Hollins (top) became a business tycoon, creating Cypress Point and Pasatiempo. Molly Gourlay broke into the all-male world of golf architecture, working alongside the brilliant Tom Simpson. (Right: Courtesy of collector Bruce Chalmers)

Eleven

MATCHLESS

G LENNA Collett was at Hunstanton Golf Club in the spring of 1928, continuing her quest to win the British Ladies' Championship, when she heard the news about Joyce Wethered. The following May, for the first time in two decades, the tournament would make a historic return to the Old Course at St Andrews, and Wethered would be playing. Like everyone else in golf, Collett was overjoyed to hear the news, and the truth is that it could not have come at a better time. The two years since the glories of 1925 had seen Glenna slip into something of a slump. She didn't win any of the major events in 1926, faltering in both the North and South and Eastern Amateurs, before losing her title as national champion by falling to Virginia Wilson in the third round of the US Amateur at Merion Cricket Club.

The following season was better. She won the North and South and Eastern Amateurs for the fourth time each, but again faltered in the national championship, losing in the second round to the woman she had dismantled two years earlier at St Louis, Alexa Stirling. Collett's overseas ventures hadn't gone much better. She had travelled to Wales for the 1926 British Ladies' at Harlech – a course she'd taken the trouble to scout before flying home the previous season – but a general strike foiled her plans to compete. The strike forced the Ladies' Golf Union to postpone the tournament for a month, and according to Eleanor Helme, 'Miss Collett's father took such alarm at the articles contributed to the American press by Mr Lloyd George that a cable demanded her instant return.'

In 1928, when Glenna crossed the Atlantic once more to compete at Hunstanton, on England's Norfolk coast, Eleanor Helme thought she looked sharper than ever. 'There was something really professional about the nip she put into the swing,' she wrote. Collett got off to a tremendous start in the tournament. In the first round, she came up against reigning champion Simone de la Chaume, the same woman she had beaten in 1925 to win the French Open. Collett took her measure again, winning by 3 and 1, then went on to defeat her old rival Gladys Ravenscroft in the next round.

Still, when Collett played in the British Ladies', something always seemed to go awry. Her fourth-round match, against Yorkshire veteran Mabel Wragg, was played in weather Helme described as 'more villainously wet and windy than anything in championship annals since the day when Miss Leitch had beaten Miss Stirling at Turnberry'. Glenna was knocked out by 3 and 2. In the end, for the second year in a row, the British title went to a Frenchwoman, this time Nanette Le Blan.

The trouble with Collett's game during those years traced to her long-time Achilles heel, putting. Cecil Leitch, who covered the championship at Hunstanton for Britain's version of *Golf Illustrated*, summed up Collett's game this way: 'She is a beautiful golfer, and her wooden club play in particular is a joy to watch. During her previous visit – in 1925 – there was a weakness in her iron play, but this has almost entirely disappeared, and the only part of her game which one could criticise adversely is her putting. On the green there is an absence of the smooth and accurate hitting of the ball so noticeable in every other department of her play.' Dorothy Campbell Hurd, writing for *Golf Illustrated* during the 1926 US Amateur, was far harsher. 'The fact remains,' she wrote, 'that Miss Collett's victories were gained in spite of the fact that her putter stroke has always been a little less good than that of the average nine-handicap player.'

Poor putting was not the only issue Collett was facing in those lean years after 1925. Women's golf was seeing the emergence of new challengers who had grown up inspired by Stirling, Hollins and Collett – among them Midwesterner Virginia Van Wie and New Yorkers Helen Hicks and Maureen Orcutt, all of whom would prove to be formidable opponents. Perhaps more importantly, for the first time in her life, Collett had off-the-course activities to distract her. She was now 23 years old, and given the enormous expense involved in playing amateur golf year-round, Collett was feeling the pressure to earn a bit of money. In 1926, capitalising on having shot to the top of American golf with her second Amateur title at St Louis, Collett published *Golf for Young Players,* a thin volume of instruction, which she followed up two years later with a second book *Ladies in the Rough.* Long after she had retired, Glenna confided to an interviewer that both books helped to defray expenses.

The following year, Collett took her first real job, working as an associate to Devereux Emmet. He was creating a women-only golf club near Greenwich, Connecticut similar to the one her friend, Hollins, had opened a few years earlier on Long Island. It was to be called the Ladies Golf and Country Club of Westchester, and Collett served as membership director, announcing her plans in a January 1927 article she wrote for *Golf Illustrated.* By 1925, after her teacher Alex Smith left Belleair in Florida for Rye, New York's Westchester-Biltmore Country Club, Collett had begun spending her winter seasons at Pinehurst instead. She loved the outdoor life, especially riding horses, trap shooting and training sporting dogs, and there she could indulge in those pursuits alongside her golf. During those winters spent in Pinehurst, in another attempt to help her parents defray expenses, Collett tried her hand at selling real estate, although as a naturally shy person that turned out not to be a job she enjoyed doing and she quickly gave it up.

The news that Wethered would be returning to championship golf after an absence of four years – setting up the tantalising possibility that Collett would meet her again at St Andrews – apparently was just the tonic Glenna's faltering game needed. In the autumn of 1928, coming off a victory over Van Wie in the high-profile Buffalo Invitational, Collett turned up in Hot Springs, Virginia, for the US Women's Amateur playing like the golfer who had swept all before her from 1922 to 1925. Lucille MacAllister, writing for *Golf Illustrated*, took note of the change that had come over Collett. She was driving the ball farther than ever, bombing tee shots 250 yards or more, and performing the way a two-time champion should on the greens. 'Those who saw her at Hot Springs felt that she had her fighting spirit back,' MacAllister wrote. 'She was sinking her putts with all the confidence of old and she showed more studied care and precision than in the past.'

The result was a triumphal procession into the final for Collett, including an 8 and 7 shellacking of Virginia Wilson, the woman who had knocked her out of the national championship two years earlier, and a 3 and 2 victory over Mrs G. Henry Stetson, the national champion of 1926. In the final, Collett came up against the rising star who had emerged as her chief rival, 19-year-old Virginia Van Wie, who earlier that season in the Mid-South Open at Pinehurst had become the only player ever to have beaten Glenna twice in succession. Perhaps Collett thought it was time to square accounts because she never gave Van Wie a chance. Glenna roared through the first nine holes of the final in 36, taking a 7-hole lead as her battered foe stumbled out in 47. By lunchtime, Collett had extended her lead to 10 holes, finishing the round with a record score of 76 over William Flynn's crafty Cascades Course. The outcome was such a foregone conclusion that MacAllister didn't bother documenting what happened in the afternoon. 'From there on,' she wrote, 'there is no point in recording difficulties.' Collett prevailed by 13 and 12, at that time the largest margin of victory ever recorded in the US Women's Amateur. It would not be surpassed until 1961, when Anne Quast Sander won by 14 and 13 at Tacoma Golf and Country Club in the state of Washington.

A pattern was developing with Collett's appearances in the Amateur final. When she had made it to the championship match, she did not simply win, she won big – 5 and 4 over Margaret Gavin in 1922, 9 and 8 over Alexa Stirling in 1925 and now the 13 and 12 humbling of Van Wie. That enormous margin of victory guaranteed two things. The first was that Collett would be playing with renewed confidence when she sailed to St Andrews for the 1929 British Ladies' Championship. That became especially true after Glenna won her fifth North and South Amateur over the tough Pinehurst No 2 course just before leaving, including posting a brilliant qualifying score of 75 in a gale of wind and rain. The second thing Collett's razor-sharp form guaranteed was this: she would arrive in Britain more feared than ever.

CHANGE OF HEART

Joyce Wethered cringed at the prevailing notion that she had been lured out of retirement to compete in the British Ladies' at St Andrews by a sense of duty to repel the threat represented by Glenna Collett. 'It has often been attributed to me that I entered for this event in a purely patriotic spirit, with the expressed intention of preventing any of the American invaders from winning our championship,' she wrote. 'I really must protest against this rather pretentious statement.' The notion clashed with Wethered's understanding of the sporting ideal that guided amateur golf in that age – a viewpoint that would continue to influence her decisions as international golf became all the rage in the years ahead.

'A championship in my opinion is an event originally instituted solely for private enterprise and for the best player to win,' she wrote, 'and it seems to me a pity that it need necessarily be converted into an international match on a larger scale.'

Wethered had entered the championship for one reason only – it was being played over the Old Course at St Andrews, the venue over which every golfer of consequence dreams of winning. Those childhood days in Dornoch had bred in Wethered a deep passion for Scottish golf. Every year between the end of the Great War until her retirement in 1925, Wethered had competed for the Ladies' Silver Medal at Dornoch, winning in 1919, 1920, 1921, 1923 and 1924. She might well have stepped away from championships after her third victory in the British Ladies' at Portrush in 1924 had it not been for the reality that the 1925 championship was to be conducted over the ancient links of Troon in Ayrshire. 'With me there were never any reservations as to which country I looked forward to the most,' she wrote. 'Scotland has something about her golf finer and more characteristic than any other country, as is only fitting and natural for the land of its birth.'

Still, Wethered could do nothing to control the narrative about her 'patriotic act' as exemplified by a British newsreel that proclaimed, 'Miss Joyce Wethered re-enters golf lists once again to prevent cup going to America!' Al Laney, the well-known tennis correspondent of *The New York Herald Tribune* sent to cover Collett's championship bid, admitted he was aware of Wethered's protestations, but ignored them. 'It made a good story,' he wrote, 'and we all went along with it.' Given what was going on in the wider world of golf, it was inevitable that such a narrative would develop. The years since the war had seen a changing of the guard in the men's game. Americans were decidedly in the ascendancy, especially in the Open Championship.

Every year since 1921, with the exception of Arthur Havers' victory at Troon in 1923, the Claret Jug had been spirited across the Atlantic to the United States. It was some consolation that two of the eight winners – St Andrean Jock Hutchison in 1921 and Cornishman Jim Barnes in 1925 – were expatriates who learned their golf in Britain before moving to America. Still, there was no denying that darkness had settled over British men's golf, after Open wins by Walter Hagen in 1922, 1924, 1928 and 1929 – just a week before the start of the British Ladies' at St Andrews – interspersed with two wins by Bobby Jones. The Claret Jug would not remain on home soil until 1934, when Henry Cotton brought Britain back into the light at Royal St George's. In 1926 even the Amateur Championship trophy was carried across the ocean as Jess Sweetser became the first American-born player to win it. By 1929, the only cup that had never gone to America was the one awarded to the winner of the British Ladies', so it was only natural that Wethered was hailed for doing her bit in stepping up to defend it.

When she retired from championship golf in 1925, Wethered hardly disappeared from view. By then she was as famous as Harry Vardon and cricket star W.G. Grace, often called upon to preside at village fetes, garden parties or the opening of a new golf club. While she devoted more time to tennis, squash, salmon fishing, skiing and other favourite pursuits, she never stopped playing golf, turning out for her powerhouse Surrey team and regularly showing up to compete at the game's premier social events. She won both the London Foursomes and *Golf Illustrated* Gold Vase in 1925, and over the next four years racked up two victories in the Worplesdon Mixed Foursomes. She and Cyril Tolley prevailed in 1927 over her brother, Roger, and Simone de la Chaume, and the following autumn Joyce and John Morrison claimed the fourth of her eight victories in that event.

Nor did Wethered cease her pursuit of the perfect swing. In fact, it was during these years, as she became acquainted with the worldwide star of amateur golf, Bobby Jones, that Joyce put the finishing touches on the classically powerful move for which she would be forever remembered. Jones made his first appearance in British golf in 1921 – an undistinguished debut in which he tore up his card in frustration on the Old Course – but he soon began to win Amateur and Open championships on both sides of the Atlantic at a superhuman clip. Nearly every competition Jones entered overseas – whether it was the Open, Amateur or the newly established international competition between the US and Great Britain and Ireland known as the Walker Cup – also featured Joyce's brother, Roger. As any leading figure in the game would have been, Jones was welcomed into the Wethereds' inner circle and became a friend of the family, a relationship cemented in 1930 when Bobby and Roger served on opposite sides as playing captains in the Walker Cup.

Joyce came to idolise Jones, not simply because he had a near-perfect swing, but also because after his temper tantrum at St Andrews in 1921 he had learned to behave like a perfect gentleman on the golf course, in both victory and defeat, and came to represent the personification of the amateur ideal that Wethered so cherished. A person who learned by imitation, Wethered made a practised effort to mimic Jones's swing – a long, flowing, seemingly effortless move through the ball. Her success in doing so was remarkable. Years later, Wethered allowed Canadian Hal Rhodes to take a stop-action film of her swing. Rhodes had previously done the same with Jones and made a detailed study of the amateur superstar's every position, from the start to the finish of his move through the ball. What he found was that Wethered's swing matched Jones's almost frame by frame, despite the reality that she was two inches taller than her idol.

It was this swing Wethered brought to St Andrews in 1929, but even still she was apprehensive about how she would perform after four years away from championship competition, especially given the dominant display Collett had recently put on in America. Whatever happened in the championship, it would be a chance for Wethered to renew acquaintances with Collett, and the new correspondent on the block, Al Laney of the *Herald Tribune*, immediately picked up on the bond between the two champions. 'She and Joyce seemed to be very friendly,' Laney wrote. 'They were together a lot, two very attractive young women, and the two best golfers of their sex in the world.'

The draw placed Wethered and Collett in opposite halves, and everyone hoped and expected that they would meet in the final, but Glenna began the week playing scratchy golf. She barely survived early matches she ought to have won with ease. Those struggles seriously dented Collett's confidence, and calmed the fears of Wethered's legion of fans. 'The British public had almost ceased to bother its head about the American invasion,' wrote Eleanor Helme. 'They had gone out in all humility to watch Miss Collett. They had come in lulled into a false sense of security.' On Thursday evening, two days before the championship final was to be played, Collett dined with the Wethered family at Rusacks Hotel, where they were staying for the week. 'I watched her as she walked over from the Grand Hotel, a charming and striking picture in blue and gold against the grey buildings,' Wethered recalled. 'She was not particularly happy that evening, a little dispirited with the course, and rather depressed and dissatisfied with her golf; up till then only flashes of her true form had been visible in the matches she played.'

Wethered, meanwhile, had been playing the brand of flawless golf for which she was famous, mercilessly dispatching one opponent after another. Even that did not stop her from fearing the worst when Collett found her game on Friday and crushed two formidable golfers to make her way to the final against her friend and dinner partner. 'She showed such convincing form in both these matches that I ruefully, and truthfully, prophesied that evening that there was trouble brewing for me on the morrow,' Wethered wrote.

BLACK MAGIC

The scene that greeted Collett and Wethered on the first tee the following morning was something to behold. Thousands of fans swarmed around them as they awaited instructions from the starter, with thousands more encircling the first green out beyond the Swilcan Burn. The crowd would only become larger as the day wore on, given that it was customary in Scotland, when an important tournament was in town, for businesses to declare a half-day holiday, so everyone could witness the final 18 holes of the championship match. Women's golf had not experienced such a frenzied scene since Troon in 1925, and the way fans dashed helter-skelter after every shot, buffeting the players as they ran, added coping with that chaos to the difficulty of playing championship golf.

Wethered and Collett wore nearly matching outfits for the occasion – both decked out in a skirt, blouse, sweater and cloche hat, although perhaps in a nod to the importance of the occasion, Glenna had accented her ensemble with a string of pearls. Before they hit their opening tee shots, there was the usual speculation about what manner of test the two women would face that morning over the Old Course, based on how far back the Ladies' Golf Union had set tees for the final. By 1929, the course stretched to 6,569 yards from the back tees, too far even for the Union's aggressive inclinations. Helme said the tees were set, on average, 10 to 20 yards in front of those used for men's championships, meaning the links played between 6,300 and 6,400 yards.

From the moment the match began, on a grey, nearly windless Saturday morning that was ideal for golf, it was clear that Wethered's fears of trouble on the morrow were well founded. Collett outdrove her from the opening tee, and then watched as Wethered hit a rare wayward approach shot that landed right of the green. Collett's answer found the putting surface, and she took the first hole when Wethered needed three putts. Wethered appeared poised to get the hole back at the second, where Collett sprayed her approach right, but the opportunity vanished when Joyce left her first putt six feet short. Glenna didn't do any better with her approach – it ran 12 feet past the cup – but she calmly holed the second as Wethered missed again to go 2 down.

Joyce described that 36-hole final as a match 'of extraordinary vicissitudes', and here was one of them. The player for whom putting had always been the weak link was rolling them in like a champion, while the woman acknowledged as the game's best on the greens weakly three-putted. Wethered did get a hole back at the third, with a brilliant birdie three. The fourth was halved in fours, and both players found the green with their third shot at the long Hole O' Cross, Collett's ball stopping 15 feet from the cup, Wethered's a bit further away. Joyce putted first, and again she faltered, sending the ball racing past the cup. Collett calmly drained another one, going 2 up again after just five holes had been played. Matters were about to become bleaker still for British fans. Wethered barely escaped the sixth with a half, and stumbled again at the seventh when the hole seemed hers to win. Collett's approach at that hole sailed long into a pot bunker. Wethered's landed short of the green. Glenna dug her ball out, but was still a dozen feet from the cup. Joyce's run-up left her another knee-knocker of just over a yard. Collett holed hers, but Wethered remained stone cold with the putter, missing the short one to go 3 down.

That was nothing compared to what happened at the eighth, the only short hole on the outward nine. Wethered's tee shot was safely aboard, but Collett's barely reached the green. She was some 75 feet or more from the cup as she surveyed the monstrous putt. Miraculously, Collett knocked it in, convincing stricken British fans that she was a woman possessed. 'It was black magic, ghastly, horrible but true,' Darwin wrote in *The Times*. Wethered's brave attempt at a half stopped a hair short, and it was 4 down. On the ninth, a rattled Wethered found a bunker from the tee, but played out beautifully and had a chance to save par. To the mortification of her fans, however, she three-putted again for a dreadful six. Collett made four, and the outward nine ended with Joyce a shocking 5 down. 'Now,' wrote Helme, 'we quaked in our shoes. We might be hot with the exertion of trying to see in a crowd not much smaller than Troon four years earlier, but we were cold with horror.'

On her way to the 10th tee, Wethered made the mistake of casting a glance at Darwin as he followed the match. The *Times* correspondent was living up to his reputation for fanatical partisanship, and 'his dark, angular face was as black as thunder,' she recalled. Darwin had not seen a crowd so grimly silent since 1904 at Royal St George's, when the Australian-turned-American Walter Travis wielded a scorching-hot putter to become the first golfer from outside Britain to win its Amateur Championship. Indeed, the most oft-told story of that forlorn morning in St Andrews, one Wethered recounted in her memoir, was of the town's postman passing a complete stranger on the street and mournfully reporting, without having been asked, 'She's five down!'

Collett had gone around the outward nine in a scintillating 34 strokes – making eight fours and a two. 'It was overwhelming golf worthy of any male champion,' Darwin declared. Pleased as she was with her game, Collett laboured under the strain of a crowd that, while perfectly civilised, was rooting passionately for Wethered. 'When I was winning,' Collett confided to an interviewer years later, 'the silence was deafening.' The greatest of champions dig deepest when their backs are to the wall, and that is precisely what Wethered did coming home. The first sign that a rally might be afoot came at the 10th. Joyce hit a stellar approach and appeared set to get a hole back until her putt dipped into the cup and cruelly popped out again, allowing Collett to escape with a half.

The famed 11th, which Darwin called 'the most fiendish short hole in existence', was halved in threes, and then at the short 12th came the turning point of the match. Both women reached the green in two, and as she had been doing all morning, Wethered left her first putt woefully short and missed the next. Collett faced a putt of just four feet to go 6 up – a lead even Wethered thought might be insurmountable – but Glenna shocked herself and the crowd by pulling it left, the first putt of consequence she had missed since the two of them teed off that morning.

Having watched Collett's impressive wins on Friday, *New York Herald Tribune* correspondent Al Laney was confident that, at the end of the day, he would be sharing with his readers the story of America's first victory in the British Ladies' Championship. He was standing beside the 12th green when Wethered missed her second putt, and was so confident that Collett would make hers and go 6 up that he was on his way to the 13th tee when he caught sight, over his shoulder, of the ball sliding past the cup. 'I stopped still, and I must have exclaimed too, as the crowd let out the kind of noise that always accompanies unexpected failure – half gasp, half shout,' he wrote. 'I thought, "Good Heavens! How could Glenna have been so careless?" Then I had the first faint glimmer of foreboding.'

That was the opening Wethered needed to restore her confidence, and it showed on the very next green. At the 13th, she again left her approach putt absurdly short, but this time she holed the 12-footer to save her skin, and the rally was decidedly on. At the next, the Long Hole, Wethered was the one who managed a five, while Collett put the first six of the day on her card. That cut the lead to four. The 15th was halved, but the 16th again went to Wethered as she made four and Collett needed five. Just three holes down now. Both women made careful fives at the treacherous Road Hole, and on the final green it was Wethered who putted better. Glenna had five feet for par, but missed. Joyce knocked hers in from just over a yard away and reduced the once daunting lead to a mere 2 up. 'There was a great sigh of relief,' wrote Darwin, as if the crowd was saying in unison, 'It's all right; she's got her now.'

SURPASSING GREATNESS

Wethered came out for the second round full of confidence, and she showed it on the first green by sinking an 18-foot putt for a birdie three, cutting the lead to a single hole. That set the tone for the afternoon, one that would see the greatest of women golfers at the absolute peak of her powers. 'Miss Collett never cracked or looked like cracking,' Darwin wrote, 'but she was putting iron shots a little farther from the hole than in the morning, and she had become an ordinary, uninspired mortal on the greens. So the fours turned to fives, and fives were no good here.'

The second hole was halved, but when Wethered played the third and fourth perfectly, and Collett needed five at both, Joyce squared the match and then took her first lead of the day. Glenna showed no sign of quitting, making a four at the long fifth hole to tie things up again. It would prove, however, to be short-lived relief from Joyce's onslaught. Wethered played the next three holes in par as the strain began to show on Collett. She hooked her tee shots into bunkers at the sixth and seventh and three-putted the eighth, losing all three and finding herself 3 down with just 10 holes left to play. Wethered made matters worse by knocking her approach to the ninth stiff for a three and reaching the turn 4 up.

It had been a classic Wethered charge – going from 5 down to 4 up over 18 holes – during which she posted the astonishingly low score of 73. By comparison, when Bobby Jones won the Open Championship two years earlier over the same course, playing from tees set slightly farther back, his scores for the four rounds were 68, 72, 73, 72, good enough to beat the field by a full six strokes. 'Four up at the turn and all seemed over,' wrote Darwin. 'Little did we imagine we were yet to suffer tortures. Now was the time of Miss Collett's supremely courageous counter attack.'

Collett did the 10th and 11th holes in three, one birdie and one par. Wethered could do no better than par on 10 and made bogey on 11 when her tee shot found the Hill bunker. That cut the lead to 2 up with seven holes remaining, keeping America's hopes very much alive. At the 12th, Collett looked as if she might give a hole right back, but she drained a critical putt to save a half. Wethered did pick one up at the next, however, as Glenna sliced her second shot into trouble and made a six to Joyce's five. At the 14th, the Long Hole, the strain of the afternoon seemed to hit both players at once. They found trouble on every shot, Collett somewhat less so as she managed to win despite making a dreadful seven. Wethered, shockingly, made eight.

The 15th proved to be the supreme moment of what had been a brilliant match. Collett played the hole perfectly and her ball lay next to the cup in three. Wethered pushed her drive, left her approach short, and only half-hit her run-up shot, leaving herself a putt of nearly 20 feet to avoid losing a hole at a critical moment. As she stood over that putt, Wethered later acknowledged, she was having flashbacks to Troon in 1925, when she had allowed her lead over Cecil Leitch to slip away late, forcing her to pull the match out of the fire with an heroic effort on the 37th hole. The *Tribune*'s Laney, still hoping to write about a glorious American victory, was on tenterhooks. 'One down with three to play seemed certain now,' he wrote, 'and with Miss Wethered playing so nervously, anything might happen. What did happen was that Miss Wethered holed that putt and undoubtedly won the match then and there.' The roar that went up from the crowd when that putt dropped said it all, and it was a sound that would still be ringing in Collett's ears some 60 years later. 'When she started to win,' Glenna recalled at the age of 84, 'there was a noise like I had never heard.'

Wethered needed only two halves to win now, and she got one of them at 16, which both played in perfect fours, leaving the match to be decided at the most feared hole in golf, the dangerous 17th. Collett did not show her best there, requiring four shots to find the green, and leaving herself a testing putt for a five. Wethered, playing perfectly, hit her third on to the green and left her approach putt less than a yard from the cup. When Glenna missed for five, Joyce knocked hers in, and the match was over, with Wethered prevailing by 3 and 1. By the time Joyce stood over that last putt, the enormous crowd that had assembled that afternoon – nearly 10,000 souls – was gathered around the 17th green and along the famous road that runs beside it, ready to let loose its pent-up excitement. 'When the moment finally came, it threatened very nearly to destroy us,' Wethered remembered. 'Glenna and I were torn apart and became the centre of a squeezing, swaying and almost hysterical mob, shouting and cheering themselves hoarse.'

The match that afternoon at St Andrews would be remembered as one of the most electrifying in the history of golf – as brilliantly played as the fabled battles between Young Tom Morris and Davie Strath, and as nail-bitingly exciting as the 1899 Amateur Championship final between Scotland's Freddie Tait and England's John Ball Jr. Darwin had covered golf for two decades by then, and for the first time in that storied career, the brilliance he witnessed that afternoon on the Old Course was beyond his powers of description. 'Many epithets will be used to describe the fluctuations of the match and the quality of the play,' he wrote in his opening paragraph for the following morning's *Times*. 'I feel unequal to the effort and will let stark figures without adjectives speak.' He then went on to lay out, in plain numbers, how that matchless duel unfolded. Darwin was unstinting in his praise of both Collett and Wethered. 'America can be every bit as proud of the lady champion who has come here and lost as she is of her various male champions who have come here and won,' he wrote of Collett. 'As to Miss Wethered, if she prefers now once more to retire into private golf she can do so with the knowledge that she has given as complete a proof of surpassing greatness as any game player of either sex that ever lived.'

Twelve

THE GRAND STAGE

GLENNA Collett would never have a more bitter pill to swallow than that loss to Joyce Wethered in what Al Laney described as 'The Greatest Women's Match Ever Played', especially given her hot start. The gracious way in which she accepted her fate did nothing but affirm her reputation as one of the finest sportswomen of her age. How many golfers were capable of recognising that their greatest accomplishment in the game had come in defeat? It was living proof of what Collett had written in 1928 for the *Sacramento Union*. 'There is an ideal far and beyond the goal of mere winning,' she explained in the newspaper, 'and it is the art of yielding gracefully to an opponent in the moment of defeat.' It was that attitude, no doubt, that enabled Collett to do precisely what she had done after her loss at Troon in 1925 – return to the United States and resume winning golf championships.

Four months after that epic match in St Andrews, 96 women gathered at Oakland Hills Country Club in Michigan for the 33rd playing of the US Women's Amateur Championship over the long and difficult South Course designed by Donald Ross.

For the first two rounds of that tournament, Collett was at her indomitable best, sweeping aside both of her opponents without having to play beyond the 13th hole. That included a 7 and 5 victory over the formidable Maureen Orcutt, who had taken over the correspondent's duties at *Golf Illustrated* from the now 50-year-old Dorothy Campbell Hurd. In the third round of the championship, however, Collett experienced one of those baffling days when she simply could not find her game. Her opponent was Dorothy Higbie, a strong local player, but not one who would have been expected to pose a serious threat.

Still, when Collett needed 44 strokes on the outward nine, she found herself two holes down. By the time they reached the 14th, her back was against the wall – four down with four to go. The golf gods have a way of repaying misfortunes, and that's what happened to keep Collett from being knocked out of the tournament. Her putt for a half was going to miss, but deflected off Higbie's ball and into the cup, keeping the match alive. Collett no doubt found that just compensation for the lucky break Mary K. Browne received in 1924 to rob Glenna of a chance to compete for the title. Collett played par golf from there on in to pull the match out of the fire on the 19th, then defeated Opal Hill 3 and 2 in the next round to make her way into yet another championship final.

Over the 36 holes against Leona Pressler, Collett wielded a hot putter, draining 15- and 20-footers as her opponent missed several short ones that might have affected the outcome, enabling Glenna to cruise to a comfortable 4 and 3 victory. Collett was now breathing rarefied air. She had won as many Amateur titles as Bobby Jones, the player universally acknowledged as the greatest golfer in the world. Not only that, she had as many national championships to her credit as both Joyce Wethered and Cecil Leitch, and she had eclipsed her childhood hero, Alexa Stirling.

The following season, as Jones mesmerised the world with his march to the Grand Slam, it would be Wethered's turn to burnish the legend she had established the previous autumn at St Andrews. That year, 1930, was a red-letter one for the Wethered family, as Roger had been named playing captain of Britain's Walker Cup team, with Jones serving as his opposite number for America. Given that Roger's golf was a family affair for the Wethereds, Joyce would have a front-row seat for Jones's attempt at the greatest feat in the history of golf – winning the Amateur and Open championships of both Britain and America in a single season.

It was a good thing Joyce so idolised Jones as it might otherwise have been a dreary few months for her family, beginning with the Walker Cup at Royal St George's in May. Roger and Cyril Tolley did win their foursome over George Voigt and George Von Elm – the only victory for Britain in that session – but Wethered proved no match for Jones in the singles. Roger went down meekly, losing by 9 and 8. With only one player on his team, Tony Torrance, prevailing in singles, Britain were shellacked by the Americans, 10 to 2.

The results of the Amateur Championship a week later at St Andrews were not much more heartening for the Wethereds. The final there came down to Bobby and Roger as well, after Jones survived a number of tough scrapes, among them a death struggle against Tolley that Bobby won only by virtue of a stymie on the 19th hole. Once safely into the final, Bobby turned up in one of his invincible moods and rolled over poor Roger again, this time by 7 and 6, to secure the first of the four titles that comprised what one sportswriter grandly called The Impregnable Quadrilateral.

It was while Jones was in St Andrews, making his preparations for the Amateur, that he and Joyce played the game that left the greatest of all golfers feeling humbled. One afternoon, she was invited to join a friendly best-ball match with Jones, her brother, Roger, and Dale Bourne, the reigning English Amateur champion. It was played from the men's championship tee in brisk wind, with Joyce and Bobby as partners against her brother and

Bourne. Jones was so impressed by his partner's game that he was moved to write an article about her for *The American Golfer*. He started by noting that Joyce had not taken a club in hand for a fortnight before that afternoon, which only redoubled his amazement at the way she played. 'Miss Wethered holed only one putt of more than five feet, took three putts half-heartedly from four yards at the 17th after the match was over, and yet she went around St Andrews in 75,' wrote Jones, who finished only a stroke lower than his partner. 'She did not miss one shot; she did not even half miss one shot,' Jones marvelled, 'and when we finished I could not help saying that I had never played golf with anyone, man or woman, amateur or professional, who made me feel so utterly outclassed.'

Jones noted that when he hit the ball properly, he outdrove Joyce by 20 or so yards, but when it came time to play to the green with irons, none of the three men was able to match her. She was closer to the hole than any of them on the majority of approach shots. As far as Jones was concerned, Wethered had turned golf's eternal problem on its head. She had not simply closed the gap with men. She had surpassed them, at least in mastery of technique. 'I have no hesitancy in saying,' he concluded, 'that, accounting for the unavoidable handicap of a woman's lesser physical strength, she is the finest golfer I have ever seen.'

For the rest of that season, Jones would be the focus of the sporting world as he continued his march to the Grand Slam – winning the Open at Hoylake, the US Open at Interlachen and the US Amateur at Merion, where he had debuted as a 14-year-old boy. In her own inimitable way, however, it was Collett who put the finishing touch on golf's year on the grand stage. Two weeks after Jones wrapped up the Slam, she delivered a performance for the ages at Los Angeles Country Club in the 1930 US Women's Amateur, the first held in California.

Collett turned up at the George Thomas Jr. masterpiece in razor-sharp form and proved unstoppable from start to finish.

Only one of the five opponents she faced, Peggy Wattles, gave Glenna any trouble, taking her to the 17th before succumbing by 3 and 1. Along the way, Collett had a chance to settle a score that must have been gnawing away at her, as over the previous 18 months she had lost three consecutive encounters to the rising star from New York, Helen Hicks. From the outset of their semi-final match, Collett made it abundantly clear that the result would be different this time. She started with a birdie and rolled over Hicks 5 and 3, earning another chance to face her familiar rival, Virginia Van Wie, in the 36-hole final.

In the opening round, Collett took just 76 strokes over that 6,400-yard layout – five over men's par of 71 – setting a new women's course record and sending her into the lunch break sitting on a 5-hole lead. Van Wie fought back in the afternoon round, winning two of the first three holes, but Collett was not backing down. She finished Van Wie off on the 13th by 6 and 5 for another dominant victory in the final. For the second consecutive season, Collett had placed herself on a pedestal beside Jones. With the win in Los Angeles, she matched his five US Amateur victories – and, in so doing, surpassed the four national championships won by Leitch and Wethered. She had also accomplished a feat that had eluded even Jones and Joyce, winning the championship for the third year in succession – joining Lady Margaret Scott, Beatrix Hoyt, Leitch and Stirling as the only women to have reached that magic number.

DREAM REALISED

Even before she won that fifth Amateur to stand shoulder to shoulder with Jones, Collett recognised that she was singularly well positioned to help women realise a dream they had harboured since the days of Issette Pearson – and she seized the opportunity. In the spring of 1930, months before she headed to California again to defend her title in the championship, Collett crossed the Atlantic for the fifth time in pursuit of the British Ladies' Championship. This time, however, she had a larger mission in mind – to promote an international competition between the women of America and Great Britain to rival the men's Walker and Ryder Cups.

Collett arranged an informal match between the two nations at Sunningdale Golf Club in advance of the British Ladies' at Formby. Hers was one in a long line of efforts to generate enough interest in such a match to overcome the obstacles in the way – namely time, travel and money. Pearson, ever a forward-thinking woman, had broached the idea of such a match as early as 1898, but the first steps towards making it a reality were taken by the Curtis sisters of Boston. In 1905, when they joined a contingent of American women crossing the ocean to compete in the British Ladies' at Cromer, Margaret and Harriet Curtis arranged an informal match between the two countries. Even the 6-to-1 drubbing the Americans received did nothing to diminish their enthusiasm for launching a formal competition, and the Curtis sisters would remain passionately devoted to the cause all their lives.

In 1909, the USGA offered to donate a cup for international competition, and over the next four years two other informal matches were conducted – one at Portrush in 1911 and one in the US in 1913 when Gladys Ravenscroft came to claim the Women's Amateur. None of that proved enough to make the match a reality, however, and when war intervened in 1914, thoughts of an international competition between the women of America and Great Britain were put aside. Curiously, when the dust of war had settled, it was men who would establish the first competitions between the world's leading golfing nations, with the Walker Cup for amateurs making its debut in 1922 and the Ryder Cup for professionals following in 1927. It speaks volumes about the challenges women faced in that age that men were the first to establish a formal competition between the golfers of America and Great

Britain and Ireland. Women had embraced international competition long before them.

During the 1895 British Ladies' at Portrush, a match was arranged between England and Ireland. It quickly evolved into the annual Home Internationals, with Scotland and Wales also battling it out for the International Shield donated by Thomas H. Miller. Those matches continue to this day. Men did not embrace international competition until 1902, when the first match between England and Scotland was played at Royal Liverpool, creating such a sensation that it was followed the next year by a similar event for professional golfers.

The excitement generated by the Walker and Ryder Cups renewed interest in a women's international match, a subject discussed endlessly in *Golf Illustrated* and by members of the USGA Women's Committee. In 1927, the year the Ryder Cup made its debut, the Curtis sisters donated a simple Revere bowl as a prize 'to stimulate friendly rivalry among the women golfers of many lands'. They envisioned a day when an international match would include not simply the United States and Great Britain – as would turn out to be the case – but also France, Canada and perhaps even South Africa and Australia, where women's golf was growing rapidly. The following year, Margaret Curtis sent a private letter to her friend, Cecil Leitch, offering to address the principal obstacle – money. Curtis told Leitch that she was prepared to donate $5,000 per match to cover expenses for the first 10 international competitions, a total of $50,000, or nearly $1 million in today's currency. Her only stipulation was that the donation remain strictly anonymous.

That was the momentum Collett was riding when she brought her team of 14 golfers to Sunningdale in May 1930 for a match in which only 10 would be able to compete at a time. It must have pained Collett that her friend Wethered showed no interest in international competition. Joyce was, naturally, offered the captaincy of the British side, but turned it down. That was the year Roger was captain of the Walker Cup team – with her idol Jones as his American counterpart – and Joyce would never have missed that or wanted to create a distraction for the family as her brother was enjoying his big moment. It was more than that, however, as Wethered's biographer Basil Ashton Tinkler explained: 'Joyce was not at all enthusiastic about the proposal for international matches,' he wrote. 'Apart from the tricky subject of finance, she seemed to think it would not be good for the amateur status of the game. She thought that the winning would become more important than the playing, and feared that commercial matters would intrude and take over.'

In truth, Wethered's response is hardly surprising, given that she had always been a step removed from the circle of women who dominated the Ladies' Golf Union. She regularly ran afoul of the Union's guidelines for submitting handicap scores as she could not be bothered to compete in events that did not interest her simply to post a number. And, while she was unfailingly gracious and courteous, Wethered seldom mixed with other women at events in which she competed. Enid Wilson, who would win three consecutive British Ladies' titles after Wethered retired and go on to become one of the game's most distinguished correspondents, described Joyce's approach to championships this way: 'From a quiet house or secluded part of an hotel, she would come to the first tee, smile charmingly at her opponent when they met at the commencement of their game, and then, almost as if in a trance, become a golfing machine,' Wilson wrote. 'The match concluded, Miss Wethered would vanish and be seen no more until the starter called her name for the next round.' Wethered suggested Molly Gourlay as her replacement, and it was she who selected and led the side at Sunningdale – a match that would prove to be another triumph for the British, as all three of the previous informal international matches had been.

Characteristically, Collett's focus as American captain was as much on making sure every woman along for the journey got a chance to compete as it was on winning, and as her partner in the opening foursome she chose an unheralded player named Marion Bennett. They went down 4 and 3 to the powerhouse British duo of Gourlay and Wilson, but America still managed to halve the morning matches, 2½ to 2½, with victories from the teams of Maureen Orcutt and Hazel Martelli and Helen Hicks and Lee Mida. In the afternoon singles, Collett went around Sunningdale in a sparkling 76, but even that was not enough to defeat an inspired Gourlay, who carried the day by 1 up on the 18th green. Britain went on to win the match 8 to 6, and the passionate response from the crowd of 5,000 that swarmed Sunningdale, as well as the enthusiastic coverage in the press, all but guaranteed that the moment had, at last, arrived for the birth of a formal women's international match.

It helped, of course, that British women had succeeded when their men so consistently failed. That year, for the sixth consecutive time, Great Britain and Ireland had been thrashed by America in the Walker Cup – a reality that became the focus of *The Scotsman*'s report from Sunningdale. 'British women have retrieved some of the lost golfing honours of the country, for today at Sunningdale they defeated a team of the strongest women golfers America could produce,' the newspaper crowed, declaring that the victory would 'make a glorious page in golfing history'. The joy of that triumph, however, did nothing to diminish fears that an American might, at last, win the Ladies' Championship the following week at Formby. 'We were honestly terrified,' wrote Eleanor Helme. 'Even after beating the Americans at Sunningdale we were not altogether happy, for they had been out of practice there, fresh from a life on the ocean wave, and they all had beautiful swings.'

Those fears only heightened as Collett began another inexorable march towards the championship final, and especially after she survived a desperate match with the hero of Sunningdale, Gourlay. Their third-round encounter was a pitched battle that saw Collett arrive at the 14th with a 2-up lead. Bravely, Gourlay dug in and squared the match at 16. When the next two holes were halved, the 'agonisingly exciting' match entered sudden death. Gourlay appeared on the edge of defeat at both the 19th and 20th – miraculously saving herself first with an up-and-down and then with a seven-yard putt – before Collett finally put her away at the 21st. That afternoon, Collett faced the woman many in Britain considered their last line of defence, the formidable Wilson. Near panic set in when she developed a wicked hook with her irons that enabled Glenna to close her out on the final hole. 'English faces grew long as they realised that the American lady had beaten our best two players and was now into the final,' wrote Helme.

Before 1929, no woman from the United States had ever competed in the championship match of the British Ladies'. Now Collett had a second consecutive chance to carry off the most cherished trophy in women's golf. Her opponent in the final was 19-year-old Diana Fishwick, a former British Girls' Champion who would emerge as a first-class player but was not then viewed as a match for a veteran like Collett. Glenna, however, was not herself that day. She had lost her touch with the putter – that old Achilles heel resurfacing – and with it any hope of victory. Collett was 5 down by lunchtime and fell to Fishwick 4 and 3, her most disappointing defeat in the Ladies' Championship. 'British breasts might swell with pride, but British hearts also beat with sympathy,' wrote Helme, for one who had come so faithfully to compete in their championship and accepted the tough breaks without complaint.

It is a testament to her extraordinary resilience that four months later, Collett was lifting the Robert Cox Trophy before a cheering throng in Beverly Hills. Four times she had faltered in pursuit of the British Ladies' title, and four times she had returned home undaunted to win her own national championship. Collett also had the comfort of knowing that the match she arranged at Sunningdale had accomplished just what she had hoped. In 1932, the Curtis sisters would finally get a chance to give away their cup at a competition starring the two greatest players women's golf had ever known – this time on an international stage.

THE CURTIS CUP

The sensation created by the match at Sunningdale convinced even the reluctant Joyce Wethered that international matches were the way of the future in women's golf. 'Today,' she acknowledged, 'we see the beginning of a new era when British lady golfers will be crossing swords and oceans to settle the vexed question of supremacy.' In March 1931, when it was announced that the first Curtis Cup would be contested in England the following spring, Wethered put aside her reservations and agreed to serve as captain of the British side. She played the same role that autumn at another new international event, the Vagliano Cup, a competition between France and Great Britain. The two sides met in October at Oxhey, near London, where Wethered won both her matches and led the way to an easy victory by 8½ to ½.

Collett might well have been Wethered's opposite number on the American Curtis Cup side had it not been for a momentous change that unfolded in Glenna's life during the previous season. In June 1931, Collett married Edwin H. Vare Jr., the son of a wealthy and powerful State Senator from Pennsylvania. A construction engineer by trade, Vare was a fine golfer himself and, fittingly, a man with a reputation for driving the ball nearly as far as the woman he married. Settling into life at their new home in Philadelphia left Collett too busy to lead the US side, as she had at Sunningdale. In her place, America chose a non-playing captain, Marion Hollins, a decision that turned out to be pivotal.

Hollins brought to the Curtis Cup the same hard-charging attitude that helped her strike oil in California and create two temples of American golf at Cypress Point and Pasatiempo.

Having concluded that Collett's team for the 1930 match arrived too late to be effective, Hollins had her side settled in days before the match began at Wentworth Golf Club in Surrey. Wethered welcomed her American visitors at Waterloo train station – dressed for the occasion in an elegant suit, a decorated cloche hat, a string of pearls and a luxurious fox fur – and saw them safely to the Grand Fosters Hotel near the golf course. The following morning, to the shock of the British, Hollins had her team out on the East Course at Wentworth practising foursomes – the format for the Cup's opening session and one with which Americans were largely unfamiliar, then and now. Hollins was not only introducing her players to the course and this relatively unfamiliar game, she was also trying out different combinations to see which players paired up best together in the tricky alternate shot format.

Wethered took a laissez-faire attitude towards the proceedings, asking her team simply to show up the day before the match in time for afternoon tea. Years later, she admitted that she never warmed to team competitions, and especially not to being the kind of aggressive captain represented by Hollins. 'To be honest,' Wethered said, 'I no more liked ruling others than I liked to be ruled myself. Things such as team practices appalled me. I preferred to do things in my own good time and in my own way.' Nor did Wethered consider it her responsibility to look after the needs of her players. That job, as she saw it, belonged to the Ladies' Golf Union. When British players came in for lunch after the morning foursomes, they found that no tables or food had been set aside for them. What food had been provided was gone, gobbled up by spectators attending the match. Wilson, a star player on Britain's side, said she was left with no choice but 'to go round the dining room and find bits of discarded bread roll and bits of cheese'. Hollins, perpetual host that she was, saw to every aspect of her side's care and feeding and had them served lunch between rounds in the comfort of their hotel.

Given that Britain had won all of the previous friendly encounters between nations, it was heavily favoured to claim the inaugural Curtis Cup, and as Wethered saw it, her principal job as captain of the side was to make sure of that by winning her two matches. The format consisted of three 18-hole foursome matches in the morning – a game in which the British were considered to have a major advantage – followed by six singles in the afternoon, with each worth one point. Play began that morning, Saturday 21 May, in glorious sunshine before a hyped-up crowd of some 10,000 fans – the largest ever seen at a women's tournament in Britain. The size of the throng made it all but impossible to see the action. 'It was a mad, scampering crowd,' reported *The Glasgow Herald*, 'some carrying step ladders, others using periscopes, women taking mirrors from their vanity bags, and men and women seeking every vantage point, even to climbing trees.'

The two greatest women golfers in the world – Wethered and Collett – naturally led their sides into battle in the opening match. Joyce was accompanied by the young English champion Wanda Morgan and Glenna by veteran Opal Hill, a notoriously tough customer who was by then a three-time winner of the Western Amateur. The opening holes unfolded as expected. Wethered and Morgan took a 2-up lead as they reached the turn, but with Collett playing beautifully all morning, she and Hill were well within striking distance when events took an ominous turn for the British beginning at the 12th. On that hole and the next, the massive crowd following the match saw the rarest of sights, the incomparable Wethered making one mistake after another. At 12, she dumped her approach into a bunker. At 13, she missed the green. Britain lost both holes, and now it was all square with five to play.

Perhaps feeling the pressure of international competition, Hill mirrored Wethered's mistakes at 12 and 13 with a poor approach of her own at the 14th, handing the lead right back. Wethered and Morgan's reaction to that gift, however, was hardly what the mob of fervent fans expected. On the 15th green, Joyce faced a three-foot putt to put her side 2 up and all but secure Britain's first point. But, horror of horrors, she missed it. Nor was that the only misery the home crowd had in store. Morgan's putt at the 16th was too strong, running five feet past the cup, and again Wethered failed to get down the next. Suddenly, the entire lead had vanished.

A half at the next left all to play for on 18, where both Wethered and Collett smacked perfect drives into the middle of the fairway. Facing a dangerous shot to a flag tucked just behind a bunker, Morgan wilted under the pressure and topped her brassie, leaving Wethered to bear the burden of sticking it tight with everything on the line. 'Miss Wethered went for a champion's shot,' the *Herald* wrote, 'and the tragedy of it was that although she hit the ball well it just caught the top of the bunker, and there in the sand British hopes were buried.' The Americans prevailed 1 up, securing what would turn out to be the winning point in the match. That must have been an extraordinarily gratifying moment for Collett – the first time, in any competition, that she had beaten the player she considered the greatest golfer in the world.

The correspondent for the *Herald* was as stunned by the result as everyone else at Wentworth. 'The invincible Joyce Wethered, the British captain, playing in partnership with Miss Wanda Morgan, was perhaps for the first time in her life, the weakness of her side,' the newspaper wrote. The shock of that loss rippled through the field as America made a clean sweep of the foursomes. Virginia Van Wie and Helen Hicks beat Enid Wilson and Charlotte Watson 2 and 1, as Maureen Orcutt and Leona Cheney outlasted Molly Gourlay and Doris Park 1 up on 18. Even Wethered had to concede that all the preparation Hollins had done in conducting practice sessions over the Wentworth course and mixing and matching foursome pairings had paid off. 'We were both surprised, I remember, to find out how the foursomes had been arranged, as we had both much too ingeniously predicted something quite different from the opposite side,' she wrote. 'As events were to prove, Marion Hollins certainly made the wiser choice of the two.' With the Americans having swept the board in the morning, 'Britain was faced with the seemingly hopeless task of winning five of the six singles' that afternoon, the *Glasgow Herald* noted.

It was not to be. Wethered, as might be expected, came out in a mood to take no prisoners. She played the brand of golf Britain expected of her, sweeping Collett aside 6 and 4 – the worst beating Glenna had ever received at the hands of her friend. Two others on Britain's side also racked up victories that afternoon – Wilson defeating Hicks 2 and 1 and Diana Fishwick beating Orcutt 4 and 3 – but the day was saved for America by Hill and Van Wie. Van Wie started slowly, falling 2 down by the turn, but she played superbly coming home, winning three consecutive holes and dispatching Morgan 2 and 1. Hill stuck doggedly to Gourlay, also coming back from a 2-hole deficit at the turn, and managed a critical half. The final American point was provided by Leona Cheney, who easily beat Elsie Corlett 5 and 3. Cheney had formerly competed as Leona Pressler, finishing second under that name to Collett in the 1929 US Women's Amateur, but she had since divorced and remarried. The match ended 5½ to 3½ in favour of the Americans. For the first time since Irish star Rhona Adair laid down the challenge all those years ago, the US had broken through the seemingly impenetrable citadel of British women's golf. In the years ahead, just as men from America had done, they would come to dominate the women's game.

The *Glasgow Herald* seemed positively stricken. 'America has gained many sensational victories in golf over Britain,' the newspaper wrote, 'but none so surprising, so overwhelming and so humiliating as that they scored on the course of the Wentworth Club on Saturday.' It was fitting that Collett and Hollins were together to celebrate America's breakthrough victory, as pioneers who had paved the way for a new generation of hard-hitting players. What satisfaction it must have given them to see the Curtis

Cup – which their sisters in America had championed for so long and worked so tirelessly to establish – cement its place as one of the most important competitions in amateur golf.

Wethered would never compete in another international match, but for Collett the Curtis Cup would remain a lifelong passion. She would lead the American side as a player or its captain well into her forties. That first Curtis Cup match might have been the last time Wethered and Collett ever battled on a golf course were it not for the storm clouds that had been gathering worldwide since the day the American stock market crashed in October 1929. The fallout of that financial disaster would bring radical change to the lives of Wethered and her family – so much so that for the first time in her life, Joyce's thoughts would turn to America.

Thirteen

SWAN SONG

SINCE the moment she faced Joyce Wethered at Troon in 1925, Glenna Collett had wished for nothing more passionately than a visit to the United States by the world's greatest woman golfer. Collett wanted the men and women of her country to witness what she had seen, to marvel at Wethered's rare combination of grace, power and imperturbable temperament. 'It is futile for me to attempt to tell what a golfer she really is,' Collett wrote. 'I want to have you see her in action. She is as near perfection as I ever dreamed of being when I sat in the deep-seated rocker on the front porch in the cool summer evenings years ago and dreamed my best dreams.' No one, however, would have wished for the circumstances that made Collett's wish come true.

The generational wealth on which the Wethereds had lived so comfortably throughout Joyce's life, money earned from mining coal and spinning yarn, was heavily invested in US stocks, with the family's annual income provided by the returns. In the years since Black Friday – as the 1929 market crash came to be known – Newton Wethered's holdings, like those of countless other wealthy men worldwide, had all but evaporated. He and his family were forced to retrench. Wethered sold their lavish arts and crafts-style home at Tigbourne Court, moving to far more modest quarters a few miles away in Brook. Roger had already left home, having married in 1925 and begun work as a stockbroker.

Now Joyce also had to find work, taking a job in February 1933 as manager of the golf department at Fortnum & Mason, the famed department store in Piccadilly. She was paid £600 a year, a salary that enabled Joyce to move out of the house as well. She took a flat in Grosvenor Place, a mile east of the store. Within months, Wethered was fielding offers to sell clubs under her name from both A.G. Spalding & Co. and Kinghorn Ltd. In addition to working at Fortnum & Mason, Wethered added money to the till by writing *Golfing Memories and Methods*, published in 1934. The first half of the book is devoted to recounting her experiences in championship golf, the second half to instruction. The book demonstrated, once again, Wethered's singularly deep understanding of the golf swing, and her extraordinary gift for explaining its intricacies clearly, as she had done previously in articles for golf magazines and with her brother Roger in *Golf from Two Sides* and the 1931 Lonsdale Library book titled *The Game of Golf*.

The most curious development in Wethered's life during this period – and one that, perhaps, reveals the extent of the financial strain facing her family – came in an announcement that appeared on 9 November 1931 in the 'Forthcoming Marriages' section of *The Times*. That morning the newspaper reported that Joyce had become engaged to Major Cecil K. Hutchinson, a friend of her father who had served with both the Coldstream Guards and Royal Scots and who was a prominent amateur golfer and noted golf architect. In many respects, Hutchinson was an ideal match for Joyce, as a family friend, jovial dinner companion and a member of the golfing royalty in which she felt most comfortable. Trouble was, Hutchinson was old enough to be her father – 24 years older to be exact. An intensely private person, Wethered never spoke about the proposed match, or why the engagement was eventually called off. One cannot help but wonder if marrying Hutchinson simply seemed a safe choice at a time when financial calamity was engulfing her family and irrevocably changing the only life she had ever known.

By the middle of 1934, when *Golfing Memories and Methods* was making its debut, Wethered received an offer from America that would both resolve her financial problems and cement her reputation as a golfer. Alexander Findlay, golf adviser to the John Wanamaker Department Store in Philadelphia, wrote to Wethered and Fortnum & Mason proposing to sponsor her on an exhibition tour of the US and Canada as a way of promoting the new clubs being sold under her name. Findlay was no stranger to the business of sponsoring tours. It was he who had arranged – again on behalf of Wanamaker stores – Harry Vardon's year-long excursion to America in 1900, during which he competed in 98 exhibition matches and won the US Open. Tours of that sort represented the mother lode for British golfers. Vardon is estimated to have earned an extraordinary £2,000 from his visit. While Wethered's trip would not be anywhere near as long as Harry's, her proceeds would be more than twice that amount.

As she did with all things, Wethered had firm ideas about how a trip to the US should unfold. She wanted a tour befitting a champion. She had no interest in anything that smacked of a sideshow. No hitting balls into New York Harbor. No performing for crowds at baseball stadiums. Nor did she want to exert herself to the extent Vardon had. Wethered found the rigours of his 1900 tour intimidating, as she explained in an April 1935 letter to Findlay. For herself, she imagined a tour of two months or so, involving perhaps 30 exhibitions. 'I don't think that I can undertake as many matches a week as you suggest,' Wethered wrote. 'I should prefer that you made an average of three a week, and that perhaps it will be possible to fit more in after I arrive out. You see I am not sure yet how I shall find the heat conditions. Also, I should imagine that the distances to be covered will entail a great deal of travelling. Harry Vardon seems to have been very active!'

In the end, Wethered would spend most of four months in North America – leaving England in late May and returning home in mid-September – playing 53 exhibitions in all, receiving $200 for each game and 40 per cent of the profits made from charging for admission. Weeks before she signed on the dotted line, Wethered began to work on her game in earnest. Having been retired from championship competition for the better part of six years by then, Joyce wanted to be certain that Americans saw her at her best. The timing was right for a return to the public eye, given that Wethered had spent so much time in deep thought about her swing as she composed *Golfing Memories and Methods*. In March, she turned out for the Sunningdale Foursomes, teaming up with her Worplesdon mate John Morrison to win the event over Pam Barton and Leslie Barnett by 3 and 2.

A month later it was on to the men vs ladies match at Stoke Poges, where the women were to receive nine bisques that season. No man on earth could give that many strokes to Joyce Wethered, as poor Jack McLean was fated to learn that afternoon. He reached the turn in a sparkling 34 strokes, only to find that he was 3 down. Indeed, McLean managed to win only two holes before Wethered closed him out 5 and 4 – once when he made birdie on a long par four and once when he drove the green of the 295-yard 10th. Afterwards, McLean told the assembled reporters that no golfer could give Wethered strokes and win, let alone the full complement of nine bisques awarded that year at Stoke Poges. Joyce went on to add an exclamation point to her performance by teaming up with Surrey pal Molly Gourlay to win her foursome match as well.

She was ready now. On 22 May 1935, accompanied as any proper Englishwoman would be by a chaperone named Dorothy Shaw, a 33-year-old, prematurely greying Wethered boarded the SS *Bremen* for New York and a nation buzzing in anticipation of her visit. The excitement was stoked, in part, by multiple major champion Gene Sarazen, who had pulled off a miraculous victory that spring in a new event that was already attracting considerable attention, an invitational at Augusta known as the Masters. He had issued a statement congratulating Wanamaker Stores 'for its momentous contribution to the advancement of the Royal and Ancient pastime in the United States by sponsoring the first exhibition tour of Joyce Wethered, which will supply a unique and highly important chapter in the already glittering annals of American golf'.

TOUR DE FORCE

Had it not been for the financial catastrophe facing her family, it is a safe bet that Wethered would never have agreed to take a golfing tour of the United States and Canada. She was a shy, reserved woman; showing herself off in that way simply was not her style. Still, once she had agreed, Wethered looked forward with great enthusiasm to seeing North America and rubbing shoulders with the golfing royalty of the US and Canada. Above all, she wanted the world to see why America's sporting hero, Bobby Jones, described her as 'the finest golfer I have ever seen'. She also looked forward to playing again with Glenna Collett and to renewing acquaintances with players like Marion Hollins and Alexa Stirling.

Wethered's tour would see her travel some 15,000 miles to 21 US states and three Canadian provinces. Along the way, she would compete with and against many of the game's finest – Walter Hagen and Gene Sarazen, Francis Ouimet and Tommy Armour, Alexa Stirling and Ada Mackenzie, Leo Diegel and Horton Smith. Playing in a new country, Wethered faced the same kind of obstacles that confronted women who crossed the Atlantic to try their luck in the British Ladies' Championship. Most of her rounds were played in searing heat unlike anything she had experienced back home. She had never seen any of the courses over which she competed. And she had to play with the larger American ball, which did not fly as far as the British ball did.

Nearly every match in which Wethered participated was four-ball featuring teams of men and women, both playing from the back tee. Wisely, the promoters had players putt out on every hole, even though it was match play, so scores could be recorded and compared. Despite getting off to a slow start – in five of her first 10 rounds, she posted scores higher than 80, including one dismal 85 – Wethered's performance during the tour was simply astonishing. Her side won or halved two of every three matches she played – including contests against teams featuring such luminaries as Bobby Jones, Gene Sarazen, Francis Ouimet and Billy Burke. In 44 of her 53 rounds, Wethered went around in the 70s – often the low 70s – producing an average score for the trip of 76.9, a brilliant record considering the challenges involved and her long layoff. In 34 matches, Wethered set a new women's course record – although some of her scores did include conceded tap-ins – and she nearly broke 70 once, missing a seven-foot putt on the final hole for a 69. She had done that a handful of times back home, at courses as challenging as Royal Dornoch, Lossiemouth and Gullane No. 1.

The tour's opening match, played on 30 May, needed to be a barn burner, and Alexander Findlay had outdone himself by lining up a star-spangled foursome – Wethered and Jones vs Collett and Sarazen at the Women's National Golf and Tennis Club, the course Marion Hollins founded on Long Island. It is difficult to imagine a match that would generate more excitement than that one, but, alas, it was not to be. Just before the match, Jones was afflicted by a bout of recurring appendicitis and had to be replaced by amateur Johnny Dawson of Chicago. Wethered must have been terribly disappointed, but despite the loss of Jones, some 2,000 fans turned out to see the two sides fight to a draw. Sarazen came in with 72, Dawson with 75 and Wethered with 78. Collett did not complete one hole, but had gone around the 17 holes she did finish in 75. Joyce was displeased with her score, mostly the result of poor putting on greens far slower than those she was accustomed to at home. Nevertheless, the crowd and the writers covering the match were in awe of her game, as Collett had always known they would be. Wethered's drives were phenomenally powerful and straight as a rope – nearly always longer than Collett's and usually within 10 yards of Sarazen's – but it was her swing that mesmerised the crowd, as it would everywhere she travelled. 'That graceful, fluid swing epitomised the effortlessness of art,' George Trevor wrote in *The Sportsman* magazine. 'Here, visualised in the flesh, was a living picture of everything the textbooks and theorists had written about the perfect golf swing.'

The first month of Wethered's tour was something of a reunion with Collett, whose life had changed dramatically since she and Joyce had last met at the Curtis Cup in 1932. Glenna now had two infant children, and had largely stepped away from championship golf. Her daughter, also named Glenna, was born in 1933, her son, Edwin, a year later. For part of the tour, Wethered stayed at Collett's home in Philadelphia, a palatial residence originally built by the famous art collector Alfred Barnes, and where Glenna's friend and fellow golfer, Betty Jameson, said the family enjoyed 'a rather grand lifestyle'.

Joyce and Glenna would compete together five times that first month – four times against one another and once as a team. Three other matches would follow in July and August, when Wethered returned to the Northeast after jaunts through the Midwest and South. The results were about the same as they had always been. Wethered and Collett brought the best out of one another, but Joyce was nearly always just a few strokes better. Glenna defeated Joyce only once in a match, in August at Collett's home course, Point Judith Country Club in Narragansett, Rhode Island. That day, both played with another woman as a partner and posted a score of 78. Joyce's side lost by 2 and 1. Only once did Collett score lower than Wethered, posting an 82 to her 83 when they were beaten 2 and 1 by Sarazen and Jess Sweetser in the second match of the tour at A.W. Tillinghast's famed Winged Foot Golf Club in Mamaroneck, New York.

As thrilled as Joyce was by her reunion with Glenna, the highlight of her trip was, unquestionably, a make-up game Jones arranged at his home course – East Lake Country Club – to compensate for having been forced to withdraw from the tour's opener. Given that the match was squeezed in at the last minute, Wethered and her companion, Dorothy Shaw, opted to take their first aeroplane ride to Atlanta, an experience both thoroughly enjoyed. On every other occasion, they had travelled by train. That evening they dined in Atlanta with Jones and his biographer, O.B. Keeler, as Bobby and Joyce discussed changes she was making to her putting grip to adapt to the slower American greens.

The match unfolded the next morning, Wethered and Georgia collegiate champion Charlie Yates facing Jones and a promising 15-year-old from Atlanta named Dorothy Kirby. All four played from the back tee, with the course stretching to 6,600 yards. From the outset, it was clear that Jones and Wethered – whom Keeler considered the two finest players in the world – were giving everything they had in the match. 'I have watched many exhibition matches, but none quite like this one,' he wrote in *The American Golfer*. Keeler and the crowd were flabbergasted by Joyce's length from the tee. 'Miss Wethered's driving was simply tremendous,' he wrote. 'The wind was coming up, and when facing it she was hitting a low, raking drive of great carry and astonishing run,' sometimes even outdriving Jones and Yates when they had hit a cracker. Jones reached the turn in 34 to Wethered's 36 and was holding on to a slim 1-up lead in both matches – the game between the two teams and the one between him and Joyce, the only thing fans cared about. Wethered was playing so marvellously that it wasn't until the 14th hole – where Joyce sailed a bunker shot over the green, leading to a bogey – that Charlie Yates's score on a hole figured in the match. A bemused Yates told Keeler he had never played so many holes as a woman's partner without contributing. 'Well,' he joked, 'as long as she's carrying me around on her back, I'll just try not to let my feet drag.'

The team match was all square as they came to the 18th, an unusual finishing hole given that it was a par three stretching 200 yards across a lake from an elevated tee to a hilltop green. Wethered played first, knocking her tee shot on to the green, 20 feet short of the flag. Yates hit his shot about the same distance past the pin, while both Jones and Kirby fell short of the putting surface. Wethered and Yates narrowly missed their attempts for a two, which would have won the match, and it came down to the 15-footer Jones left himself after pitching on to the green. Champion that he was, Bobby drained it, and the game ended all square. The individual contest between Wethered and Jones had concluded on the 17th, where Bobby closed Joyce out 2 and 1. His score for the 18 holes was 71. Hers was 74, while Yates had come in with a 76 and young Dorothy Kirby with an 84. 'Miss Wethered's play was beyond praise,' Keeler wrote. 'On Bermuda greens, which she then saw for the first time, she had needed three putts twice, and she had been a trifle off-line with two drives. And that was all that stood between Joyce Wethered and a level 70, the first afternoon she had seen the 6,600-yard East Lake course.'

During the match, Jones was followed around the course by his doctor – the problem with his appendix persisted – and two days after the match he was in the hospital having it removed. Wethered was keenly aware of Jones's situation, and when Keeler walked alongside her down the 16th fairway, she expressed her gratitude towards Bobby and explained how determined it had made her to deliver her best golf in front of him. 'I had to play well here,' she told Keeler. 'Bobby arranged the match, you know. And he's said and written so many kind things about my game. And then he was ill, and then he insisted on playing. I wish I were sure he *should* be playing, now. It's – it's the most sporting thing I've ever known. I had to play well at East Lake. I couldn't let Bobby down, you know.' 'Yes – I knew,' Keeler concluded. 'I know too that I saw something that afternoon at East Lake that will stand out as the prettiest picture of a lifetime in sport – the two greatest golfers, playing all they knew in every shot, in generous and gallant complement to one another, in the greatest match I ever witnessed.'

THE BABE

For Wethered, the remaining highlights of her tour included visiting California as a guest of Marion Hollins and reuniting with Alexa Stirling in Canada, but that was hardly true for American golf fans. They wanted to see how she fared against the Babe. In the 1932 Olympic Games at Los Angeles, 21-year-old Babe Didrikson had taken the sporting world by storm – winning gold medals in javelin and the 80-metre hurdles and a silver medal in the high jump. In the process, she set four new world records, a performance reminiscent of the great British athlete Lottie Dod.

Didrikson's friend, the sportswriter Grantland Rice, had recently introduced her to golf – a game at which she would, in time, amass one of the greatest records in history, including becoming the first American woman to win the British Ladies' Championship in 1947. In 1935, despite her athletic gifts, the Babe was still raw and unschooled at golf, and she proved no match for Wethered on either of the two occasions on which they met. The first of those unfolded on 7 July at Oak Park Country Club in Chicago, where a crowd of 4,000 – the largest of the tour – assembled to watch a match pitting Didrikson and Gene Sarazen against Wethered and Horton Smith, winner of the inaugural Masters the previous season. Wethered and Smith waxed them, needing only 11 holes to close out Didrikson and Sarazen 8 and 7. Both men came in with 71, and Joyce posted a 78 to the Babe's 88.

The story would be much the same when the two clashed again on 24 July at Meadowbrook Country Club in Buffalo, this time with Wethered playing alongside the local professional, Elwyn

Nagell, against the team of Didrikson and Sarazen. This match, played before a crowd of 2,500, was scored by points, with one point awarded for the low ball of the four and another for the team with the lowest aggregate score on the hole. Again, Wethered and Nagell won easily, beating the Babe and Sarazen by four points. And again, Joyce had the lower of the two scores – a 77 to Didrikson's 81 – as Sarazen came in with 72 and Nagell with 73.

Given her distaste for the boisterous scene that surrounded Cecil Leitch, one can imagine how Wethered felt about the sideshow that was Babe Didrikson, then three years away from marrying professional wrestler George Zaharias. Babe spent both matches showing off and clowning around with spectators, adding what journalists called 'colour' to the proceedings. Joyce no doubt found her behaviour off-putting, but was too polite to say anything – or to respond to Didrikson's boasts about how much farther she hit the ball. Wethered preferred to let their scores speak.

Most of the month after that final match against the Babe was spent in California as the guest of Hollins, the creator of Cypress Point and doyenne of Pasatiempo. Hollins took Wethered to many of the greatest courses on the west coast – among them Wilshire Country Club in Los Angeles, San Francisco Golf Club and the American course that most impressed Joyce, Pebble Beach on the Monterey Peninsula.

The final leg of Wethered's North American adventure involved a journey across Canada, which she had visited earlier with a quick stop in Toronto during one of her East Coast swings. Her first stop was Jericho Golf Club in Vancouver, where Wethered and the great Canadian amateur, Ada Mackenzie, teamed up to halve a match against two local male professionals, Dave Black and Alec Duthie. From there, it was a long haul by train across the picturesque landscape of Canada to its capital city, Ottawa, and a reunion with the woman who had caused such a stir in 1921 at Wethered's first British Ladies' Championship, Alexa Stirling. By then, Stirling had been married for a decade to Dr

Wilbert G. Fraser, and was busy raising three children – Sandra, Glen and Richard – but she was still a strong enough golfer to have claimed the second of her two Canadian Amateur championships the previous season.

Wethered played the final two matches of her tour against Stirling – the first at Rivermead, Alexa's home course, and the second at Marlborough Golf Club in Montreal – with both women taking men as their partners. Wethered finished in style as her side won both times with consummate ease, taking the first match by a whopping 15 points and the second 3 and 2. In both cases, she outscored Stirling, coming in with 73 to her 83 the first time around and 75 to her 85 in the second match.

It had been an exhausting grind of matches and travel, and thrilled as she was by the tour, Wethered was happy to be headed home. 'I'm glad it's all over now,' she told a reporter, 'but it has been a fine experience, and I wouldn't have missed it for the world.' Decades later, in a letter to tour organiser Alexander Findlay's grandson, Wethered added that 'being able to meet your top American golfers was a great privilege I enjoyed. I was a special fan of Bobby Jones!' Findlay himself was convinced that the journey he planned for Wethered would do for women's golf in the United States and Canada what Harry Vardon had for the men's game with his visit to North America in 1900. 'It is no overstatement to say that thousands of American women who never played the game before, or played it only casually, were turned into enthusiasts by Miss Wethered's visit,' he told a newspaper reporter. 'Her game was a revelation, not only to women but to men also.'

ONE LAST TIME

Perhaps it was her reunion with Joyce Wethered, or perhaps it was simply that the competitive fire never stopped burning within Glenna Collett. Whatever it was, by the summer of 1935, she had developed an itch. Five times now, she had seen her given name engraved on the Robert Cox Trophy, the glittering prize awarded to the winner of the US Women's Amateur Championship. It was high time, she told her friend Betty Jameson, for a new name to be placed alongside it – that of Mrs Edwin H. Vare Jr., as she had been known since her marriage in 1931 to the Philadelphia engineer. Less than a month after Wethered set sail for home, Collett was on her way to Interlachen Country Club in Hopkins, Minnesota, for her 14th attempt to win the women's national championship, which began that season on 26 August.

It was not the first time Collett had returned to the national scene since she stepped away from golf in 1933 after the birth of her first child. She had competed in the 1934 Amateur, losing in the semi-final to her old nemesis Virginia Van Wie by 3 and 2. That year, Van Wie would go on to win her third consecutive national championship – placing her name alongside the greats – before announcing her retirement from golf.

At Interlachen, Collett faced a field of 94 players, among them the rising stars of a new generation who had grown up admiring and imitating America's greatest woman golfer. For the eighth time in her 14 attempts at the national championship, Collett made her way into the final against a leading light of this new crop of golfers – a red-headed, freckle-faced, 17-year-old from Minnesota by the name of Patty Jane Berg. She was, of course, the home-town favourite, but for the throng of 7,000 that followed the final – paying $1 a ticket during the height of the Great Depression – Collett was the sentimental choice. 'If there is something a doting public loves to witness, it is to see a noble figure emerge from the shadows of the past and return to head the parade,' wrote Bernard Swanson, correspondent for *The American Golfer*.

No doubt because she had spent much of the summer playing against the world's finest woman golfer, Collett came into the tournament feeling confident in her game. While she thought she had lost a bit of length from the tee, that was more than compensated for by the reality that her golf was more consistent than it had been even in her halcyon days. As Swanson saw it, Glenna would never have won the championship otherwise. 'It took Collett at her best to stand off the challenge of a youngster, in fact, to stand off a coterie of youngsters virtually new to national tournament play,' he wrote, singling out not just Berg but also Jameson. Years later, Berg admitted that she found it intimidating to compete against her idol in that final, especially given that the ordinarily charming Collett became such a stoic on the course.

Having made it to that 36-hole championship match on the strength of phenomenal putting, Berg suddenly found herself struggling on the greens. By the time they had reached the turn during the second and final round, she had fallen 4 down. Gamely Berg fought back, winning both the 32nd and 33rd holes to be just 2 down, but that was as close as she would get. Collett calmly rolled in her putt for four on the 34th, as her young opponent could do no better than five, and claimed her sixth national championship, 3 and 2. 'I thought it'd be 8 and 7 or 9 and 8, or something like that, so I really felt that I did OK,' Berg told an interviewer in 2010, on the 75th anniversary of Collett's historic victory.

Collett now stood alone in American golf. No player in the United States – not even Bobby Jones – had ever won six Amateur championships, and chances are no one ever will. JoAnne Gunderson came closest, winning five in the 1950s and 1960s before turning professional. In all of history, only one golfer has won more amateur championships than Glenna Collett, and that is John Ball Jr. of Royal Liverpool Golf Club who won an unimaginable eight. Swanson, for one, was impressed. 'It isn't everyone who, playing in their fourteenth national championship, is still good enough to cope with the next generation on their own field of sports,' he marvelled. 'And fewer still who could win.'

Fourteen

ENDURING LEGACY

———•∘●●∘•———

THE years between Joyce Wethered's ascent at Sheringham and Glenna Collett's passing of the torch at Interlachen would be remembered as a transformative age for women's golf. During those 15 years, Wethered and Collett set a new standard for performance, building on the legacy of the fierce swingers who had preceded them, Britain's Cecil Leitch and America's Alexa Stirling. Both left records likely to stand for all time – Wethered's five consecutive victories in the English Ladies' and Collett's six wins in America's national open. Along the way, both repeatedly posted scores once considered unthinkably low for women – playing over the game's classic courses from the back tees or very close to them.

Wethered was capable of such bursts of brilliance that her matches rarely lasted long enough for her to post a full score – the classic example being her scintillating opening nine of 33 at Troon in 1925 to demolish Gladys Ravenscroft in 13 holes. Few players could withstand such an onslaught. Those who did only inspired Wethered to greater heights, as Collett learned at St Andrews when she played the first 11 holes in 41 to take a 5-up lead, only to see Joyce turn the tables by playing an 18-hole stretch in a mind-boggling 73. Across the Atlantic, where stroke play was more dominant, Collett regularly tamed America's most brutish courses with scores that would have done any man or woman proud – among them 75s at Belleair, Pinehurst No. 2 and St Louis Country Club.

During their reign atop the world of golf, Wethered and Collett scored so low so often that even famous sportswriters like Grantland Rice agreed that the endlessly discussed gap between men and women was narrower than it had ever been or, perhaps, would ever be. How fulfilling it must have been for Issette Pearson, Mabel Stringer and the other pioneers of the Ladies' Golf Union that they lived to see women challenge the hegemony of men. Rare was the golfer who could give Collett the six bisques she believed separated the best men and women, as she demonstrated in high-profile exhibitions and The Gold Ball Tournament. Wethered proved an even tougher proposition. The succession of men she brushed aside at Stoke Poges and elsewhere tended to agree with Jack McLean that only the greatest golfers in the world could give Joyce even a single bisque and prevail.

After watching Wethered at Troon – four years before her miraculous display at St Andrews – Bernard Darwin was already prepared to crown her as the finest player ever seen. 'I hereby declare,' he wrote, 'that more flawless golf than Miss Wethered's has never been played by anybody, man, woman or demi-god.' Darwin was hardly alone. Every leading golfer and writer who watched or competed with Wethered during her tour of the US and Canada walked away awed by her gifts, and by the notion that she could post an average score of 76.9 during a gruelling trip on which she played over 53 courses she'd never seen in her life. Typical among them was Gene Sarazen, by then a winner of seven major championships and the career Grand Slam. He played with Glenna Collett against Wethered and Johnny Dawson in the tour's opening match, and competed against her side on three other occasions, twice with the great Olympian, but novice golfer, Babe Didrikson as his partner. In advance of the tour, Sarazen assured writers that he knew Joyce would present a formidable challenge. 'If anyone thinks I am taking her lightly, they have another guess coming,' he said. 'I'll probably have to be right at the peak in order to top her by a stroke or two, and if I'm off my game – well I can only hope she doesn't lose her sea legs too quickly after getting off the boat. I blush easily.'

As it turned out, Sarazen needn't have worried. He outscored Wethered comfortably every time – the closest she came was within five strokes – even though he lost both of his matches with Didrikson, halved with Collett and only prevailed when playing against Joyce and Glenna with Jess Sweetser, a winner of the US and British amateurs. Still, Sarazen was mightily impressed by what he saw from Wethered. In his memoir, *Thirty Years of Championship Golf*, Sarazen devoted a chapter to ranking the great men and women of his time, which of course extended well beyond the careers of Wethered and Collett. He placed women golfers in three classes. Wethered and Collett stood alone at the top. Next came Virginia Van Wie, Babe Didrikson, Pam Barton and Louise Suggs, followed on his third tier by Patty Berg, Helen Hicks, Betty Jameson, Maureen Orcutt and Alexa Stirling. 'There is one note I would like to add on this ranking,' Sarazen wrote. 'Joyce Wethered, the English star, struck me, as she did most critics, as being in a class by herself. At the same time, anyone who has won six National Championships, as Glenna Collett did, cannot be ranked in anything but the top category.'

Walter Hagen, the other leading American professional of the 1920s and 1930s, came to a similar conclusion after seeing Wethered play while he was in Britain to compete in the Open. 'As I watched her,' Hagen wrote in 1934, a year before Joyce's tour of the States, 'I thought there wasn't a male golfing star in the world who wouldn't envy the strong, firm type of stroke she played.' Brilliantly as they performed during their 15-year reign as the Empresses of Golf, the lasting memory of Wethered and Collett would always be the scintillating display they put on at St Andrews in 1929. Even today, nearly a century later, many historians would agree that their 36-hole final in that British Ladies' remains what *New York Tribune* correspondent Al Laney proclaimed it to be in his report on the championship – the greatest women's golf match ever played.

THE PERFECT GOLFER

In the aftermath of that epic clash at the Home of Golf, the cognoscenti began to seriously contemplate the notion that one day the game might produce a perfect golfer. That was only natural given the scores Wethered and Collett posted that afternoon. Still, the notion that perfection might be achieved in golf got a far bigger boost the following season as Bobby Jones marched to the Grand Slam, a goal no player had previously had the audacity to set for himself. Even before he had completed the Slam, however, Jones had played 18 holes of golf as flawless as any the game had ever witnessed. In qualifying for the 1926 Open, Jones went around Sunningdale in 66 strokes – 33 shots and 33 putts, with nothing but fours and threes on his card. 'He simply went on and on with exact perfection,' marvelled Darwin, who struggled to believe what he had seen, as did the crowd that followed Jones every step of the way.

The year after the Grand Slam, in 1931, the concept received an in-depth exploration in a book by Herbert Newton Wethered titled *The Perfect Golfer*. In his preface, Wethered acknowledges that his children, Joyce and Roger, had originally been approached as the writers, but she, at least, was far too modest to style herself as anything close to faultless. Curiously, Wethered opens his book with an acknowledgement that perfection is unattainable – and, indeed, undesirable. If the perfect golfer came along, he writes, 'golf would have ceased to function as a game, or to have any meaning as a sport. There would be no fun in it.'

Still, Wethered asserts that during the course of history, three players had emerged who came close enough to perfection 'to have brought the cup to the lip' – Tom Morris Jr., Harry Vardon and Bobby Jones, an assessment few historians would challenge. One chapter of the book is devoted to the question Alexander Doleman posed all those years ago when he was awestruck by the play of Lady Margaret Scott in the first British Ladies' – could a woman ever master golf sufficiently to win a men's championship? Wethered concedes that, beyond the difference in physical strength, there is no reason why that should not come to pass one day, given the remarkable progress women had made during those years between wars. 'Within an incredibly short space of time scores have come down with a rush,' he notes, 'the play has opened up; no distinction of style now exists from that of men; there is a difference of power, but the gap is closing up chiefly by the application of greater skill and artistry. In fact, if some phenomenal putter were to arise whose play in other departments of the game was equally efficient, there is no knowing what might happen.'

Newton Wethered goes on to single out the three women he believed had come closest to mastering golf at a level comparable to the immortals of the men's game: Cecil Leitch, Glenna Collett and his daughter, Joyce. 'Here again it will be noticed that by an accident of history a trio has arranged itself in harmony with the various triumvirates that have arisen,' he writes. 'They are each of them individualists who have the nearest reached perfection and succeeded in monopolising during their careers the majority of the championship honours.'

It is puzzling that Wethered did not include Alexa Stirling in his line-up of breakthrough women golfers, given the splash she made in 1921 and that her impact was as transformative in America as Leitch's was in Britain. Collett would be the first to acknowledge that it was Stirling who taught American women to lash at the ball. Perhaps it was simply a fascination with triumvirates in the years following the reign of Harry Vardon, John Henry Taylor and James Braid. Or, perhaps, Wethered perceived a chink in Stirling's armour that left her a notch below the other three, as Sarazen clearly had. A woman of frail constitution, Stirling was never as effective over 36 holes as she was in a single round, and in Britain that is considered the all-important test of a champion. Nor was she able to defeat men at Stoke Poges, as Collett had done, or to return to America as champion of another nation, as Glenna had in winning a title in France.

Nevertheless, it seems a shame to have overlooked a player who paved the way for her fellow American women and placed her name alongside the immortals by winning three consecutive US Women's Amateurs. Even if Stirling had been given her due alongside Leitch, there is no denying that during their careers, Wethered and Collett separated themselves from those two and all other women golfers – Joyce as the perfect technician, Glenna as the perfect competitor.

Wethered came of age at a time when stop-action photography, and later slow-motion film, made it possible to dissect the golf swing position by position, from takeaway to follow-through. In 1931 and 1932, Joyce's idol, Bobby Jones, made a series of instructional films that proved beyond any shadow of doubt what had already been declared by acclamation – that he had as fine a golf swing as any ever seen. No wonder, then, that Wethered's reputation for surpassing greatness was only redoubled when Hal Rhodes's film showed her move to be a mirror image of the great amateur's. Grantland Rice, America's leading sportswriter, was so mesmerised by Wethered's action as he followed her 1935 tour that he devoted an article in *The American Golfer* to 'The Secrets of Miss Wethered's Golf' – from the way she held the club to the way she effortlessly transferred her weight during the backswing and downswing. Rice was also deeply impressed with Wethered's ability to discuss the golf swing in intricate detail, and to clearly articulate her own methods – a gift she had demonstrated over and over in instructional books and articles that constitute a legacy of their own.

Wethered's North American tour, her record of nine victories in a dozen championships and her gorgeous swing combined to earn her a lasting reputation as the greatest of all women golfers – and, in Jones's assessment, the finest player of either sex the game had ever produced. That was only reinforced by an article British golf writer Leonard Crawley published in January 1944, in which he pointed out that Wethered's lifetime winning percentage exceeded 90 per cent – 152 wins, two halves and only a dozen losses in 166 matches. It is true that Wethered competed far less frequently than her peers. Collett, for instance, played as many matches in three seasons as Wethered did in her entire career. Nevertheless, Crawley asserts that 'taking everything into consideration, I do not know of a record in the annals of sport so utterly consistent or so absolutely convincing.' Even as late as 1975, when he was writing his seminal history *The Story of American Golf*, Herbert Warren Wind was not prepared to declare any woman superior to Wethered – and that was well after he had witnessed the dazzling golf of Mickey Wright and Babe Didrikson. Wethered's swing, Wind insisted, was 'the most correct and loveliest golf has ever known'.

Collett never did have the classically beautiful swing of Wethered, but she had the perfect temperament for championship golf, a competitive fire that burned brightly all her days, and a graciousness in both victory and defeat that endeared her to a generation. The wild, scampering crowds, the enormous pressure of a tournament's defining moment – all the things that made Wethered happy to put championship golf behind her – were an elixir to Collett, who never tired of the thrill of being in the arena, win or lose.

Perhaps the defining fact about the life of Glenna Collett is this. Her home course, Point Judith Country Club in Rhode Island, held an annual invitational, and Collett competed in the event for 62 consecutive years, playing into her eighties, even as her handicap rose to 15. Collett's son, Edwin, learned the hard way just how competitive his mother was. In the 1950s, they played together as a team in a mixed foursomes event. He lost track of the score, and made the mistake of asking his mother where the match stood. 'What do you mean, how do we stand?' she snapped. 'Why am I playing with you? This is why we're here, to beat these people. We're three up and we're going to get four up.'

Indeed, the record Collett assembled in championship golf knows few rivals in all of history – men or women. During her career, she played every season in three major championships, the Eastern Amateur, the North and South Amateur, and the US Women's Amateur. She won each of them six different times – a record in both the Eastern and US Women's Amateurs and second-best in the North and South, behind Estelle Lawson's seven victories in the 1930s and '40s. When it came time to write the first history of American golf, published in 1936, the year after Collett's sixth and final US Amateur victory, there was no question in the mind of author H.B. Martin about who deserved the title of 'queen of the American links'. It was the young woman from Rhode Island whom he had introduced to Scotsman Alex Smith in 1919, just three years before her ascent to the top at White Sulphur Springs, Virginia, in the 1922 US Women's Amateur. 'It was,' Martin wrote, 'the start of a glorious reign of links supremacy that has carried her to the greatest heights in women's golf.'

NEW ERA

The legacy of Joyce Wethered, Glenna Collett and the other luminous stars of women's golf during that age between two wars extended far beyond riveting championship finals and otherworldly scores. No entrepreneur with an eye for profits could fail to notice the size of the crowds that had begun to assemble for major events in women's golf. The two championship finals between Wethered and Collett – at Troon in 1925 and St Andrews in 1929 – had drawn crowds approaching 10,000, as did the first Curtis Cup three years later. Even more fans, some 15,000 in all, had swarmed Interlachen Country Club – paying $1 a ticket at the height of the Great Depression – over the six days of the 1935 US Amateur.

Numbers that large did not fail to attract the attention of those interested in creating professional opportunities for women golfers, first among them L.B. Icely, chief executive of Wilson Sporting Goods. In 1935, the year of Wethered's North American tour, Icely signed the former US Women's Amateur champion Helen Hicks to a professional contract to promote Wilson equipment. A handful of lesser-known women had already turned professional to be able to give lessons or work in golf shops. By the late 1930s, the ranks of women professionals had swelled to include such famous players as Opal Hill, Collett's first Curtis Cup partner, and the megastar of Olympic fame, Babe Didrikson. A handful of women's tournaments – the Western Open, the Titleholders in Augusta, the Asheville Invitational and the Women's Texas Open – had also begun allowing professionals to enter alongside amateurs.

Together, these developments created a groundswell of interest in a formal women's professional tour, but by 1939 the world was again engulfed in war, and no progress could be made until hostilities ceased in 1945. The first attempt to launch a professional circuit was begun that very year by Hope Seignious, who had just been hired as head golf professional at North Shore Country Club in Milwaukee, Wisconsin. Using her own money, supplemented by support from her father, a cotton broker, Seignious founded the Women's Professional Golf Association. Several notable stars immediately signed on, among them Hicks and another US Amateur champion, Betty Jameson, a close friend of Collett's.

Initially, the WPGA made considerable progress. It added a handful of tournaments to the schedule, among them the Hardscrabble in Arkansas and the Tam O'Shanter in Chicago, and in 1946 launched the US Women's Open, with sponsorship from the Spokane Athletic Round Table. Seignious may have had the vision to foresee the future, but she did not have either financial resources or the promotional skills required to make her dream of a thriving women's professional golf tour a reality. The inevitable result was internal squabbling among members of the WPGA and, in December 1949, the closure of the tour.

That's when L. B. Icely and Wilson Sporting Goods came to the rescue. Icely asked Fred Corcoran, a member of his staff who was already managing the career of Didrikson, to help launch a new organisation for professional women golfers. The following year, in 1950, the new Ladies' Professional Golf Association was launched, with Corcoran as its commissioner and 13 women as founders: Didrikson, Patty Berg, Louise Suggs, Betty Jameson, Helen Hicks, Opal Hill, Helen Dettweiler, Alice and Marlene Hagge, Sally Sessions, Marilynn Smith, Shirley Spork and Bettye Danoff. Half those women had competed alongside Glenna Collett – and all of them had grown up idolising her, Joyce Wethered, Marion Hollins, Alexa Stirling, Cecil Leitch, Molly Gourlay and the other women who had blazed a trail that made their new lives as professionals possible.

With Didrikson as its shining star and Corcoran at its helm, the fledgling LPGA was positioned to survive the long and rocky road to becoming the thriving organisation we know today. By 1952, for instance, the new tour had already amassed 21 events. It would be another generation before women's professional golf arrived in Britain, where the amateur ideal had deeper roots and more staying power. The Ladies' European tour was not launched until 1978.

Neither Collett nor Wethered ever expressed the slightest interest in professional golf. Even when financial necessity forced her to take a job in golf and tour North America, Wethered never had any intention of using her new status to compete in professional tournaments. Collett felt the same way, and said so in her 1928 book *Ladies in the Rough*. 'As for me,' she wrote, 'I like to play the game for the mere fun of it. It is not, and I hope it never will be, a religion with me. When it becomes a purpose in life, a means to an end, a weakness rather than a strength, I shall announce my retirement from amateur sport.'

Nevertheless, Collett could see that the world of sport was changing, and that the ideals she and Wethered had grown up with were fading fast in a post-war age increasingly captivated by sport and driven by men and women ambitious to capitalise on every opportunity. 'The amateur is a vanishing figure in American life,' she wrote. 'Even in England it is not easy to find amateurs who can give their time freely to sporting pursuits. All of which means that the amateur is on the brink of oblivion. Look on him while you may.'

Collett's own beliefs, however, never stopped her from being an encouraging mentor to many of those 13 pioneers who set out to create a life for themselves in professional golf, in particular to Betty Jameson. Born in Oklahoma but raised in Texas, Jameson was something of a child prodigy. She won her first event, the Texas Public Links Championship, at 13, and two years later, in 1934, she claimed the Southern Amateur title. That same year she came east to compete in her first US Women's Amateur at Whitemarsh Valley Country Club in Chestnut Hill, Pennsylvania. There she first met her idol Collett, by then a married woman returning to competition after the birth of her two children. It was the beginning of a friendship that became increasingly intimate as the years passed. In a 1992 interview with the USGA, when she was approaching her 73rd birthday, Jameson described the relationship she developed with Collett one of the great joys of her life. 'I was accepted in her home and as part of her family,' Jameson explained in an oral history interview with the USGA. 'That was the most beautiful thing about my relationship with Glenna.'

In 1952, two years after the founding of the LPGA, Jameson made certain that Collett's name would be remembered forever by women in professional golf when she donated a trophy to be awarded annually to the player who compiled the lowest scoring average over the season. It was christened the Vare trophy – honouring the name under which Glenna competed after her marriage, Mrs Edwin H. Vare Jr. – and first awarded during a March 1954 ceremony at the Augusta Country Club, where the annual Titleholders Championship was being played.

Collett, then aged 51, was on hand to present the trophy to the very player she had defeated in 1935 when she claimed her sixth and final US Women's Amateur – Patty Berg. Berg had completed the 1953 LPGA season with a scoring average of 75, exactly the sort of number Collett and Wethered posted regularly enough during their primes to demonstrate to all the world that a new age had arrived for the women's game. Collett's remarks on the occasion reveal an awful lot about a woman whose gift for golf made her among the biggest stars of America's Roaring Twenties, but whose natural shyness always left her feeling squeamish when she was in the limelight. Her speech was brief – 168 words – but typically gracious. She took care to thank Jameson for bestowing this honour upon her and to congratulate the woman who had come closest to Berg in the race for low scoring average, sweet-swinging Louise Suggs. Then she turned to Berg, with whom she had become close friends, and lavished praise on the 36-year-old who had gone on from Interlachen to win the first US Women's Open Championship in 1946. 'I have known Patty for a long time,' Collett told the crowd. 'I beat her once when she was too young to know better. We have been partners in two Curtis Cup matches. Patty has grown up to be a leader in women's golf and has helped the game more than anyone in her teaching, in her clinics and in charity matches. Her wit, leadership and sportsmanship have endeared her to a vast and idolising public.' Then Collett did the most classically Glenna thing of all. 'It gives me great pleasure,' she said, 'to present the Betty Jameson Trophy for the first time . . . and to Patty Berg.' Everyone in that room was well aware that Collett was the greatest woman golfer America had ever known and, perhaps, ever would know, but she was still far too modest to publicly acknowledge her own accomplishments by using the award's proper name – the Vare Trophy.

Fifteen

AFTERLIVES

———•●●●•———

FEW people earn everlasting fame in more than one endeavour. Joyce Wethered was one of those. In the years after 1935, as the game that had dominated her life returned to being a mere pastime, Wethered developed a new passion – gardening – and pursued it with the same relentless quest for perfection that she had applied to mastering the golf swing. Over the years, Wethered became such a renowned gardener that she was awarded the Victoria Medal, the highest honour given by the Royal Horticultural Society, and invited to contribute a chapter to a book titled *The Englishwoman's Garden*.

Not surprisingly, Wethered found her way into this new life through golf. One Saturday in 1936, she was invited to play a game at Royal North Devon organised by a friend named Dickie Hull. He had arranged for their party to include a decidedly eligible bachelor, 42-year-old Sir John Heathcoat-Amory, the second member of his family to inherit the title of baronet that had been awarded to his grandfather in 1874 by Queen Victoria. Hull had a hunch that Wethered and the baronet might hit it off, and when he saw them together on the links, he became certain of it. That afternoon, he bet a friend £5 that Wethered and Heathcoat-Amory would one day be wed. He cashed that wager when the golfer and the baronet became engaged three months later at Royal West Norfolk and married on 6 January 1937 at St George's Church in London. As a wedding gift to the woman now known as Lady Heathcoat-Amory, Sir John commissioned a nine-hole putting green designed by celebrated architect Tom Simpson, a friend of the Wethered family. It was laid out in front of Knightshayes Court, Heathcoat-Amory's grand estate in Tiverton, Devon, and opened in June 1938 with a gala whose attendees included Joyce's parents, Roger and Elizabeth Wethered, Bernard and Eily Darwin and Tom and Edith Simpson.

Heathcoat-Amory led the typical life of an English gentleman. Educated at Eton and Oxford, he played cricket for Devon, maintained a single-figure handicap at golf, demonstrated a keen eye for trap shooting, and served as Master of the Tiverton Hounds, as well as in various local positions, including High Sheriff of Devon. From his father, Heathcoat-Amory had inherited the textile factory that provided his family's wealth. By all accounts, he and his predecessors were model owners, paying decent wages, providing inexpensive housing for employees, giving their children a proper education, and even offering pension plans long before those had become the fashion. Sir John and Joyce, who was seven years younger than her husband, were just three years into their new lives at Knightshayes Court when, on 3 September 1939, Great Britain declared war on Germany in response to its brazen invasion of Poland.

For the next six years, Knightshayes became a rest home for US airmen, the family business made parachutes for the war effort, Sir John became a major in the Home Guards, and Joyce became an inspector in their factory. One night, in the midst of all the horror of bombings during the Blitz, Heathcoat-Amory turned to his wife and said: 'If we get through this war, let's make a garden together.' And that they did. Even before the war broke out,

Wethered had become enchanted by the beauty of the formal garden Edward Kemp laid out in front of Knightshayes when it was built during the late 19th century, as well as its ancient Walled Kitchen Garden. When hostilities ended in May 1945, she threw herself into the new project with characteristic zeal, reading countless books and periodicals on the subject to develop ideas of her own and reaching out to prominent gardeners throughout the nation for advice.

A man with a passion for collecting and the money to buy whatever he desired, Heathcoat-Amory ordered new plants by the score. Wethered took great joy in arranging them in an ever-evolving garden, aided from 1963 by a head gardener named Michael Hickson. From its original 12 acres, their garden at Knightshayes grew to be more than four times that size, especially after the Heathcoat-Amorys became devotees of Dame Sylvia Crowe's notion that gardens should harmonise with the surrounding countryside. To Knightshayes' formal garden and topiary of a fox and hounds, they added a great garden in the wood of rare plants and trees arranged along shady paths leading to stunning vistas. The Walled Kitchen Garden, which provided fruit and vegetables for the household, lasted until the 1960s, when it became unprofitable to maintain and was allowed to go fallow. It has since been restored by the National Trust.

Sir John would be the first recognised for the couple's contributions to gardening, receiving the Royal Horticultural Society's Victoria Medal in 1967, with Joyce receiving that same honour in 1982. It was in the following year that Joyce was invited to contribute to *The Englishwoman's Garden*, and the chapter she wrote demonstrates the same skill in explaining the intricacies of gardening that she had shown in writing articles and books about how to play golf. 'Gardening has been full of excitement for me,' Wethered wrote in the book. 'I know at heart I am a plantswoman, and in company with all those who are devoted to horticulture.'

Even as she dived into her new passion, Wethered did not entirely abandon her first love. In 1951 she became the first president of the English Ladies' Golf Association, a position in which she was largely a figurehead, as she had been during the early 1920s when she served in the same role for the Girls' Golfing Society. Nevertheless, in 1984, aged 83, Wethered admitted in an interview with correspondent Lewine Mair that she sometimes felt guilty about not becoming more involved in golf after she stepped away from the game. 'For my own part, I never got caught up in administration,' she said. 'I hated such things as committee meetings, but looking back, I feel perhaps that I should have done more.'

She also continued to play golf for fun and to compete in the Worplesdon Mixed Foursomes, winning for the eighth and final time in 1936, with Thomas Coke, the 5th Earl of Leicester, as her partner. Wethered and her husband reached the final together in 1948, but Sir John proved to be one of the few men she was unable to drag across the finish line, and they lost by 5 and 4 to Wanda Morgan and Eustace Storey.

The latter part of Wethered's life saw another development that leaves one wondering about the true nature of an intensely private woman. She became a devoted Christian Scientist, the only member of her family to join a church widely viewed as a cult. Founded in the United States by Mary Baker Eddy in 1879, the church teaches, among other things, that there is no such thing as illness, and that the cure for sickness is not medicine but prayer. Wethered was no casual devotee. She contributed generously, was a First Reader at its services in Exeter, shuttled local children to and from church in her Jaguar, and, on the rare occasion when she was ill, took up residence in a Christian Science nursing home. If nothing else, Wethered's devotion to Christian Science demonstrates that she was a woman with an iron will and a mind of her own, and once she'd made it up, there was no convincing her otherwise.

Wethered was 71 years old when her husband died peacefully at Knightshayes on 22 November 1972 at the age of 78. They had been married for 35 years. The following year, Knightshayes and its elaborate gardens were turned over to Great Britain's National Trust, which continues to operate the estate today as a popular tourist attraction. Joyce lived on at Knightshayes for another 25 years, helping Hickson tend its gardens, although later in life she developed inner ear problems that kept her from pursuing her passion for digging in the soil. After Sir John's death, a small room in the mansion was devoted to Wethered's glorious career in golf, no doubt as a way of satisfying the curiosity of visitors. Peter Alliss flew home from the 1989 Masters in Augusta, Georgia, to preside at the opening ceremony. Reflecting Wethered's modesty, it is a small room, 15 feet by 15 feet, that features, among other items, scrapbooks she kept of news clippings, displays of her books, a watercolour of Joyce painted by her father, and various medals she won, especially from Worplesdon.

Curiously, for a woman who prevailed in so many championships, there is but one trophy on display. Wethered had most of the prizes she won melted down by silversmith Omar Ramsden and reconstructed as one large cup, whose base is inscribed with a list of events she treasured winning most. They include her four British Ladies' titles, her five English Championships, her triumph in the *Golf Illustrated* Gold Vase, her three victories in the London Foursomes, her four Surrey championships and, of course, her eight wins in the Worplesdon Mixed Foursomes.

Wethered outlived every one of her contemporaries in women's golf. Issette Pearson passed quietly as World War II was raging. She died on 25 April 1941, aged 79, at her home in Singleton Park, Lancashire, where she had lived since the death of her husband, Thomas H. Miller, in 1916.

Mabel Stringer lived to see one last moment of glory for British women's golf, a victory in the 1956 Curtis Cup, before passing away on 10 February 1958 at her cottage in Kent, where she had installed electric lighting with the £160 gift the union's many 'nieces' had given their beloved Auntie Mabel upon her retirement in 1924.

Eleanor Helme kept writing into her golden years, publishing a series of wildlife books and the wildly popular story of Jerry the Exmoor pony as she lived with her sister, Vera, in Luccombe, West Somerset. Age and infirmity eventually forced both to move to a nursing home in Minehead, where Helme passed away on 13 March 1967, aged 80.

Molly Gourlay lived nearly as long as Wethered did, devoting most of her time to Surrey golf before retiring to quiet life in Camberley, where she died at the age of 92 on 1 October 1990.

Cecil Leitch turned her energies to business and recreation after stepping away from the game, first in antiques and then as the director of Cinema House, which brought foreign films to Britain. She also worked with the Kent County Playing Fields Association, the Central Council of Physical Recreation and the YMCA. In 1976, when the British Ladies' Championship was at last played over her beloved links at Silloth, Leitch was there to present the trophy. A year later, on 16 September 1977, the first great woman golfer died at her home, Chatsworth Court, in London. She was 86.

As she aged, Wethered would receive every honour available to a golfer. In 1988, *Golf* magazine included her on its list of the 100 Heroes of the First Century of Golf in America, and in 1975 Wethered was inducted into the newly created World Golf Hall of Fame. But she was perhaps most proud of the Joyce Wethered Trophy, a small bronze statue presented annually to the best British woman golfer younger than 25.

Wethered continued to watch men's and women's professional golf on television – she was a particular fan of Jack Nicklaus – and in the 1970s attended the LPGA's Women's Masters at Hilton Head, North Carolina, where she marvelled at the casual attire women wore and the remarkable skill they had developed at putting. Passionate as she had become about gardening, it was golf that Wethered returned to on nights when she had trouble falling asleep. At such times, she told Lewine Mair, she would imagine going once again around the Old Course at St Andrews, where she had enjoyed the most glorious afternoon of her illustrious career. That was a memory she would savour until 18 November 1997, the day after her 96th birthday, when the greatest of women golfers died peacefully of old age at Knightshayes.

FOREVER GOLF

In 1938, three years after her final victory in the US Women's Amateur, Glenna Collett and Edwin Vare bought a home overlooking a cove of Narragansett Bay in Rhode Island. They had already been married for seven years, and would be together for another 37 as they raised young Glenna and Edwin, then aged five and four, in the state where Collett had spent her own childhood. Maintaining that old, white house by the bay was always a massive job, but Collett would not have had it any other way. 'It really is home to me,' she told an interviewer in her 85th year, even as she struggled to drive out a family of racoons nesting in her attic. During those years, Collett devoted more time to her passions outside golf – raising dogs and cats, skeet shooting, playing bridge and entertaining her many friends. But she never wandered far from the game, remaining deeply involved with the USGA and the Curtis Cup and competing in her beloved Point Judith Invitational.

Not surprisingly, Collett devoted much of her service to the USGA to helping guide the future of the women's game, serving on the organisation's Women's Committee from 1941 to 1950 and the Girls' Junior Committee from 1951 to 1988. Collett was also passionately devoted to preserving the history of golf in America, especially the extraordinary progress the women's game made during her lifetime, and served on the USGA's Museum Committee for half a century, from 1938 to 1988.

Her driving passion in those days, however, remained the Curtis Cup. She participated in the international match five more times after its debut in 1932, the year she and Opal Hill scored America's winning point against Joyce Wethered and Wanda Morgan. In 1934, following the birth of her son, Edwin, Collett did not take the field, but she nevertheless led the US side to a dominant 6½ to 2½ victory over Great Britain and Ireland as its non-playing captain. Two years later, she returned as America's playing captain, earning a half in her foursome match and a full point in singles to lead her side to a 4½ to 4½ draw that enabled the US, as the holder, to retain the Cup. In 1938, Collett did not serve as America's captain – the honour went to Frances Stebbins that year – but she contributed to another 5½ to 3½ victory by winning her singles match to make up for a surprising loss in foursomes with Patty Berg as her partner.

The coming of war meant no matches for 10 long years, but when the competition resumed in 1948, a 45-year-old Collett was once again at the helm of the American side, winning her foursome with Dorothy Kirby en route to another dominating 6½ to 2½ victory. Collett's final appearance in the Curtis Cup came in 1950, as the side's non-playing captain. It must have been especially satisfying for her to come away with the most dominant victory yet – a 7½ to 1½ drubbing of the team led by Diana Fishwick, the woman who had denied her the British Ladies' Championship in 1930 at Formby. Even today, 75 years later, Collett's four victories as a Curtis Cup captain remain a record for the event, one unlikely to be broken. Her own performance in the competition was also stellar – four wins, one half and two losses in the seven matches she played.

Like Wethered, Collett was destined to outlive her husband, Edwin. He passed away quietly at their home in Narragansett on 29 November 1975 at the age of 75. During her golden years, as she had done when she was an up-and-coming star, Collett divided her time between Rhode Island and Florida, spending winters at a home in Delray and commuting back and forth in a Cadillac Fleetwood, her Norwich Terrier Jimmy at her side. In 1986, as she was approaching her 83rd birthday, writer James Dodson paid Collett a visit in Narragansett after reading that she was about to take part in her 62nd consecutive Point Judith Invitational, as it turned out her final appearance in that event. By then, The Great Glenna's game had become entirely ordinary. Few players who have achieved at such an exalted level can bear to play golf like a weekend hacker, but Collett went on, year after year, competing even as her handicap rose to 15. 'My game is very bad now,' she lamented. 'I'm really no good at it.' Dodson, as it happened, had the exact same 15 handicap, and he sheepishly admitted to Collett 'that's one of the reasons I came. I had it in my mind that it would be fun to play a round together. A head-to-head match.' To which Collett replied curtly, 'You must be dreaming.'

Collett did share with Dodson that many of her friends at the Gulfstream Country Club near Delray, where she played in the winter, had already given up the game. 'The membership is so old that people in their 50s are considered teenagers,' she joked. 'They've quit playing golf, some of them, taken up gourmet cooking ... At parties, that's all they talk about now, gourmet cooking. Not one word about golf anymore. I either had to join them or be left out. So now, I'm a gourmet cook, too.' Collett had apparently applied herself to cooking with the same zeal she brought to golf, as Dodson learned when she served him a steaming hot bowl of her latest specialty, tomato-barley soup.

In the aftermath of her 62nd consecutive Point Judith Invitational, Collett at last decided to give up the game, exasperated by her inability to summon the shots she once made with consummate ease. She still watched professional golf, preferring the men's game just as Wethered did, partly because she was so often disgusted by the way LPGA events were presented on television. Commentators, she noted, never explained how far a woman had driven her ball, or from what distance she was approaching the green with her 6-iron. 'I think some of the men look down their noses at the women,' Collett observed. 'I don't like that at all.'

A visitor to Collett's home would have been just as puzzled as any guest at Knightshayes by the absence of trophies in the home of a woman who carried them off by the score. She, too, had nearly all her cups melted down and refashioned into a large silver tray on which were engraved the names of important tournaments she won. Like Wethered, Collett would be showered with honours as she aged. Her name was also on that 1988 list of the 100 Heroes of the First Century of Golf in America, and in 1975 she too was inducted into the Hall of Fame. A decade earlier, she received the Bob Jones Award, given annually by the USGA to a golfer who demonstrates the same spirit, character and respect for the game as the Grand Slam winner. Collett's final moment of recognition came in 1982 at Jack Nicklaus's Memorial Tournament, where she was the first woman to be honoured with a re-release of her 1928 classic *Ladies in the Rough*. Collett told the crowd she was thrilled to be recognised, 'especially since I am still alive' – a line that got a laugh even from comedian Bob Hope.

As Wethered did, Collett outlived the vast majority of her contemporaries. Marion Hollins, the brightest light of that generation, met an especially tragic end. By 1937, between the Great Depression and her extravagant spending, she was in serious financial trouble. The situation became untenable that December when her convertible was hit by a drunk driver as she was returning to Pasatiempo. Hollins suffered a severe concussion, the beginning of a decline that led to her death on 28 August 1944 at a nursing home in Pacific Grove. She was 51 years old.

Alexa Stirling lived the rest of her days in Canada, raising her three children, enjoying her music, making tongue-and-groove furniture and playing the game she loved. Over the years, she won the ladies' championship at Royal Ottawa Golf Club nine times. In 1950, when the Women's Amateur was played at East Lake, she paid a visit to Bobby Jones, by then crippled by a rare spinal disease. When Stirling saw him propped up on two canes, 'I felt as if a steel band had suddenly been clamped around my chest.' It was the last time those childhood friends would meet. Jones died on 18 December 1971. Six years later, on 15 April 1977, Stirling passed away in Canada. She was 79 years old.

Edith Cummings retired from tournament golf in 1926, and eight years later married wealthy Detroit businessman Curtis B. Munson, who had earned a fortune in coal and lumber. Beyond travel and philanthropy, her principal interests became big-game hunting and fishing in the Yukon. Cummings died on 20 November 1984, five years after her husband, at Decatur House, their home in Washington, DC.

Only Virginia Van Wie would live longer than Collett. The American with the sweetest swing retired in 1935, following her three consecutive victories in the Women's Amateur, and went on to spend more than three decades teaching golf in Chicago. She died on 18 February 1997.

In her waning years, Collett contracted lymphoma, but even as she suffered with cancer she remained as stoic as she had always been on the golf course, never once complaining about the hand fate had dealt her. Collett was at her home in Delray on 2 February 1989, just months away from her 86th birthday, when the friends and family who had joined her for a dinner party noticed a change coming over her. It was mid-afternoon, a time when the sun shines so brightly in Florida that Collett ordinarily had the curtains drawn. Her daughter, Glenna, her sister-in-law and her dear friends Betty Jameson and Mary Lena Faulk were all surprised to hear her say, 'Turn the lights on. It's dark in here.' 'She was really just going on her way,' Jameson remembered. 'And I went home that night, and the next morning when I called and asked how Glenna was, they told me she had died.' Collett left behind two puppies she had taken in after Jimmy's passing – a dachshund named Willie and a shih-tzu called Sammy – both of whom were adopted by her closest friend, Betty Jameson.

THE ETERNAL STRUGGLE

Events that unfolded in the aftermath of Collett's death provided a stark reminder that women's golf had developed alongside the struggle women waged to earn their rightful place in a man's world – and that the battle was still a very long way from being won. Days after her passing, Collett's children received a call from the president of the Metacomet Golf Club in Rhode Island, where on that long-ago afternoon, in the company of her father, Collett struck her first drive and awed the assembled crowd. The club wanted to create a memorial to honour Metacomet's most famous golfer, and asked her children, Glenna and Edwin, for memorabilia to include in the display. They donated an early trophy their mother had won – one she valued enough that it was not melted down for the creation of her silver tray – and both were invited to present it during a ceremony at the club on 30 October 1991.

Just before the ceremony, one of Edwin's friends invited him and Glenna's husband into the grill room for a drink. Collett's daughter and the wife of another friend were not invited in. They were left to wait outside on a bench, as women were not permitted in the men's grill at Metacomet. 'I was angry,' Glenna later told a reporter, and so was her brother, especially as the wait went on and on. 'It had never occurred to me that I was a second-class citizen.' In the days afterwards, Edwin explained, he and his sister could not stop thinking about how their mother would have reacted. 'Our mother would never have stood for such treatment,' he said. 'And had she known about Metacomet's policies towards women, she would not have donated anything to honour such a club.'

The club's president sought to explain, arguing that women at Metacomet had their own locker room and their own grill and better access to tee times than other clubs provided. That was not enough for Glenna and Edwin. They told the president that they would give Metacomet time to change its policy, but if the club was unwilling to do so, Collett's trophy would have to be returned. It arrived days later by registered mail, without comment from the club.

If Metacomet's attitude was a distressing reminder that achieving genuine equality remained an eternal struggle for women, and always would, the response of Collett's children was, at least, a testament to the progress society had already made. It was progress born of the indelible mark women had made in fields ranging from politics and literature to science and sport – not infrequently moving men to preserve forever the memory of accomplishments so extraordinary that they might never be witnessed again.

The transcendent golf Collett and Wethered brought out of one another during the generation between two wars was exactly that sort of manifest genius, capped by their dazzling performance at St Andrews in 1929. On that May morning – standing on the shoulders of a succession of women that stretched from Lady Margaret Scott and Beatrix Hoyt through May Hezlet and Rhona Adair to Cecil Leitch and Alexa Stirling – they played a game as sublime as any seen in five centuries of golf over the Old Course. The lustre of that matchless performance has not dimmed in the decades since, and as long as golf is played it will keep alive the memory of Joyce Wethered and Glenna Collett, two women who stood astride their sport as few players, men or women, have ever done in any game.

NOTES ON CHAPTERS

This book, in keeping with its predecessors *Monarch of the Green* and *The Long Golden Afternoon*, is a narrative history. Its ambition is to tell the story of a transformative age in women's golf without straying from the documented record of the times. Below readers will find the source material that is the basis of quotations and statements of fact in this book, as well as the scenes that unfold during the telling of the story.

Writing about women during this age presents a unique challenge – addressing the reality that most changed their names after marriage. This raises two issues, confusion for the reader and loss of identity for the woman. Keeping track of characters and their accomplishments becomes impossibly difficult if their names change midway through the story. For these reasons, the author has chosen to refer to women throughout the text by their given names, even after marriage.

The only exceptions involve competitors mentioned in passing. Often, it was not possible, without an unprofitable expenditure of effort, to determine their given names. In such cases, those women are referred to in the text only by their married name, as was convention at the time.

ONE
EMPRESSES OF GOLF

The full-page presentation about Joyce Wethered and Glenna Collett headlined 'Empresses of Golf' appeared in the August 1924 issue of *Golf Illustrated* magazine in the United States.

Recollections by Collett and Wethered of their match at Troon in 1925 are from their respective memoirs, *Ladies in the Rough* and *Golfing Memories and Methods*, supplemented by contemporary news accounts.

The statement that their play at St Andrews in 1929 left golf correspondent Bernard Darwin at a loss for words is drawn from his account in *The Times* of London, as preserved in the collection *Mostly Golf*, edited by Peter Ryde.

Information about the history of the suffragette movement is drawn from two books, *Suffragettes*, edited by Joyce Marlow, and *The Woman's Hour*, by Elaine Weiss.

Information about the birth of the US-based Ladies Professional Golf Association is drawn from Rhonda Glenn's *The Illustrated History of Women's Golf* and the 2016 documentary film, *The Founders*.

TWO
LADIES ON THE LINKS

The report of women playing over Bruntsfield Links in 1738 is drawn from an article by David Hamilton and Neil Millar in the journal, *Through the Green*, published by the British Golf Collectors Society.

Information about the evolution of women's golf at Musselburgh and St Andrews is drawn from *A History of Golf*, by Robert Browning, *The St Andrews Ladies Putting Club* by Seonaid McAinish and *The Life of Tom Morris*, by W.W. Tulloch.

Information about the formation of the North Devon Ladies' Club and the subsequent growth of women's golf in England is drawn from *The Great English Golf Boom*, by Michael Morrison, as well as *The Royal North Devon Golf Club*, a centenary history.

Information about the childhood of Issette Pearson is drawn from her entry in the *Oxford Dictionary of National Biography*.

Information about the founding of the Wimbledon Ladies Golf Club, Pearson's relationship with Dr William Laidaw Purves, the founding of the Ladies' Golf Union and the first Ladies' Championship, is drawn from a variety of sources. These include: *Golfing Ladies*, by Rosalynde Cossey; *The Story of Ladies' Golf*, by Malcolm Crane; *One Hundred Years of Women's Golf*, by Lewine Mair, and *The History of Royal Wimbledon Golf Club*.

The statement by a journalist describing Pearson as 'despotic as the Czar of Russia' is repeated in all three of the previously mentioned histories of the women's game by Cossey, Crane and Mair.

NOTES ON CHAPTERS

The quotes from Purves' speech at the founding meeting of the Union are from *Ladies Golf*, by May Hezlet, where the speech is preserved in its entirety.

Pearson's quote about now knowing whether other women were playing when she learned the game on Barnes Common is from *Our Lady of the Green*.

Information about the growth of the women's game around the globe is from Browning's *History of Golf*; *From Green to Gold: The First 50 Years of The Australian Ladies' Golf Union*; *The History of Royal Melbourne Golf Club in Australia*, published on its 125th Anniversary; online histories of women's golf in South Africa; James Barclay's *Golf in Canada*, and Glenn's *Illustrated History*.

The story of France Boit's visit to Boston, and the developments that followed, is from H.B. Martin's *Fifty Years of American Golf*, supplemented by Glenn's *Illustrated History*.

Information about the founding of the USGA and the first women's championship is from Martin's history, as well as *Golf in America*, by George B. Kirsch, The Story of American Golf, by Herbert Warren Wind and Glenn's *Illustrated History*.

THREE
AUNTIE MABEL AND THE CZAR

The story of Mabel Stringer's life and her meeting with Issette Pearson is from her memoir, *Golfing Reminiscences*, as well as her entry in the *Oxford Dictionary of National Biography*.

Information about the charges filed against Henry Stringer, Mabel's father, was discovered in research by noted historian Gillian Kirkwood and shared with the author. The New Romney Public Library tracked down the results of the case, in which Stringer was acquitted of all charges.

Information about the growth and development of the Ladies' Golf Union is from the histories by Mair, Cossey, Crane and Glenn, along with Stringer's *Reminiscences* and Eleanor Helme's memoir, *After the Ball*.

Information about the founding of women's golf associations in America is drawn from online histories of the groups mentioned. Information about early tournaments for women – and the Orange Blossom Circuit in Florida – is drawn from Glenn's *Illustrated History*.

Pearson's quote about handicapping is from *Our Lady of the Green*. Information about the specifics of the handicapping system developed by the Ladies Golf Union is from Cossey's *Golfing Ladies*.

The statements about women's golf by Lord Wellwood are quoted from Cossey's *Ladies Golf*. The quotes from Genevive Hecker are from her book *Golf for Women*.

Stringer's descriptions of the various clubhouses mentioned are from her memoir.

Descriptions of the clothing women wore are from Stringer and Helme's memoirs, as well as the histories by Cossey and Mair.

Stories about women's early involvement in sport are from *The Gentlewoman's Book of Sports*, edited by Lady Violet Greville.

Lottie Dod's life story is from *Little Wonder*, by Sasha Abramsky.

The history of the suffragette movement is summarised from the works of Marlow and Weiss, supplemented with scholarly articles by John Ellwood of Moray Golf Club and historian Jane Kay. The quote from Lilian Lenton and the story of Emily Wilding Davison are from Marlow's *Suffragettes*.

The story of Pearson hiring boy scouts to patrol a golf course is quoted from Crane's *The Story of Ladies' Golf*.

Stringer's quote about suffragettes is from her memoir.

Qualifying scores made by women and men in US Amateur Championships are from the records of the USGA, supplemented by details in Martin's *Fifty Years of American Golf*. Similarly, records of British men are from the Royal and Ancient Golf Club of St Andrews.

Information about records set by women golfers is drawn from Cossey's *Golfing Ladies*, as well as *The Golfing Annual*. Details about the length of Woking Golf in 1895 are from the club's history, *A Temple of Golf*.

May Hezlet's quote about Rhona Adair is from her book, *Ladies Golf*.

Information about Rhona Adair's matches against Old Tom Morris is drawn from W.W. Tulloch's *The Life of Tom Morris*, as well as from reports in the following newspapers: *The Morning Leader* of 31 July 1900 and 16 August 1901; *The Lancashire Evening Post* of 16 August 1901; *The Daily Telegraph* and *Courier* of 16 August 1901 and the *St Andrews Citizen* of 4 August 1900.

Adair's quote about American women and their driving ability is from Genevive Hecker's *Golf for Women*.

FOUR
SHE IS FIERCE

The notion that conducting the Ladies' Championship at St Andrews was like visiting Mecca, as well as the subsequent quotes from Mabel Stringer about the event's place in history, the invitation to visit the Royal and Ancient, and her meeting with Old Tom Morris are all drawn from her memoir.

The descriptions of the play in the tournament by Maud Titterton, Dorothy Campbell, Cecil Letich and others are drawn from multiple sources, including *The Golfing Annual*, Stringer's memoir, Leitch's memoir *Golf*, and Helme's memoir.

Helme's assessment of what Leitch taught women golfers also from her memoir.

Leitch's quotes reflecting on her experiences at St Andrews are from her memoir.

Details of Leith's childhood in Silloth are from multiple sources, including her memoir, her entry in the *Oxford Dictionary of National Biography*, *Golf at Silloth, a club history* by Peter Cusack and John Pearson, and a pamphlet Pearson wrote about Leitch for the club.

The story about Cecil hacking away from the heather as her sister May looked on is told in Leitch's memoir. The description of her golf swing is drawn from *Golf at Silloth*.

Leitch's specific quotes about her early golf at Silloth, including the tales of visits by Eustace White and Mrs Archibald Smith, are all from her memoir, as are her recollections of the way Issette Pearson nurtured her during her early years in the game.

Stringer's memoir notes that she provided news coverage of the 1908 Championship at St Andrews to newspapers in New Zealand and the United States, and includes her description of Leitch as the 'girl-child from Cumberland'.

Leitch's memoir, along with the previously mentioned histories of the women's game, note how Pearson changed eligibility rules for the International Match to allow Cecil to join the English side and later to enable her to play County Golf for Hertfordshire.

Leitch's record score of 72 is quoted from *Golf at Silloth*. Other tales of Leitch's troubles during her lean years are drawn from her memoir, supplemented by the histories of women's golf written by Cossey and Crane.

Details of Leitch's loss at Royal North Devon in 1910, as well as her quote, are from her memoir, supplemented by the memoirs of Stringer and Helme, as well as the various histories of the women's game.

Information about the careers of Dorothy Campbell and Gladys Ravenscroft is drawn from the histories by Mair, Cossey and Crane, Leitch's memoir and the memoirs of Stringer and Helme.

Leitch's assessments of why she struggled during her lean years, as well as her recollections of her breakthrough at Hunstanton, are all drawn from her memoir, supplemented by the histories of the women's game and by the memoirs of Stringer and Helme.

FIVE
AMERICA'S ANSWER

Information about Alexa Stirling's winning of the medal in the first Southern Amateur Championship is drawn from records kept on the website of the Southern Women's Golf Association.

Information about Stirling's performance in the 1914 US Amateur Women's Championship is drawn from reports in the US magazine *Golf Illustrated*.

Information about Stirling's childhood is drawn from multiple sources, principally Linton Hopkins' book *East Lake: Where Bobby Learned to Play*, supplemented by O.B. Keeler's *The Bobby Jones Story*, Jones' memoir *Down the Fairway* and James Barclay's *Golf in Canada*.

Stirling's quotes about her love of carpentry and the violin are from a 1920 story in *Canadian Golfer* entitled 'The Glorious Golfing Girl'.

The quote by Grantland Rice is from a 1919 story in the *New York Herald Tribune*.

Stewart Maiden's quote about Alexa's devotion to the violin is drawn from *Women's Golf's Greatest Forgotten Champion*, an article published on the website of the Ladies' Professional Golf Association.

The story of Jones and Stirling competing for a cup at East Lake as youngsters is from Hopkins' book on East Lake, as well as Keeler's biography and Jones' memoir.

Stirling's memories of Jones's temper tantrums are from an essay she wrote for *Readers Digest* in April 1960 entitled 'The Most Unforgettable Character I've Met'.

Information about America's boom years in golf is from *Golf in America*, by George B. Kirsch, *50 Years of American Golf*, by H.B. Martin and *The Story of American Golf*, by Herbert Warren Wind.

Information about the formation of the Southern Women's Golf Association and the staging of the first Southern Amateur at East Lake in 1911 is from the association's website and *Golf Illustrated*.

Information about Stirling's performances in the 1915 Southern and Women's Amateur championships is from *Golf Illustrated* and the website of the Southern Women's Golf Association.

Stirling's own assessment about the strength she had developed in her wrists is from the *Canadian Golfer* article 'The Glorious Golfing Girl'.

Coverage of the 1916 Southern and Women's Amateur championships is drawn from *Golf Illustrated*, *The Boston Herald* and *The American Golfer*, supplemented by details from Keelers' biography, Hopkins' book on East Lake and Glenn's *Illustrated History*.

Information about Bobby Jones performance in the US Amateur is from his memoir, *Down the Fairway*, and Keeler's *The Bobby Jones Story*.

Information about Cecil Leitch's activities during the war is drawn from newspaper accounts kindly supplied to the author by Paul Fowler, of *The Golfing Herald*, supplemented by research shared with the author by historian John Pearson, as well as his pamphlet *Cecil Leitch: Champion Golfer*.

Information about Stirling's activities during the war is drawn from Keeler's *The Bobby Jones Story*, *Down the Fairway* and Hopkin's book on East Lake.

Information about women gaining the right to vote during and just after World War I is from Weiss's *The Woman's Hour* and Marlow's *Suffragettes*. Women's firsts were drawn from Basil Ashton Tinkler's biography of Joyce Wethered, entitled *The Great Lady of Golf*, as well as the online US website history.com

SIX
CORONATION AT PRINCE'S

Bernard Darwin's quote about the dominance of Cecil Leitch is from 'The Ladies', an essay in his book *Golf Between Two Wars*.

Information about the women's English Amateur Championship of 1919 and the British Ladies Championship of 1920 is drawn from multiple sources – the memoirs of Leitch, Stringer and Helme, supplemented by coverage in *The Scotsman*, Barclay's *Golf in Canada*, and summaries of the event in the histories by Crane, Mair and Cossey.

NOTES ON CHAPTERS

Information about Joyce Wethered's childhood and her early development in golf is from multiple sources, including Tinkler's biography, Joyce's memoir, and her entry in the *Oxford Dictionary of National Biography*, supplemented by the various histories of women's golf in Britain and notes supplied by Royal Dornoch Golf Club.

Information about the 1920 Women's English Amateur Championship at Sheringham is drawn from multiple sources, among them the memoirs of Wethered, Leitch, Stringer and Helme, supplemented by coverage of the event from the *Times of London*.

The exchange between Wethered and a reporter about the passing train is from Roslalynde Cossey's *Golfing Ladies*, supplemented by recollections from Leitch's memoir.

Information about the American invasion of Britain in 1921 is from multiple sources, among them the memoirs of Leitch, Helme and Stringer, John Behrend's history *The Amateur*, and online records of The Open Championship kept by the Royal and Ancient Golf Club.

Information about Stirling's performances in 1919 and 1920 is drawn from multiple sources, among them *Golfers Magazine*, *The American Annual*, *Glenn's Illustrated History*, Hopkins' book on East Lake, Keeler's biography of Bobby Jones, and Barclay's history of golf in Canada.

Information about the 1921 British Ladies' Championship at Turnberry is drawn from multiple sources, among them coverage in *Golf Illustrated*; the memoirs of Stringer, Helme, Leitch and Wethered; Darwin's *Golf Between Two Wars*; Tinkler's biography of Wethered; the histories by Glenn, Cossey, Crane, and Enid Wilson's *A Gallery of Women Golfers*.

Information about the French Open at Le Fontainebleau is from the memoirs of Leitch and Wethered, as well as a biography of Leitch compiled by *The Golfing Herald*.

Joyce Wethered's comments about how Cecil Letich was the better player in 1921 are drawn from her memoir.

Tinkler's quote about Wethered is from his biography of her.

Information about the 1921 English Amateur Championship is drawn from multiple sources, among them the memoirs of Stringer and Helme, the histories of women's golf and Tinkler's biography.

Information about Cecil Leith's trip to America and Canada drawn from her memoir, Barclay's *Golf in Canada*, and historian Pearson's pamphlet on Leitch.

Information about the 1922 British Ladies' Championship at Prince's is drawn from coverage in *The Scotsman*; the US and UK editions of *Golf Illustrated*; the memoirs of Stringer, Helme and Wethered, and the various histories of the women's game. The specific detail about the referee retiring from the field in tears is from Glenn's *Illustrated History*.

SEVEN
THE GREAT GLENNA

Information about Glenna Collett's early experiences in golf is drawn principally from her book, *Ladies in the Rough*. Supplementary sources include Herbert Warren Wind's *The Story of American Golf*; George Kirsch's *Golf in America*; Bill Fields's article 'A Place in Time', from the collection *Arnie, Seve and a Fleck of Golf History*, and an article from the LPGA archives by Kikue Higuchi entitled 'Reluctant Legend'.

The story of how Collett came to take lessons from Alex Smith, of Carnoustie, is drawn from Martin's history of American golf, as are his quotes about watching her play in the 1919 Eastern Amateur Championship. Smith quotes about Collett are as Martin recalls them in his book.

Information about the life of Alex Smith is drawn from *The Book of Golfers*, by Daniel Wexler, and the website *antiquegolfscotland.com*, a compendium of well researched histories of Scottish golf club makers and professionals operated by Douglas MacKenzie.

Information about the influence of Scots in shaping golf around the globe is drawn from the author's previous work, *The Long Golden Afternoon: Golf's Age of Glory, 1864–1914*.

Collett's memories of Smith and his teaching are drawn from her memoir.

Herbert Newton Wethered's observations about Collett's swing are from his book, *The Perfect Golfer*.

Information about Collett's performances in the tournaments she entered in 1919, 1920 and 1921 are from multiple sources – coverage in *Golf Illustrated*, *The American Annual* and *The American Golfer*, along with recollections in Collett's memoir.

Collett's specific memory of receiving a swing tip from Stirling is from *Ladies in the Rough*.

Information about the 1922 US Women's Amateur Championship is drawn from coverage in *Golf Illustrated*, *The American Golfer* and *The American Annual*, as well as from Collett's memoir.

EIGHT
INHUMANLY GOOD

Joyce Wethered's recollections about her experiences in the 1923 British Ladies' Championship – and the family's subsequent trip to Deal – are from her memoir.

Additional information about the 1923 Ladies' Championship is drawn from Helme's memoir, Tinkler's biography of Wethered and accounts in *Golf Illustrated*.

Information about the 1924 British Ladies' Championship is drawn from Helme's memoir, Tinkler's biography, Wethered's memoir and *Golf Illustrated*.

Information about Collett's 1923 and 1924 seasons is drawn from coverage in *Golf Illustrated* and *The American Annual*, as well as recollections in her memoir.

NINE
LEVIATHANS AT TROON

Information about the long-running battle between the English and Scots for supremacy in golf before the first World War is drawn from the author's previous work, *The Long Golden Afternoon*.

Information about the advanced coverage of the 1925 Ladies' Championship at Troon is drawn from *Golf Illustrated*, *The Glasgow Herald*, Dawin's *Golf Between Two Wars* and the various histories of the women's game.

Information about the golf course at Troon is from R.A. Crampsey's club history, *The Breezy Links o' Troon*.

Information about the match between Wethered and Collett at Troon in 1925 is drawn from multiple sources, among them coverage in *Golf Illustrated*, *The Glasgow Herald* and *The Scotsman*; Tinkler's biography of Wethered; Darwin's history and the memoirs of Helme, Collett and Wethered.

Information about the match between Wethered and Leitch at Troon in 1925 is drawn from multiple sources, among them coverage in *The Glasgow Herald*, *The Scotsman* and *Golf Illustrated*; Helme's memoir; Darwin's history; Tinkler's biography of Wethered, and Wethered's memoir.

The quote from Wethered about Leitch, in which she stated that 'People either adored Cecil or they didn't,' is from a 1984 interview with correspondent Lewine Mair, which was originally published in *Golf Monthly* and reprised in Mair's history of ladies' golf.

Darwin's quote about the crowd wishing the title of champions could have been shared by Wethered and Leitch is from his essay, 'The Ladies', in *Golf Between Two Wars*.

Collett's memories of her trip abroad are drawn from two sources – her memoir and a 1925 article she wrote for *Golf Illustrated* entitled 'Experiences Abroad'.

Information about the 1925 US Women's Amateur Championship is drawn from multiple sources, including *Golf Illustrated*, *The American Annual*, Collett's memoir, and *St Louis Country Club: A Legacy of Sports*.

Information about the changes in Stirling's life since her 1920 victory in the US Women's Amateur Championship was drawn from Hopkins' history of East Lake Golf Club, as well as Barclay's *Golf in Canada*.

The information that Collett's friends bought her a blue Mercer raceabout is drawn from a profile of the champion by Niven Bush Jr that was published in the New Yorker on 17 September 1927 and collected in the *The Great Women Golfers*.

TEN
THE ETERNAL PROBLEM

Collett's observations about the relative strengths of men and women in golf are drawn from the opening chapter of her memoir entitled 'Golf We Women Play'.

Grantland Rice's remarks on the low scores posted by Collett and Edith Cummings at Belleair are from an article published in *The American Golfer* magazine in March 1922 and collected in Charles Price's book of the same name.

William D. Richardson's article on the improvement in women's golf is from the *New York Times*'s edition of 23 September 1928.

The comparison of qualifying scores made by men and women in the US Amateur championships is based on records held in the online archives of the United States Golf Association.

Dorothy Campbell Hurd's article on the improvement in women's golf between 1914 and 1929 is preserved in the scrapbook of Eleanor Allen held by the archives of the USGA – although the specific date of the clipping is not preserved in that collection.

Mabel Stringer's recollection of the first women v. men match at Claygate Club in 1898 is from a chapter of her memoir entitled 'Odds and Ends'.

Information about the Gold Ball Tournament at The Country Club of Fairfield in Connecticut is drawn from coverage of the event in the *New York Times* during the years 1924–1929.

Helme's observations about 'Ladies v. Men' are from a chapter of that title in her memoir.

The quote about how Wethered was able to shepherd men to victory at Worplesdon is from a December 1931 article in *Golf Illustrated*.

Wethered's comment about playing as the partner of Bernard Darwin is from her interview with Lewine Mair.

Information about the 1923 match involving Collett, Stirling, Walter Hagen and Gene Sarazen is drawn from *Ladies in the Rough*.

Information about the life and work of Marion Hollins is drawn principally from David Outerbridge's biography, *Champion in a Man's World*, and supplemented by coverage from *Golf Illustrated* during the 1920s and 1930s, as well as the various histories of the women's game.

Information about Molly Gourlay and her work with Tom Simpson is drawn principally from Simson & Co., Fred Hawtree's examination of the life and work of the famed Golden Age architect. It is supplemented by Wexler's *The Book of Golfers*, *The Shell Encyclopedia of Golf* and articles Gourlay wrote for *Golf Illustrated* in 1938 and 1939. Those pieces have been preserved on the website of *The Golf Chronicle*, operated by Lee Patterson.

ELEVEN
MATCHLESS

The news that Wethered would return to compete in the 1929 British Ladies' Championship at St Andrews was published by *Golf Illustrated* as part of its coverage of the 1928 event at Hunstanton, England.

Information about Collett's performance during the 1926, 1927 and 1928 golf seasons is compiled from numerous sources, principally her memoir and coverage in *Golf Illustrated*, although it is supplemented by Helme's memoir and Glenn's *Illustrated History*.

Leitch's observations about Collett's game were made in a May 25, 1928 article in the British editions of *Golf Illustrated*.

Collett's admission that her two books helped to defray the expense of travelling and competing year round were made to Rhonda Glenn in a 1985 interview and noted in an article about Glenna that she wrote for The USGA in 2010, on the 75th anniversary of Collett's sixth and final victory in the US Women's Amateur.

The statement that Collett's 13 and 12 victory was the largest margin of victory up to that point in the US Women's Amateur is based on a review of scoring records kept by the USGA.

Wethered's statements refuting the notion that she entered the 1929 British Ladies' Championship out of a sense of patriotic duty to keep the trophy on home soil are from her memoir.

The information about Wethered's performances in the Ladies' Championship at Royal Dornoch Golf Club was kindly supplied to the author by former Club captain David Bell.

Wethered's comments about her love for Scottish golf are also from her memoir.

The remarks by *New York Herald Tribune* correspondents Al Laney – regarding both Wethered's patriotism and her friendship with Collett – are from the essay 'The Greatest Women's Match Ever Played', which appears in the *Classic of Golf* book entitled *Following the Leaders*.

Information about Wethered's activities following her 1925 retirement from championship golf are from her memoir, as well as from Tinkler's biography of her.

Information about the filming of her swing by Hal Rhodes is from Tinkler's biography and contemporary reports in the Canadian press.

Wethered's quotes about dining with Collett on the Thursday evening of the championship, as well as her concerns that she might be facing trouble in the final, are drawn from her memoir.

Information about the match between Collett and Wethered in the final of the 1929 British Ladies' Championship at St Andrews is drawn from multiple sources. These include Helme's memoir; Darwin's coverage in the *Times of London*; Laney's remembrance of covering the tournament for the *New York Herald Tribune* and reports in *The Scotsman*.

Wethered's remembrance of casting a glance at Darwin as she made the turn during the championship final, when she was 5-down to Collett, is from her interview with Mair.

Collett's memories of that afternoon are drawn from an interview with Rhonda Glenn, which were included in the article she wrote for the USGA on the 75th anniversary of Collett's final victory in the US Women's Amateur.

Darwin's description of the 11th at St Andrews as 'the most fiendish short hole in existence' is from his book *The Golf Courses of the British Isles*. All other quotes are from his coverage of the match in the *Times*.

TWELVE
THE GRAND STAGE

'The Greatest Women's Match Ever Played' is the title of Al Laney's essay about the 1929 match between Collett and Wethered in Following the Leaders.

The quote from Collett about being a gracious loser is from an article she wrote that was published on 14 October 1928 in the *Sacramento Union*.

Wethered's quote about Collett's sportsmanship is from her memoir.

Information about the 1929 US Women's Amateur Championship is drawn from coverage in *Golf Illustrated* and *The American Annual*.

Information about Bobby Jones Grand Slam year and his appearances in the Walker Cup is drawn from Keeler's *The Bobby Jones Story*; *Bobby Jones and the Quest for the Grand Slam*, by Catherine M. Lewis; Tinkler's biography of Wethered and coverage in *The Scotsman* and *The Glasgow Herald*.

Information about the friendly match played in St Andrews involving Jones, Joyce and Roger Wethered and Dale Bourne is drawn from Tinkler's biography and an article that Jones wrote for *The American Golfer* in 1930, which is collected in Charles Price's book of the same name.

Collett's participation in the exhibition match that opened Pasatiempo was reported both in *Golf Illustrated* and in Outerbridge's biography of Hollins.

Information about the 1930 US Women's Amateur Championship at Los Angeles Country Club is drawn from coverage in *Golf Illustrated* and *The American Annual*.

Information about the early history of the Curtis Cup is drawn from the various histories of the women's game by Cossey, Glenn, Wilson, Crane and Mair.

Information about the birth of the Home Internationals for women is drawn from those histories, as well as from the memoirs of Stringer and Helme.

The letter written by Margaret Curits to Cecil Leitch is quoted from Glenn's *Illustrated History*.

Information about the International Match at Sunningdale in 1930 was drawn from *Golf Illustrated* and *The Scotsman*.

Information about the 1930 British Ladies' Championship at Formby is drawn from Helme's memoir and coverage in *Golf Illustrated* and *The Scotsman*.

Wethered's quote about the future of international matches in the women's game is from her memoir.

Collett's plans to marry Edwin H. Vare Jr were announced in the *New York Times* on 29 May 1931, and the wedding took place on 25 June.

Information about the inaugural Curtis Cup competition in May 1932 is drawn from reports in *The Glasgow Herald* and *Golf Illustrated*, supplemented by the Outerbridge's biography of Hollins, Tinkler's biography of Wethered, and the histories of women's golf written by Cossey, Crane, Mair and Wilson, and records of the United States Golf Association.

Wethered's admission that she never warmed to team competitions – and liked neither ruling nor being ruled – are from her interview with Mair.

Enid Wilson's statement about foraging for food at the Curtis Cup is from an interview she gave to the Ladies Professional Golf Association in 1991 that is quoted in Tinkler's biography of Wethered.

Wethered's quote about the foursome pairings arranged by her opposite number Hollins is from *Golfing Memories and Methods*.

Results of the various Curtis Cups are quoted from records of the USGA.

THIRTEEN
SWAN SONG

Collett's remarks about her desire for Americans to see Wethered play are quoted from her memoir.

Information about the financial decline of the Wethered family – and the various steps family members took to address that – is drawn from Tinkler's biography.

Information about Wethered's engagement to Cecil K. Hutchinson is drawn from reports in *The Times*, supplemented by Tinkler's biography and mentions of the planned match in the various histories of the women's game.

Information about Harry Vardon's tour of the United States in 1900 is drawn from *Vardon in America*, by the late Bill Williams, supplemented by the author's own book, *The Long Golden Afternoon*.

Wethered's exchange of letters with Alexander Findlay – along with a scrapbook of clippings kept by his family – was kindly shared with the author by historian William J. Casto, who has written a biography of Findlay.

Information about Wethered's performances at Sunningdale and Stoke Poges in preparation for her North American tour is drawn from Tinkler's biography.

Gene Sarazen's statement congratulating Wanamaker Stores on Wethered's US tour is included in the Findlay family scrapbook.

Information about where, when and with whom Wethered competed during her tour of North America – including her win-loss record and the scores she posted during the trip – is drawn from Tinkler's biography, the Findlay family scrapbook and contemporary news reports.

The quote from George Trevor about the perfection of Wethered's swing is drawn from an extensive excerpt of his piece in *The Sportsman* that was reprinted in Tinkler's biography.

Information about the match between Jones and Wethered at East Lake – including Wethered's own comments about the contest – is drawn from a 1935 article by Keeler in *The American Golfer* that is reprinted in Charles Prices' collection of the same name, supplemented by Tinkler's biography and the Findlay family scrapbook.

Information about the life and career of Babe Didrikson is drawn from Susan Clayeff's biography, Babe.

Wethered's quote reflecting on her tour of North America is drawn from an article in the quarterly publication *Golf Lore* that appeared in the spring–summer edition for 1935 and is included in the Findlay family scrapbook.

Findlay's quote summing up the impact of Wethered's tour is from a report in *The Philadelphia Record* that is included in the Findlay family scrapbook.

The information that Collett had spoken with her friend Betty Jameson about her desire to have the name of Mrs Edwin H, Vare Jr engraved on the Robert Cox Trophy is drawn from Glenn's 2010 USGA article.

Information about the 1935 US Women's Amateur Championship at Interlachen Country Club is drawn from an article by Bernard E. Swanson published in *The American Golfer*, supplemented by Glenn's article for the USGA and her *Illustrated History*.

Patty Berg's quote about finding it intimidating to compete against Collett and her expectation that she would lose by a substantial margin is drawn from Glenn's USGA article.

FOURTEEN
ENDURING LEGACY

Information about Jack McLean's match with Wethered in the Mens v. Ladies' event at Stoke Poges in April 1935 is drawn from Tinkler's biography, as are his remarks to the press afterward.

Dawin's quote in *The Times* about Wethered's performance Troon is drawn from an extensive excerpt of his newspaper article that is reprinted in Tinkler's biography.

Sarazen's assessment of the women golfers of his age is from 'The Masters of Modern Golf', the penultimate chapter in his memoir *Thirty Years of Championship Golf*.

Walter Hagen's remarks about the quality of Wethered's swing are from an August 1934 article in *Esquire* magazine.

Darwin's quote about Jones's near-perfect performance at Sunningdale in Open qualifying is from his book, Golf Between Two Wars.

Herbert Newton Wethered's quotes and discussion of the women's game are drawn from his 1931 book, *The Perfect Golfer*, in particular from a chapter entitled 'The Perfect Amazon', a reference to the mythical race of women mentioned in Greek mythology.

Grantland Rice's article 'The Secrets of Miss Wethered's Golf' appeared in the July 1935 editions of *The American Golfer*.

Golf writer Leonard Crawley's article reflecting on the career of Joyce Wethered and compiling her matchplay record appeared in *Golf Monthly* in January 1944.

NOTES ON CHAPTERS

Collett's experiences in the Point Judith Invitational Tournament are drawn from a May 1986 article in *Yankee Magazine* by James Dodson entitled *Still Stalking Golf Courses*.

The story told by Collett's son, Edwin, about competing in mixed foursomes with his mother is drawn from an article by Bill Fields entitled 'A Place in Time', which is included in his anthology *Arnie, Seve and a Fleck of Golf History*.

Martin's comments about Collett, as well as his quote, are drawn from his history of American golf.

Details about the founding of the LPGA tour are drawn from Glenn's *Illustrated History*, supplemented by a viewing of the 2016 documentary film entitled *The Founders*, which tells the story of the 13 women who launched the Ladies Professional Golf Association in 1950.

Betty Jameson's quotes about her personal relationship with Collett are drawn from an oral history interview with her that was conducted by Alice Kendrick of the USGA on 15 January 1992.

Collett's comments at a ceremony on 14 March 1954 to present the first Vare Trophy to Patty Berg are drawn from a transcript of her remarks preserved in the archives of the USGA.

FIFTEEN
AFTERLIVES

Information about Sir John Heathcoat Amory; his marriage to Wethered, their building of a garden at Knightshayes; the honours bestowed on the couple by the Royal Horticultural Society; the construction of a room dedicated to her golfing career, and her devotion to Christian Science is all drawn from Tinkler's biography, which includes in its appendix the chapter Wethered contributed to The Englishwoman's Garden.

Information about the putting green architect Tom Simpson built as a wedding gift to Wethered is drawn from contemporary news reports, principally a story that appeared in *Golf Architecture Magazine* on 4 January 1937.

Wethered's quotes about regretting that she did do more in the administration of golf, about watching men's and women' professional golf and about thinking of St Andrews on evenings when she had difficulty falling asleep are all drawn from her interview with Mair.

Information about the afterlives of Wethered's contemporaries – Issette Pearson, Mabel Stringer, Eleanor Helme, Molly Gourlay and Cecil Leitch – is drawn from entries in the *Oxford Dictionary of National Biography*, *Shell's Encyclopedia of Golf*, *Wexler's Book of Golfers*, *The Association of Golf Writers* and *Wikipedia*.

Information about Collett and Edwin Vare's purchase of a home in Narragansett Bay, Rhode Island, as well as the details of her life there, is drawn from Dodson's article in *Yankee* magazine. It is supplemented by a subsequent interview Dodson conducted with Collett that was published in March 1989 in *Golf* magazine, a month after her passing.

Information about Collett's work with the United States Golf Association – namely her service on its various committees – is from the organisation's archives.

Information about Collett's record in the Curtis Cup – both as a player and a captain – is drawn from the archives of the USGA and supplemented by records kept at the website Golf Compendium and Glenn's *Illustrated History*.

The quotes from both Dodson and Collett about the state of her game as she aged, his proposal to play a match against her, and how her friends in Florida had given up the game and taken to gourmet cooking are all drawn from 'Still Stalking Golf Courses'.

Collett's comments about coverage of LPGA tournaments is drawn from her subsequent interview with Dodson that was published in *Golf* magazine.

Collett's decision to melt most of her trophies and to create a single silver tray recognising her many accomplishments in the game is drawn from the *Yankee Magazine* article. Information about the awards ceremony at the Memorial Tournament is drawn from Glenn's USGA article.

Information about the lives of Collett's contemporaries – Marion Hollins, Alexa Stirling, Edith Cummings and Virginia Van Wie – is drawn from Outerbridge's *Champion in a Man's World*; Hopkins' *East Lake: Where Bobby Learned to Play*; *Shell's Encyclopedia of Golf*; *Wexler's Book of Golfers* and entries on Wikipedia.

Details about Collett's passing in Del Ray, Florida – including all of the quotes used – are drawn from the oral history interview Jameson and her friend, Mary Lena Faulk, conducted with the USGA on 15 January 1992.

The story of how Collett's children withdrew a display from Metacomet Golf Club because it refused to change its policy barring women from the men's grill was first told in *The Unplayable Lie*, a 1995 book by golf writer Marcia Chambers that outlined the state of discrimination against women in golf as of that year.

BIBLIOGRAPHY

NEWSPAPERS/PERIODICALS/FILMS

The American Annual
The American Golfer
Boston Herald
Canadian Golfer
Cecil Leitch: Champion Golfer, pamphlet
The Daily Telegraph and Courier
The Field
Fifeshire News
The Founders, 2016 documentary film
The Glasgow Herald
The Golfing Annual
Golf Illustrated, 1914–35 inclusive
Golf Lore
Golfers Magazine
Golf Monthly
Illustrated Sporting News
The Ladies Field
Lancashire Evening Post
The Morning Leader
The New Yorker
The New York Herald Tribune
New York Times
Philadelphia Record
St Andrews Citizen

The Scotsman
The Sportsman
The Times
Through the Green

ARTICLES

Barclay, James, 'The Glorious Golfing Girl', *Canadian Golfer* (November, 1920).

Crawley, Leonard, 'Famous Sports-women I Have Known', *Golf Monthly* (January, 1944).

Dodson, James, 'Still Stalking Around Golf Courses', *Yankee Magazine* (May, 1986).

Dodson, James, 'Talking Golf: A Conversation with Glenna Collett Vare', *Golf* (March, 1989).

Eubanks, Steve, 'The Women's Game's Greatest Forgotten Champion', LPGA.com (March, 2021).

Fields, Bill, 'A Place in Time', *Golf World* (November, 1997).

Fowler, Paul, 'Cecil Leitch', golfingherald.com (May, 2020).

Fowler, Paul, 'Joyce Wethered: From Piccadilly to Pebble Beach', golfingherald.com (May, 2024).

Fry, Peter, 'The Great Lady of Golf: Joyce Wethered', *Finnish Golf*, Finland (February, 2008).

Glenn, Rhonda, '75th Anniversary of Vare's Final USGA Title', USGA.org. (August, 2010).

Hagen, Walter, 'Fairway Queens and Rough Cats', *Esquire* (August, 1934).

Hamilton, David, and Millar, Neil S., 'Women on Bruntsfield Links, 1738', *Through the Green* (March, 2015).

Higuchi, Kikue, 'Reluctant Legend', LPGA.com (November, 2022).

Kay, Joyce, '"No Time for Recreation Till the Vote Is Won"?, Suffrage Activists and Leisure in Edwardian Britain', *Women's History Review* (September, 2007).

Lewis, Peter N., 'Wethered, Joyce (married name Joyce Heathcoat-Amory, Lady Heathcoat-Amory)', *Oxford Dictionary of National Biography* (September, 2004).

Lowerson, John, 'Scottish Croquet: The English Golf Boom, 1880–1914', *History Today*, Vol. 33, No. 5 (1983).

MacKenzie, Douglas, 'Alec Smith', antiquegolfscotland.com (June, 2024).

Mair, Lewine, 'Gentlemen Only, Ladies Forbidden – A History', *Women's Golf Journal* (2015).

Mair, Lewine, 'Looking Back: Lady Heathcoat-Amory', *Golf Monthly* (March, 1984).

Mallea, John R., 'The Victorian Sporting Legacy', *McGill Journal of Education* (1975).

Millar, M. S., 'Leitch, Charlotte Cecilia Pitcairn (Cecil)', *Oxford Dictionary of National Biography* (January, 2011).

Morrison, Michael, 'How Many Golfers? Part I: Men', *Through the Green* (June, 2021).

Pottle, Mark, 'Pearson (married name Miller) (Frances) Issette Jessie', Oxford Dictionary of National Biography (September, 2004).
Pottle, Mark, 'Stringer, Mabel Emily', *Oxford Dictionary of National Biography* (September, 2004).
Richardson, William D., 'The Woman Golfer Sets a Hard Pace for Man on the Links', New York Times (23 September 1928).
Rubenstein, Lorne, 'A Champion for All Time', *Toronto Globe and Mail* (April, 1998).
Stirling, Alexa, 'The Most Unforgettable Character I've Met', *Readers Digest* (April, 1960).

BOOKS: HISTORY

Balfour, James, *Reminiscences of Golf on St. Andrews Links* (Edinburgh, 1887).
Barclay, James A., *Golf in Canada: A History* (Toronto, 1992).
Baxter, Peter, *Golf in Perth and Perthshire: Traditional, Historical and Modern* (Perth, 1899).
Behrend, John, *The Amateur: The Story of the Amateur Golf Championship, 1885–1995* (Worcestershire, England, 1995).
Brenner, Morgan G., *The Majors of Golf, Vols. 1–3* (Jefferson, NC, 2009).
Browning, Robert, *A History of Golf* (London, 1955).
Clark, Robert, *Golf: A Royal and Ancient Game*, extracts from the original 1875 edition (Midlothian, 1984).
Colville, George M., *Five Open Champions and the Musselburgh Golf Story* (Musselburgh, 1980).
Darwin, Bernard, *Golf Between Two Wars* (London, 1944).
Darwin, Bernard (ed.) *A History of Golf in Britain* (London, 1952).
Geddes, Olive M., *A Swing Through Time: Golf in Scotland, 1457–1744* (Edinburgh, 2007).
Goodman, Ruth, *How To Be a Victorian* (London, 2013).
Hamilton, David, *Golf: Scotland's Game* (St Andrews, 1998).
Haultain, Arnold, *The Mystery of Golf* (New York, 1908).
Hilton, Harold H., and Smith, Garden G., *The Royal and Ancient Game of Golf* (London, 1912).
Hutchinson, Horace G. (ed.) *The Badminton Library: Golf* (London, 1890).
Hutchinson, Horace G., *The Book of Golf and Golfers* (London, 1899).
Hutchinson, Horace G., *Golf: A Complete History of the Game, Together with Directions for Selection of Implements, the Rules, and a Glossary of Golf Terms* (Philadelphia, 1900).
Hutchinson, Horace, *Golfing: The Oval Series of Games* (London, 1903).
Jackson, Alan F., *The British Professional Golfers: A Register* (Worcestershire, England, 1994).
Joy, David (compiled by) *The Scrapbook of Old Tom Morris* (Chelsea, MI, 2001).
Kerr, John, *The Golf Book of East Lothian* (Edinburgh, 1896).
Kirsch, George B., *Golf in America* (Chicago, 2009).

Labbance, Bob, *The Vardon Invasion* (Ann Arbor, MI, 2008).
Langston, Harry, *Thomas Hodge: The Golf Artist of St Andrews* (London, 2000).
Leach, Henry (ed.) *Great Golfers in the Making* (London, 1907).
Lee, James P., *Golf in America* (New York, 1895).
Lewis, Catherine, M. *Bobby Jones and the Quest for the Grand Slam* (Chicago, 2005).
Lewis, Peter N., *The Dawn of Professional Golf: The Genesis of the European Tour 1894–1914* (New Ridley, 1995).
Lewis, Peter N., *Why Are There Eighteen Holes?: St Andrews and the Evolution of Golf Courses, 1764–1890* (St Andrews, 2016).
Low, John, *Concerning Golf* (London, 1903).
Lowe, Stephen, *Sir Walter and Mr Jones* (Chelsea, MI, 2000).
Macdonald, Charles Blair, *Scotland's Gift: Golf* (New York, 1928).
Macdonald, Robert S. and Wind, Herbert Warren, *The Great Women Golfers* (Stamford, CT, 1994).
Martin, H. B., *Fifty Years of American* Golf (New York, 1936).
McPherson, J. Gordon, *Golf and Golfers Past and Present* (Edinburgh, 1891).
McStravick, Roger, *St Andrews in the Footsteps of Old Tom Morris* (St Andrews, 2014).
McStravick, Roger, *A History of Golf* (St Andrews, 2017).
Morrison, Michael, The Great English Golf Boom (Cambridge, 2002).
Oliver, Neil, *A History of Scotland* (London, 2009).
Parker, Eric and The Right Hon. The Earl of Lonsdale (eds) *The Game of Golf* (Philadelphia, 1931).
Peper, George, *The Story of Golf* (New York, 1999).
Perry, Phyllis, *From Green to Gold: The First Fifty Years of the Australian Ladies' Golf Union* (Melbourne, 1975).
Peter, H. Thomas, *Reminiscences of Golf and Golfers* (Edinburgh, 1890).
Robb, George, *Historical Gossip about Golf and Golfers* (Edinburgh, 1863).
Ryde, Peter, *Royal and Ancient Championship Records, 1860–1980* (St Andrews, 1981).
Smith, Garden G., *Golf* (New York, 1913).
Stirk, David, *Golf History and Traditions, 1500 to 1945* (Shropshire, England, 1998).
Sommers, Robert, *The U.S. Open: Golf's Ultimate Challenge* (New York, 1987).
Tombs, Robert, *The English & Their History* (London, 2014).
Wade, Don (ed.) *The U.S. Open: One Week in June* (New York, 2010).
Waterston, C. D., and Macmillan Shearer, A., *Biographical Index of Former Fellows of the Royal Society of Edinburgh, 1783–2002*, Vol. 2 (Edinburgh, 2003).
Wexler, Daniel, *The Book of Golfers: A Bibliographical History of the Royal and Ancient Game* (Ann Arbor, MI, 2005).
Williams, Bill, *Vardon in America* (Xlibris, 2016).
Wind, Herbert Warren, *The Story of American Golf: Its Champions and Its Championships* (New York, 1975).

BIBLIOGRAPHY

BOOKS: BIOGRAPHIES/MEMOIRS

Adams, John, *The Parks of Musselburgh: Golfers, Architects, Clubmakers* (Worcestershire, England, 1991).
Adamson, Alistair Beaton, Allan Robertson, *Golfer: His Life and Times* (Worcestershire, England, 1985).
Behrend, John, *John Ball of Hoylake: Champion Golfer* (Worcestershire, England, 1989).
Crabtree, Peter, and Malcolm, David, *Tom Morris of St Andrews: The Colossus of Golf, 1821–1908* (Royal Deeside, 2008).
Darwin, Bernard, *Green Memories* (London, 1928).
Darwin, Bernard, *James Braid* (London, 1952).
Darwin, Bernard, *The World that Fred Made* (London, 1955).
Garcia, John L. B., *Harold Hilton: His Life and Times* (Worcestershire, England, 1992).
Green, Robert, *Seve: Golf's Flawed Genius* (Fort Valley, GA, 2012).
Hagen, Walter, with Margaret Seaton, *The Walter Hagen Story: By The Haig Himself* (New York, 1956).
Harris, Robert, *Sixty Years of Golf* (Letchworth, England, 1953).
Herd, Sandy, *My Golfing Life* (London, 1923).
Hilton, Harold H., *My Golfing Reminiscences* (London, 1907).
Hutchinson, Horace G., *Fifty Years of Golf* (London, 1914).
Jones, Robert T. Jr, and Keeler, O.B., *Down the Fairway* (New York, 1927).
Jones, Robert T. Jr, *Golf Is My Game* (New York, 1960).
Keeler, O. B., *The Bobby Jones Story: The Authorized Biography* (Chicago, 2003).
Kirkaldy, Andra, *Fifty Years of Golf: My Memories* (New York, 1921).
Labbance, Bob, *The Old Man: The Biography of Walter J. Travis* (Chelsea, MI, 2000).
Low, J. L., F.G. *Tait: A Record* (London, 1900).
Moreton, John F., *James Braid: Champion Golfer* (Worcestershire, England, 2003).
Nicklaus, Jack, with Herbert Warren Wind, *The Greatest Game of All: My Life in Golf* (New York, 1969).
Ouimet, Francis, *A Game of Golf* (New York, 1932).
Sampson, Curt, *Hogan* (Nashville, 1996).
Sampson, Curt, *The Slam: Bobby Jones and the Price of Glory* (Emmaus, PA, 2005).
Sarazen, Gene, with Herbert Warren Wind, *Thirty Years of Championship Golf* (New York, 1950).
Stephen, Walter, *Willie Park Junior: The Man Who Took Golf to the World* (Edinburgh, 2005).
Taylor, J.H., *Golf: My Life's Work* (London, 1943).
Tulloch, William W., *The Life of Tom Morris: With Glimpses of St Andrews and its Golfing Celebrities* (London, 1908).
Vardon, Harry, *My Golfing Life* (Plymouth, England, 1933).
Williams, Bill, *Harry Vardon: A Career Record of a Champion Golfer* (Xlibris, 2005).
Williams, Bill, Ted Ray: *The Forgotten Man of Golf* (Xlibris, 2018).

BOOKS: GOLF ARCHITECTURE/GREENKEEPING

Colt, H. S. and Alison, C. H., *Some Essays on Golf Course Architecture* (London, 1920).
Cornish, Geoffrey and Whitten, Ronald E., *The Golf Course* (New York, 1988).
Cutten, Keith, *The Evolution of Golf Course Design* (Victoria, Australia, 2018).
Darwin, Bernard, *The Golf Courses of the British Isles* (London, 1910).
Dickinson, Patric, *A Round of Golf Courses: A Selection of the Best Eighteen* (London, 1951).
Doak, Tom, *The Anatomy of a Golf Course* (New York, 1992).
Doak, Tom, *The Confidential Guide to Golf Courses* (Chelsea, MI, 1996).
Hunter, Robert, *The Links* (New York, 1926).
Hutchinson, Horace G., *Famous Golf Links* (London, 1891).
Hutchinson, Horace G., *British Golf Links* (London, 1897).
Hawtree, Fred, Simpson & Co., *Golf Architects* (Ballater, Scotland, 2016).
Klein, Bradley S., *Discovering Donald Ross* (Chelsea, MI, 2001).
Kroeger, Robert, *The Golf Courses of Old Tom Morris* (Cincinnati, OH, 1995).
MacKenzie, Dr Alister, *Golf Architecture: Economy in Course Construction and Greenkeeping* (London, 1920).
MacKenzie, Dr Alister, *The Spirit of St Andrews* (Chelsea, MI, 2001, 1995).
Markham, Derek, *A Matter of Course: The Life of William Herbert Fowler, 1856–1941* (Walton on the Hill, Surrey, 2021).
Moreton, John F. and Cummings, Ian, *James Braid and his Four Hundred Golf Courses* (Worcestershire, England, 2013).
Shackelford, Geoff, *Masters of the Links: Essays on the Art of Golf and Course Design* (Chelsea, MI, 1997).
Simpson, T., and Wethered, H. N., *The Architectural Side of Golf* (Stamford CT, 2005).
Sutton, Martin H. F., *A Symposium on Golf* (London, 1912).
Thomas, George C. Jr, *Golf Architecture in America. Its Strategy and Construction* (Los Angeles, 1927).
Ward-Thomas, Pat, et al., *The World Atlas of Golf: The Great Courses and How They are Played* (London, 2008).

BOOKS: GOLF INSTRUCTION/EQUIPMENT

Armour, Tommy, *How to Play Your Best Golf All the Time* (New York, 1953).
Aultman, Dick, and Bowden, Ken, *The Methods of Golf's Masters: How They Played and What You Can Learn from Them* (New York, 1975).
Beldam, George, *Great Golfers: Their Methods at a Glance* (New York, 1904).
Boomer, Percy, *On Learning Golf* (London, 1942).
Braid, James, *Advanced Golf* (London, 1908).
Henderson, Ian T., and Stirk, David I., *Golf in the Making* (Worcestershire, England, 1979).

Hilton, Harold, *Modern Golf* (New York, 1913).
Hutchinson, Horace G., *Hints on the Game of Golf* (Edinburgh, 1886).
Jones, Ernest, with Innis Brown, *Swinging into Golf* (New York, 1941).
Jones, Robert T., Jr, *The Basic Golf Swing* (Garden City, NY, 1969).
Miller, Johnny, *Breaking 90 with Johnny Miller* (New York, 2000).
Nelson, Byron, with Larry Dennis, *Shape Your Swing the Modern Way* (New York, 1976).
Olman, John M., and Olman, Morton W., *Olman's Guide to Golf Antiques and Other Treasures of the Game* (Cincinnati, 1991).
Park, William, Jr, *The Game of Golf* (London, 1896).
Park, William, Jr, *The Art of Putting* (Edinburgh, 1920).
Penick, Harvey, with Bud Shrake, *Harvey Penick's Little Red Book: Lessons and Teaching from a Lifetime in Golf* (New York, 1992).
Simpson, Walter G., Sir, *The Art of Golf* (Edinburgh, 1887).
Stirk, David, *Golf: The Great Club Makers* (London, 1991).
Taylor, J.H., *Taylor on Golf* (London, 1902).
Travis, Walter, J., *Practical Golf* (New York, 1901).
Vardon, Harry, *The Complete Golfer* (New York, 1905)
Vardon, Harry, *The Gist of Golf* (New York, 1922).
Vardon, Harry, compiled and edited by Herbert Warren Wind and Robert S. Macdonald, *Vardon on Golf* (Stamford, CT, 2002).
Venturi, Ken, with Al Barkow, *The Venturi Analysis: Learning Better Golf from the Champions* (New York, 1981).
Wethered, H. N., *The Perfect Golfer* (London, 1931).
Woods, Tiger, *How I Play Golf* (New York, 2001).

BOOKS: GOLF LITERATURE

Bingham, Joan, and Owen, David, *The Lure of the Links* (New York, 1997).
Campbell, Patrick, *How to Become a Scratch Golfer* (London, 1963).
Darwin, Bernard, *Out of the Rough* (London, 1932).
Darwin, Bernard, *Playing the Like* (London, 1934).
Darwin, Bernard, *Golf* (London, 1934).
Darwin, Bernard, *Golfing By-Paths* (London, 1946).
Darwin, Bernard, edited by Peter Ryde, *Mostly Golf* (London, 1976).
Darwin, Bernard, with editors Robert S. Macdonald and Ian R. Macdonald, *The Happy Golfer: A Collection of Articles from The American Golfer Magazine, 1922–1936* (Stamford, CT, 1997).
Dobereiner, Peter, *Golf a la Carte* (Guilford, CT, 1991).
Dodson, James, *The American Triumvirate: Sam Snead, Byron Nelson, Ben Hogan and the Modern Age of Golf* (New York, 2012).
Feinstein, John, *The Majors: In Pursuit of Golf's Holy Grail* (Boston, 1999).
Frost, Mark, *The Greatest Game Ever Played* (New York, 2002).
Frost, Mark, *The Grand Slam: Bobby Jones, America and the Story of Golf* (New York, 2004).

Frost, Mark, *The Match: The Day the Game of Golf Changed Forever* (New York, 2007).
Jenkins, Dan, *At the Majors: Sixty Years of the World's Best Golf Writing from Hogan to Tiger* (New York, 2009).
Jenkins, Dan, *The Dogged Victims of Inexorable Fate* (Boston, 1970).
Keeler, O. B., *The Autobiography of an Average Golfer* (New York, 1925).
Laney, Al, *Following the Leaders: A Reminiscence by Al Laney* (Stamford, CT, 1991).
Leach, Henry, *The Spirit of the Links* (London, 1907).
Lema, Tony, with Gwilym S. Brown, *Golfer's Gold: An Inside View of the Pro Tour* (Boston, 1964).
McKinlay, S. L., *Scottish Golf and Golfers: A Collection of Weekly Columns from the Glasgow Herald, 1956–1980* (Stamford, CT, 1992).
Nash, George C., *Letters to the Secretary of a Golf Club* (London, 1935).
Noakes, Alistair, *Hoylake Hero* (Norfolk, England, 2018).
Plimpton, George, *The Bogey Man* (New York, 1967).
Price, Charles (ed.) *The American Golfer* (New York, 1964).
Price, Charles, *Golfer-at-Large* (New York, 1982).
Rice, Grantland, with Claire Briggs, *The Duffer's Handbook of Golf* (New York, 1916).
Ryde, Peter (ed.) *Mostly Golf: A Bernard Darwin Anthology* (London, 1976).
Sagebiel, Neil, *The Longest Shot: Jack Fleck, Ben Hogan and Pro Golf's Greatest Upset at the 1955 U.S. Open* (New York, 2012).
Shaw, Joseph T., *Out of the Rough* (London, 1940).
Silverman, Jeff (ed.) *Bernard Darwin on Golf* (Guilford, CT, 2003).
Ward-Thomas, Pat, *The Masters of Golf* (London, 1961).
Ward-Thomas, Pat, *The Long Green Fairway* (London, 1966).
Ward-Thomas, Pat, *The Lay of the Land* (Stamford, CT, 1990).
Wind, Herbert Warren, *America's Gift to Golf: Herbert Warren Wind on the Masters* (Greenwich, CT, 2011).
Wind, Herbert Warren, *On Tour with Harry Sprague* (New York, 1958).
Wind, Herbert Warren, *Herbert Warren Wind's Golf Book* (New York, 1973).
Wind, Herbert Warren, *Following Through: Writings on Golf* (New York, 1985).
Wind, Herbert Warren, *The Complete Golfer* (Stamford, CT, 1991).
Wind, Herbert Warren, *An Introduction to the Literature of Golf* (Stamford, CT, 1996).
Wodehouse, P. G., Golf *Without Tears*, originally published in Britain as *The Clicking of Cuthbert* (New York, 1919).
Wodehouse, P. G., Divots, originally published in Britain as *The Heart of a Goof* (New York, 1923).

BOOKS: CLUB HISTORIES

Bell, Blyth, and Greenway, Roger, *A Hoylake Celebration: Royal Liverpool Golf Club, 1869–2019* (St Andrews, 2019).
Behrend, John, and Lewis, Peter N., *Challenges and Champions: The Royal and Ancient Golf Club 1754–1883* (St Andrews, 1998).

BIBLIOGRAPHY

Behrend, John; Lewis, Peter N. and Mackie, Keith, *Champions and Guardians: The Royal and Ancient Golf Club, 1884–1939* (St Andrews, 2001).
Bodley, Hal, *Belleair Country Club: Florida's First Golf Course, 1897–2022* (Bellair, Florida, 2022).
Clark, Eric P., *The 150 Years: A History of the St Andrews Golf Club, 1843–1993* (St Andrews, 1993).
Connelly, James, *A Temple of Golf: A History of Woking Golf Club, 1893–1993* (London, 1993).
Crampsey, R. A., *The Breezy Links o' Troon* (Troon, Scotland, 2001).
Cruickshank, Charles, *The History of Royal Wimbledon Golf Club, 1865–1986* (London, 1986).
Cusack, Peter, and Pearson, John, *Golf at Silloth* (Silloth on Solway, 2002).
Douglas, Ian M. K., *The History of Ganton Golf Club, 1891–2006* (Ganton, England, 2006).
Everard, Harry Stirling Crawford, *History of the Royal and Ancient Golf Club from 1754 to 1900* (Edinburgh, 1907).
Farrar, Guy B., *The Royal Liverpool Golf Club* (Birkenhead, England, 1993).
Furber, F. R. (ed.) *A Course for Heroes: The History of the Royal St George's Golf Club* (Sandwich, England, 1996).
Goodban, J. W. D. (ed.) *The Royal North Devon Golf Club: A Centenary Anthology, 1864–1964* (Bideford, England, 1964).
Healy, Jim, *St Louis Country Club: A Legacy of Sports* (St Louis, 2009).
Henderson, Ian T., and Stirk, David I., *Royal Blackheath* (London, 1981).
Hopkins, Linton C., *East Lake: Where Bobby Learned to Play* (Atlanta, 2018).
Johnson, Joseph, *The Royal Melbourne Golf Club: A Centenary History* (Melbourne, 1991).
Mackie, Keith, *One Hundred Years New: A History of the New Golf Club of St Andrews* (Haddington, Scotland, 2003).
Pinnington, Joe, *Mighty Winds . . . Mighty Champions: The Official History of the Royal Liverpool Golf Club* (Wirral, England, 2006).
Pottinger, George, *Muirfield and the Honourable Company* (Edinburgh, 1972).
Shaw, James E., Prestwick *Golf Club: A History and Some Records* (Glasgow, 1938).
Smail, David Cameron (ed.) *Prestwick Golf Club: Birthplace of the Open, the Club, the Members, and the Championships, 1851 to 1989* (Prestwick, 1989).
Ward-Thomas, Pat, *The Royal and Ancient* (Edinburgh, 1980)

BOOKS: WOMEN'S HISTORY

Abramsky, Sasha, *Little Wonder: The Extraordinary Story of Lottie Dod, The World's First Female Sports Superstar* (Edinburgh, 2021).
Boys, M., and Mackern, Louie (eds), *Our Lady of the Green* (London, 1899).
Clayeff, Susan E., *Babe: The Life and Legend of Babe Didrikson Zaharias* (Chicago, 1996).
Collett, Glenna, *Golf for Young Players* (Boston, 1926).
Collett, Glenna, *Ladies in the Rough* (New York, 1928).

Cossey, Rosalynde, *Golfing Ladies* (London, 1984).
Crane, Malcolm, *The Story of Ladies' Golf* (1991, Frome, Somerset).
Glenn, Rhonda, *The Illustrated History of Women's Golf* (Dallas, Texas, 1991).
Greville, Lady Violet, *The Gentlewoman's Book of Sports* (London, 1892).
Hecker, Genevieve, *Golf for Women* (New York, 1902).
Helme, Eleanor E., *After the Ball: Merry Memoirs of a Golfer* (London, 1931).
Hezlet, May, *Ladies Golf* (London, 1907).
Leitch, Cecil, *Golf* (London, 1922).
Macdonald, Robert and Wind, Herbert Warren (eds) *The Great Women Golfers* (New York, 1994).
Mair, Lewine, *One Hundred Years of Women's Golf* (Edinburgh, 1992).
Marlowe, Joyce, *Suffragettes: The Fight for Votes for Women* (London, 2000).
McAinsh, Seonaid, *St Andrews Ladies' Golf Club: 1867–2017* (St Andrews, 2017).
Outerbridge, David E., *Champion in a Man's World* (Chelsea, Minnesota, 1998).
Sanson, Nanette S., *Champions of Women's Golf* (Naples, Florida, 2000).
Stringer, Mabel, *Golfing Reminiscences* (London, 1924).
Tinkler, Basil Ashton, *The Great Lady of Golf* (Stroud, Gloucestershire, 2004).
Weiss, Elaine, *The Woman's Hour: The Great Fight to Win the Vote* (New York, 2018).
Wethered, Joyce, *Golfing Memories and Methods* (London, 1934).
Wethered, Joyce and Wethered, Roger, *Golf from Two Sides* (London, 1922).
Wilson, Enid, *A Gallery of Women Golfers* (London, 1961).

ACKNOWLEDGEMENTS

I began this project by taking a photograph of the bookshelves at historian Gillian Kirkwood's home in Gullane. Only after I'd read all the books on women's golf history assembled there did I feel prepared to tell the story of Joyce Wethered, Glenna Collett and the extraordinary age in which they lived.

Kirkwood, who has been deeply involved in women's golf all her life, has been unfailingly helpful throughout this project, sharing research with me and, when I posed a question about Cecil Leitch, arranging for John Pearson, the distinguished former editor of Through the Green, to send an enormously helpful reply.

She and Pearson are by no means the only members of the community of historians who have helped me with this project. Michael Morrison, Roger McStravick, Peter Fry, Connor Lewis, William J. Casto and Professor Fiona Skillen all shared research with me. Paul Fowler, of The Golfing Herald website, deserves special mention as he volunteered to look into Leitch's wartime activities and delivered a treasure trove of information, for which I am deeply grateful.

I have also received considerable help from the history and

architecture enthusiasts who have formed a community on social media – many of whom shared news articles or other valuable information. They include Matthew Rose of The Golf Library, Jim Hartsell, Tim Schirmer, Keith Durrant, Ally Philp, James Woods, Simon Barrington, Jasper Miners, Joe McDonnell, Geoff Shackelford and Michael Wolf.

Of course, no author could possibly complete a book without the assistance of the game's governing bodies, the Royal and Ancient Golf Club of St Andrews and the United States Golf Association. Hannah Flemig and Angela Howe of the R&A's World Golf Museum have been unfailingly helpful in providing information and images for this project.

I'm also grateful to the staff at the USGA Library, particularly Stacy Schiff, who arranged for me to examine scrapbooks kept by three leading figures of the age. Additional assistance was provided by Katie Boyce, Jose Lopez and Elaine Bascotti.

Other librarians and archivists who pitched in include Oliver Kay of the University of California; Moira Drew of Royal Melbourne Golf Club; John Gardner of Prince's Golf Club, Sandwich; Jane Jamieson of Troon Golf Club in Scotland; Glyn Sloman of Sheringham Golf Club in England, and the research desk of the New Romney Public Library in Kent, UK.

Officials or members at golf clubs in both the US and UK also have assisted, among them Chris White at Hunstanton Golf Club; Ian Douglas at Ganton Golf Club; Glenn Deigel of Oakland Hills Golf Club; Chris Lomas of Worplesdon Golf Club and Martin Galt of St Louis Golf Club.

I am also grateful to those who read the first draft of this book and offered suggestions for improvement. They include Jim Hartsell, Dr Lauren Beatty, Connor Lewis, Jim Blankenship, Bob Proctor, David Gormley and Frank Vega.

Lee Horwich, a former journalism colleague, has my eternal thanks for his brilliant first edit of this manuscript, as does my daughter, Cori, whose technical assistance throughout this project

ACKNOWLEDGEMENTS

has been invaluable. I'm also grateful for the support of my friend Jim Stokes, who has done more for this project than he can know.

Finally, I want to thank my wife, Mara, without whom nothing I have ever accomplished would have been possible.

Stephen Proctor
Wittsend Farm
Malabar, FL

INDEX

Adair, Perry 49, 50, 60, 82
Adair, Rhona 29–31, 40, 51, 118
Adair, Thona 167
Adelaide Golf Club 13
Advanced Golf (Braid, J.) 37
After the Ball (Helme, E.) 125
A.G. Spalding & Co 170
The Age of Innocence (Wharton, E.) 61
Alliss, Peter 200
Amateur Championships 13
   1896 (Royal St George's) 8
   1898 (Royal Liverpool) 8
   1899 (Prestwick) 152
   1900 (Royal St George's) 40
   1901 (St Andrews) 40
   1904 (Royal St George's) 148
   1921 (Royal Liverpool) 71
   1923 (Royal Cinque Ports, Deal) 96–7
   1926 (Muirfield) 143
   1930 (St Andrews) 155
The American Annual 71, 72, 87
American golf
   boom years for 51–3
   formative years of 84–5
   women at war (1917-18) 59–60
The American Golfer 58, 90, 156, 176, 181–2
   'Secrets of Miss Wethered's Golf' 188–9
Anderson, Eva 59
Anderson, John 47, 54, 56, 57–8, 82–3
Anthony, Susan B. 26, 60
Apawamis in Rye, New York 83, 86
The Architectural Side of Golf (Simpson, T., and Wethered, H.N.) 66
Armour, Tommy 173
Asheville Invitational 191
Ashridge mixed foursomes (1936) 135
Associated Press 104
Astor, Nancy 61
Atlanta, Georgia 47–9, 59
Atlanta Athletic Club, East Lake 48–9
Auchincloss, Mrs Charles C. 56
Augusta Trophy 90

Baker Jr., Mrs E.H. 55
Ball, Tom 39
Ball Jr., John 12, 28, 51, 106, 152, 182
Ballybunion 135
Barclay, James 48
Barlow, Nonna 86, 87, 91
Barnes, Alfred 175
Barnes, Jim 70, 143
Barnes Brown, Lucy 15–16
Barnes Common 9–10, 13
Barnett, Leslie 172
Barton, Pam 172
Bastin, Gladys 45–6, 65, 73
Beaconsfield 125
Belleair Golf Club in Tampa 88, 89, 90, 102, 107, 123, 139, 184
Belleview Inn, Clearwater Bay, Florida 88, 102
Bennet, Marion 161
Berg, Patty Jane 181–2, 185, 194
  founder member, WPGA 192
Berthellyn Cup 89
Birkdale 42
Birkenhead 9
Bishop, Georgianna 47
Black, Dave 179
Black Friday (1929) 169–70
Boit, Frances 14–15, 51
Boston Herald 58
Bourne, Del 155
Brae Burn Country Club in Boston 50
Braid, James 37, 40, 107, 188
British Girls' Championship (1924) 117
British Ladies' Amateur
    Championships 2, 63–4, 76, 143
  1893 (Lytham and St Annes) 12, 16–17, 18
  1895 (Royal Portrush) 159
  1897 (Gullane) 12
  1899 (Newcastle, County Down) 29
  1900 (Royal North Devon) 29
  1902 (Royal Cinque Ports, Deal) 29
  1903 (Royal Portrush) 29
  1904 (Troon) 25
  1905 (Cromer) 30, 158
  1907 (Newcastle, County Down) 29
  1908 (St Andrews) 31, 32, 33–4
  1912 (Turnberry) 43
  1913 (Lytham and St Annes) 96
  1921 (Turnberry) 70–1, 179–80
  1922 (Prince's) 77–9, 93, 95
  1923 (Burnham and Berrow) 95–6
  1924 (Royal Portrush) 98–9, 105, 115, 142
  1925 (Troon) 1–2, 107–08, 111, 112, 114–15, 117, 121, 123, 142, 145, 151
  1926 (Royal St David's) 116
  1927 (Royal County Down) 118
  1928 (Hunstanton) 137, 138
  1929 (Harlech) 137–8
  1929 (St Andrews) 2–4, 141, 142–3, 145–52
  1930 (Formby) 158, 161–2
  1947 (Gullane) 178
  1976 (Silloth) 201
Brookline Country Club 14, 15, 51
Browne, Mary K. 103–04, 119–20, 154
Bruntsfield Links, women playing golf on (1738) 5
Buffalo Invitational (1924) 100, 102
Buffalo Invitational (1928) 140
Burke, Billy 174
Burton, Pam 185
Bushey Hall Golf Club in Hertfordshire 44
Byers, Eben 55

Caledonian Mercury 5, 6
Campbell, Dorothy 33, 43
  see also Hurd, Dorothy Campbell

INDEX

Canada, formation of Ladies' clubs in 14
Canadian Amateur
  at Hamilton (1924) 104
  at Mount Bruno (1923) 100
  at Rivermead (1921) 120
  at Toronto (1913) 96
Canadian Open at Rivermead 71, 75–6
Cape Golf Club in South Africa 13
Carnoustie 49, 84
Carolina Gazette 5
Carry, Margaret 93
Cascades Course at Bloomington 140–1
Catt, Carrie 60
Caverly, Mildred 56–7, 64
Central Council of Physical Recreation 201
Chambers, Doris 96, 111
Chaume, Simone de la 117–18, 138, 143
Cheltenham Golf Club 12, 27
Cheney, Leona 166
Chicago 51–2
Chicago Golf Club 15
Chiselhurst 118
Cinema House 201
Claygate Club, first men v women match (1898) 124–5
Cohan, George M. 58
Coke, Thomas 128
Collett, Ada 81
Collett, George 80, 81–2, 138
Collett, Glenna 13, 41, 111, 115, 141, 169
  Alex Smith and career of 84–5
  Amateur final appearances, pattern in 141
  American idol 100–04
  ascent to the top 93–4
  Bob Jones Award from USGA (1965) 205
  burden of reputation for 90–3
  coming of age of 21
  continental adventures 117–21
  Curtis Cup, driving passion for 203
  distinctive style of 85–6
  dream realised for women's golf, Curtis Cup and 157–63
  'Empress of Golf' 1, 2–4
  enduring legacy 183–95
  final moment of recognition for 205
  first star of American women's golf 47–8
  form worthy of 'coming champion' 89
  'golf beyond mere mortals' 104–05
  golf's 'eternal problem' of women against men and 122, 123, 125, 126, 129, 130, 133, 136, 207–08
  'Greatest Women's Match Ever Played' (St Andrews, 1929) 153
  greatness of 80–94
  Hero of First Century of Golf in America 205
  idolisation for 192
  inaugural Curtis Cup (1932) 163–8, 203
  international competition, passion for 118–21
  Leitch on future prospects of 76
  leviathans at Troon 106–10
  life after golf for 202–08
  magic at St Andrews (1929), surpassing greatness 144–52, 153
  marriage to Edwin H. Vare Jr., (1931) 163
  matches against
    Joyce Wethered at St Andrews (1929) 2–4, 144–52, 153
    Joyce Wethered at Troon (1925) 1–2, 106–10

matchless 137–42, 144–52
mentoring and encouargement from 193
Pinehurst, woman on a mission at (1922) 90–1
professional golf, lack of interest in 192–3
remarks on first presentation of Vare Trophy (1954) 194–5
service to USGA 202–03
tournaments
  Augusta Trophy at Tampa (1922) 90
  birth and early years 81–3
  Britain v US match at Sunningdale, participation in (1930) 160–1
  Britain v US match at Sunningdale, promotion of (1930) 158–60
  British Ladies Amateur, defeat again for (1930) 161–2
  British Ladies' Championship St Andrews (1929) 2–4, 144–52, 153
  British Ladies' Championship Troon (1925) 1–2
  US Women's Amateur Championship (1930) 156–7, 162
  US Women's Amateur Championship (1922) 91–3
  US Women's Amateur Championship (1929) 153–4
trial by fire for 86–9
waning years, death in 1989 and 206–07
World Golf Hall of Fame, induction into 205
Collett, Ned 81
Cooden Beach 112, 115
Corcoran, Fred 192
Corlett, Elsie 167
Cotton, Henry 143

Country Club at Brookline 51
County Golf, ladies golf progression and 20, 21
County Louth 135
Cox, Robert P. MP 16
Crawley, Leonard 189
Creek Club on Long Island 132
Crowe, Dame Sylvia 198
Cummings, Edith 71–2, 87, 123, 129, 206
  dazzling Chicago socialite 93
  and Glenna Collett at Buffalo Invitational (1923) 100–02
  and Joyce Wethered at British Ladies (1923) 95–6
  US Women's Amateur Championship (1925) 119–20
  US Women's Amateur Championship (1922) 91–3
Curtis, Harriot 14, 30, 55, 158, 162–3
  donation of Revere bowl for women golfers (1927) 159
Curtis, Laurence 14–15
Curtis, Margaret 14, 30, 107, 158, 162–3
  donation of Revere bowl for women golfers (1927) 159
Curtis Cup 3, 118
  inaugural match, Wentworth, England (1932) 3, 163–8, 175, 191, 203
Cypress Point, Sistine Chapel of American golf 132–3

Daily Gazetteer 5
Danoff, Bettye 192
Darwin, Bernard 67, 128, 197
  on Collett and Wethered, matchless at St Andrews (1929) 147–9, 150, 152
  epic Wethered/Collett final at St Andrews (1929), comments of 3–4

INDEX

Ladies v Men at Stoke Poges (1921), Wethered's loss to 125–6
Leitch as Madame Defarge, comparison by 37, 41, 112
Leitch at Hunstanton (1914), commentary on 62
on Leitch/Wethered at Troon (1925) 112–15, 184
Oxford and Cambridge Golf Society and 66
on perfect golf of Bobby Jones at Sunningdale (1926) 186
on Wethered's flawless golf at Troon (1925) 184
Darwin, Eily 197
Davison, Emily Wilding 27
Dawson, Johnny 174, 184
Dettweiler, Helen 192
Didrikson Zaharias, Mildred Ella 'Babe' 25, 133, 178–80, 185, 189, 191, 192
   founder member, WPGA 192
Diegel, Leo 173
'Dixie Whiz Kids' 60
Dobell, Temple 63
Dod, Lottie ('Little Wonder') 25, 131, 178
Dodd, Muriel ('Doddie') 96, 107
Doleman, Alexander 13, 27, 35–6, 187
Dornoch 115, 142
Down the Fairway (Jones, B.) 49
Druid Hills course in Atlanta 71
Duncan, George 123
Duthie, Alec 179
Dyer, Frank 55

Earhart, Amelia 61
East Course at Wentworth 164
East Lake Country Club 176–8
Eastern Amateur Championships 52, 137
   1919 (Apawamis) 83–4, 86
   1922 (Westchester-Biltmore) 91
   1923 (Whitemarsh) 100
   1924 (Boston) 102
Eddy, Mary Baker 199
Eldon, John Scott, 3rd Earl of 12
Emmet, Devereux 76, 132, 139
Empresses of Golf in *Golf Illustrated* 105
England v Scotland at Royal Liverpool (1902) 159
England vs Scotland at Ranelagh (1915) 59
English Amateur Championships
   1914 (Walton Heath) 44–5
   1919 (St Annes Old Links) 62–3
   1920 (Sheringham) 68–9
   1921 (Lytham and St Annes) 75
   1923 (Ganton) 97–8
   1924 (Cooden Beach) 99–100
The Englishwoman's Garden (Joyce Wethered's contribution to) 196, 198
Epsom Derby (1913) 27
Evans, Chick 51, 71
Everard, Harry 11

Fair, Talbot 11
Fawcett, Millicent 60
Fifeshire News 7
Findlay, Alexander 171, 174, 180
First World War (Great War) 1, 46, 58–61, 62, 158
Fishwick, Diana 162, 167
Fitzgerald, F. Scott 93–4
Flagler, Henry 21
Florida 88–9
   golfing centres in, development of 21
Flynn, William 140
Follett, W.H. 76
Ford, Henry 29
Fordyce, Louise 119–20
Formby 125
Fortnum & Mason 170, 171
Fownes, H.C. 91
Fownes, Mary 91

Fraser, Doris 65
Fraser, Dr Wilbert G. 120, 180
Fraser, Margaret Neill 58–9
French Open 44–5, 70, 73–4, 117–18, 138

Gardner, Robert A. 55
Garon, Marjorie 116
Gavin, Margaret 71, 87, 90, 91, 92, 100, 141
Gentlemen Golfers of Leith 6
The Gentlewoman 19
The Gentlewoman's Book of Sports (Grenville, V., ed.) 25
Gilroy, Thomas 11
Girls' Golfing Society 199
The Glasgow Herald 111, 165, 166, 167
Gleneagles 117
Gold Ball Tournaments at Fairfield Country Club (1924-1928) 125–6, 129, 184
Golf (Hutchinson, H.G.) 23
Golf (Leich, C.) 35
Golf Course Architecture, Golden Age of 66, 134
Golf du Sart Tilman in Belgium 135
Golf for Women (Hecker, G.) 30
Golf for Young Players (Collett, G.) 139
Golf from Two Sides (Wethered, J. and R.) 74, 170
Golf Illustrated 52, 109, 115, 128, 135
   Anderson's prophetic judgement 47–8
   appetite for US–British clash 107
   Cecil Leitch, full page spread on style of 53–4
   Collett's new putter, Hurd on confidence with 102
   Collett's sharpness, Hurd on 100–101
   'Empresses of Golf' feature in (1925) 1
   fundraiser for Americans to challenge British in Open (1921) 70–1
   Gold Vase Tournament 44, 143, 200
   Howard on Wethered and Leitch at British Ladies (1922) 77–8
   Hurd on Collett's game in US Amateur (1926) 139
   Hurd on Collett's Pinehurst performance (1922) 91
   Hurd on rejuvenated Collett at Shennecossett (1925) 118–19, 121
   Leitch on Collett's game at Hunstanton (1928) 138–9
   Leitch's swing, Hurd on 99
   MacAllister on change in Collet's game at US Amateur (1928) 140
   Orcutt on Collett's game at US Amateur at Oakland Hills (1929) 154
   US Women's Amateur (1925), MacAllister on 'greatest championship' ever played 119–21
   Wethered, prominent feature on (1921) 104–05
   women's international, endless discussions about 159
Golf Monthly 40
The Golfing Annual 13, 27
Golfing Memories and Methods (Wethered, J.) 170, 171, 172
Golfing Reminiscences (Stringer, M.) 19
Gosset, Isaac and William 8
Gourlay, Henry 134
Gourlay, Mary Henrietta 134
Gourlay, Molly 75, 97, 128, 131, 133–5, 172
   British Ladies Amateur at Formby (1930) 161–2

INDEX

Curtis Cup, inaugural match at
    Wentworth (1932) 166–7
death of (1990) 201
idolisation for 192
OBE award for 136
quintessential Surrey golfer 134–5
Sunningdale (1930), captaincy of
    British team at 160–1
Grace, W.G. 143
Graham, James 36
Grand Hotel in Trafalgar Square 11, 16
Great Atlanta Fire (1917) 59
Great Depression 132, 181, 191
Great English Golf Boom (1890s) 51
Greville, Lady Violet 25
Griffiths, Arthur 132
Griffiths, Molly 65, 68, 69
Griscom Cup 86
Griswold Cup 87–8, 89, 119
Guilford, Jesse 71
Gunderson, JoAnne 182

Hagen, Walter 70, 71, 84, 103, 110, 173
    British Open wins for (1922–1929) 143
    Collett/Stirling v Hagen/Sarazen, Westchester-Biltmore Country Club (1923) 130
    victory for US in Open at Royal St George's (1922) 106
    on Wethered's strength and style (1934) 185
Hagge, Alice 192
Hagge, Marlene 192
Hammond, Mrs A.G. 52
handicapping
    golf's ('eternal problem') of matches between men and women 39–40, 122–36, 207–8
    Pearson and development of 22
Hardscrabble tournament in Arkansas, WPGA and 192
Harper's Weekly 51

Harrington, Mrs George 52
Harris, Robert 97
Harvey, Florence 64
Havers, Arthur 2, 110, 142
Heathcoat-Amory, Sir John 196–9, 200
Hecker, Genevieve 23, 30
Helme, Eleanor 33, 52, 63, 134
    on Collett and American invasion of British golf 138, 145, 146, 147, 161, 162
    Collett and Wethered, golf beyond mere mortals 104
    Collett and Wethered, leviathans at Troon (1925) 108, 109, 110
    death of (1967) 201
    Leitch and Wethered, leviathans at Troon (1925) 112–13, 114
    Leitch or Wethered, comparison between 98
    Leitch–Stirling match at Turnberry (1921), comment on 72–3
    memories of Ladies v Men at Stoke Poges 125–6
    Stirling-Leitch match at Turnberry (1921), Helme's comment on 72–3
    on Wethered at British Ladies (1923) at Burnam 95, 96
    on Wethered's glorious game 69
    witness to new champion, Wethered's performance at Prince's (1922) 79
    women gaining on men, Wethered and (1925) 123–4
    Worplesdon Mixed Foursomes, victory with Tony Torrance (1921) 127–8
Hezlet, Major Charles 128
Hezlet, May 29
Hicks, Helen 139, 157, 161, 166, 167, 185, 191
    founder member, WPGA 192
Hickson, Michael 198
Higbie, Dorothy 154

Hill, Opal 154, 165, 191, 203
  founder member, WPGA 192
Hill bunker at St Andrews 150
Hilton, Harold 28, 39–41, 43, 51, 125
Hole O' Cross at St Andrews 147
Hollins, Harry 131, 132
Hollins, Marion 70, 71, 75, 88, 107, 129, 136, 139, 173, 174
  British Ladies at Royal County Down (1920) 64–5
  Curtis Cup at Wentworth (1932), non-playing American captain 163–4, 166–7
  decline and death (1944) 205
  extraordinary accomplishments 131–3
  golf, importance for 132
  idolisation for 192
  North and South Amateur at Pinehurst (1923) 100
  US Women's Amateur at Greenbriar (1922) 91, 92
  US Women's Amateur champion at Hollywood (1921) 76, 89
  Wethered in California with 178–9
  women's golf of 1920s and 1930s, significance for 131, 132–3
Hollywood Golf Club in Deal, New Jersey 76, 89
Hot Springs, Virginia 140
Howard, R.E. 77–8
Howlett, Albert 68
Hoylake 71, 106, 156
  ladies 'clubhouse' at 23
Hoyt, Beatrix 16, 28, 157
Hull, Dickie 196–7
Hulton, Blanche Martin 11
Hunnewell, Mr and Mrs Arthur 14
Hunstanton Golf Club 44–5, 137
Huntingdon Valley Country Club 89
Hurd, Dorothy Campbell 72, 92, 105, 115, 154
  on battle between Stirling and Vanderbeck (1915) 52–3
  on Collett's game in US Amateur (1926) 139
  on Collett's new putter, confidence with 102
  on Collett's Pinehurst performance (1922) 91
  Collett's sharpness, Hurd on 100–101
  on Leitch's swing 99
  on rejuvenated Collett at Shennecossett (1925) 118–19
  siminal change in women's golf, comments on 53–4, 55
  women's improvement, reasons for 124
Hurd, Jack 52
Hutchinson, Horace 22–3
Hutchinson, Major Cecil K. 170–1
Hutchison, Jock 71, 73, 106, 143

Icely, L.B. 191, 192
Illustrated Sporting News 30
Interlachen Country Club in Minnesota 181, 191
International Shield (donated by Thomas H. Miller) 159
Irish Amateur Championship (1899) 29
Irish Amateur Championship (1900) 29
Irish Ladies' Golf Union (1893) 19–20, 29
Irish War of Independence 64

Jack Nicklaus's Memorial Tournament (1982) 205
Jameson, Betty 175, 181, 182, 185, 191, 193
  founder member, WPGA 192
  USGA interview with (at nearly 73) 193–4
  Vare Trophy donation honouring Glenna Collett (1954) 194
Jericho Golf Club in Vancouver 179

INDEX

Jones, Bobby 38, 71, 82, 84, 102, 103, 110, 133, 157
 British golf, first undistinguished appearance in (1921) 143–4
 Darwin on perfect golf at Sunningdale (1926) 186
 early years at East Lake with Joyce Wethered 49–50
 'finest gentleman' and 'greatest champion' 50
 Grand Slam for (1930) 156
 'greatest golfer in the world,' Grand Slam and (1929-30) 154–5
 'Impregnable Quadrilateral' of 155
 Open Championship victory (1927) 150
 outclassed by Joyce Wethered 155–6
 perfection in golf, Jones' performances and 186–9
 Stirling's association with 51, 54–5, 60
 US and Canada exhibition tour (1935) 173, 174, 175, 177, 180, 182
 Walker Cup captain (1930) 160
 Wethered's classically powerful swing, Jones and 143–4
 Wethered's idolisation of 68, 116, 144–5, 155
Jones, Jimmy 49

Keeler, O.B. 155, 176–8
Kemp, Edward 198
Kent County Playing Fields Association 201
Kilkenny 135
King, Ginevra 93
Kinghorn Ltd 170
Kirby, Dorothy 176–7
Kit-Cat Medal 44
Knightshayes Court in Tiverton 200
 formal garden at, development of 198

Ladies' Championship 1920 at Royal County Down 64–5
Ladies' Championship at Burnham (1906) 96
Ladies' European tour, launch of (1978) 192
ladies fashions
 impediment in early days 24
 'Miss Higgins' band to control flowing skirts 24
Ladies' Field magazine 37, 40
Ladies Golf and Country Club of Westchester 139
Ladies' Golf Association 134, 199
Ladies' Golf Union 13, 18, 39, 40, 45, 63–4, 93–4
 coming of age for 19–20, 26–7
 Eleanor Helme, tireless worker for 33
 formation of 16–17, 131
 general strike and postponement of British Ladies at Harlech (1926) 137–8
 golfing world's antipathy towards 22–3
 men's hegemony, fulfilment of pioneers' dreams for women's challenge to 184
 proposal for 11
 tenth anniversary (1903) 26
 zeal to set tees back 98, 146
Ladies in the Rough (Collett, G.) 122, 130, 139, 193, 205
Ladies' Open Championship 35
Ladies' Pictorial championship at Stoke Poges (1914) 46
Ladies' Putting Club 24
Ladies' Putting Green at St Andrews (1867) 127
Ladies' Silver Medal at Dornoch 142
lady golfers
 accommodations in early days for, lack of 23–4
 convention denial and unshackling of 24–7

fashion problems for 24
restrictions on playing for 22–4
Lancaster Country Club 108
Laney, Al 142, 144–5, 149, 151, 186
Lawson, Estelle 190
Le Blan, Nanette 138
Leicester, Thomas Coke, 5th Earl of 199
Leitch, Cecilia P. ('Silloth flapper') 47, 61, 64, 67, 71, 87, 91, 93, 154
   birth and early life of 36–7
   charisma of 34
   on Collett's future prospects 76
   on Collett's game at Hunstanton (1928) 138–9
   Dickens' 'Madame Defarge,' Darwin's comparisons to 37, 41, 112
   dominance of Wethered over (1925) 111
   fate, unkindness for, Great War and 46, 62
   final bow for, Wethered's departure and opportunity for 115, 116, 118, 121
   furious swing and slashing style of 33–4, 124
   Golf Illustrated, full page spread on style of 53–4
   Great War, effect on 46, 62
   Howard on Wethered and Leitch at British Ladies (1922) 77–8
   at Hunstanton (1914), Darwin's commentary on 62
   idolisation for 192
   last stand 110–15
   later years and death of (1977) 201
   lean years for 42–5
   legacy of, building on 183
   Margaret Curtis and, Curtis Cup beginnings and 159
   matches against
      Hilton's famous match with (1910) 40–2, 125
      Ravenscroft at *Ladies' Pictorial* at Stoke Poges (1914) 46
      Wethered at Ladies Amateur Open at Prince's (1922) 77–9
      Wethered at Ladies Amateur Open at Troon (1925) 112–15, 151
      Wethered at Troon (1925), Darwin on 112–15, 184
   men vs women 39–42
   revival 45–6
   self-taught golfer 37
   swing of, Hurd on 99
   tournaments
      Berthellyn Cup in Huntingdon Valley (1921), Collett's victory over 89–90
      debut at Ladies Amateur Open at St Andrews (1908) 33–5, 37–8
      English Amateur at Cooden Beach (1924), rematch with Wethered in 99–100
      English Amateur at Sheringham (1920), defeat for 68–70
      English Amateur at Walton Heath (1914), victory for 45
      French Ladies, third consecutive victory at Fontainebleau for 74
      French Ladies at La Boulie (1914), victory for 45–6
      Ladies Amateur Open at Hunstanton (1914), victory for 44–5
      Ladies Amateur Open at Prince's (1922), defeat by Wethered in 77–9
      Ladies Amateur Open at Royal County Down (1920), victory for 63–5
      Ladies Amateur Open at Royal Portrush (1924), return for 98
      Ladies Amateur Open at Troon (1925), narrow loss to Wethered 112–15, 151

INDEX

Ladies Amateur Open at Turnberry (1921), victory for 72–3, 97, 138
Ladies' Pictorial at Stoke Poges (1914), fall to Ravenscroft 46
trendsetter in clothing 34
troubles for, broken brassie and 34–5
US and Canada, troubles touring in 75–7
wartime service 58–9
Wethered and, four national championships for each 157
Wethered and Leitch, Helme on leviathans at Troon (1925) 112–13, 114
Wethered or, Helme's comparison between 98
Wethered's attitude to boisterousness of 111–12, 179
women in golf and 61
Leitch, Dr John 36, 38
Leitch, Edith 59, 65, 75, 77, 89
Leitch, Joyce 95
Leitch, May 59
Lenton, Lilian 26
Letts, Courtney 93
Letts, F.C. 76, 91, 119–20
Littlestone Ladies' Golf Club 18, 19, 23, 25, 28, 127
London Foursomes (1925) 143
London Scottish Ladies' Golf Club at Wimbledon 9
Long Hole at St Andrews 149, 151
Lonsdale Library IX, *Game of Golf* (Wethered, J. & R. et al.) 170
Low, John 66
Lucerne Golf Club 117
Lytham and St Annes 12, 16, 18, 44, 62–3, 75, 97, 117

MacAllister, Lucille 119, 121, 140
Macbeth, Lt Allan 96
Macdonald, C.B. 51
Macdonald, Charles Blair 119, 132

Mackenzie, Ada 64, 119–20, 173, 179
MacKenzie, Alister 133
Maiden, Jimmy 84
Maiden, Stewart 49, 84, 85
Mair, Levine 112, 199
Manchester Golf Club 26–7
Marlborough Golf Club in Montreal 180
Marston, Max 129
Martelli, Hazel 161
Martin, H.B. 15, 83–4, 86, 133, 190
Massachusetts Women's Amateur 86–7, 89
Massy, Arnaud 117, 118
McBride, Molly 76
McCulloch, Jean 73
McDermott, Johnny 85
McLean, Jack 172, 184
Meador, Frank 49
Meadow Farm on Long Island 131
Meadowbrook Club in Hempstead, Long Island 15–16
Meadowbrook Country Club in Buffalo 178–9
mens' nervousness, 1920s and 122–3
Merion Cricket Club near Philadelphia 55
Metacomet Club in Rhode Island 80, 81, 83, 87–8
Miami 88–9
Mida, Lee 161
Mid-South Open at Pinehurst (1926) 140
Miller, Thomas H. 64, 159
Minoprio, Gloria 34
Moncreiff, Henry James ('Lord Wellwood') 23
Montmorency, Reymond de 125
Morgan, Wanda 165–6
Morris, Old Tom 6, 8, 29, 32–3, 35, 40, 127
Morris, Young Tom 13, 72, 98, 152, 187

Morris County Golf Club in New
    Jersey 16
Morrison, John 128, 143, 172
Morrison, Michael 9
Morse, S.E.B. 132
Musselburgh, women and children
    playing golf at (1870s) 6

Nagell, Elwyn 178–9
Narragansett Bay in Rhode Island
    202
National Championship at Merion
    56
National Golf Links of America 76
National Horse Show at Madison
    Square Garden 131
National Trust 198, 200
New American Woman 81
New York Herald Tribune 142, 144–5,
    149, 151
New York Ladies' Golf Association
    (1900) 21
New York Times 51, 123, 126
New York Tribune 186
Newport Country Club 15
North and South Amateur
    Championships 100
    1904 (Pinehurst) 52
    1921 (Pinehurst) 89, 90–1
    1924 (Pinehurst) 102
    1926 (Pinehurst) 137
    1927 (Pinehurst) 137
    1929 (Pinehurst) 141
North Devon Ladies' Golf Club 8–9
North Shore Country Club in
    Milwaukee 191
Northam Burrows 8

Oak Park Country Club in Chicago
    178
Oakland Hills Country Club 153–4
Old Course at St Andrews 32
Olympic Games at Los Angeles (1932)
    178
Onwentsia Club, Illinois 52

Open Championships 13, 28, 73,
    142–3
    1890 (Prestwick) 106
    1892 (Muirfield) 40
    1897 (Royal Liverpool) 40
    1907 (Royal Liverpool) 117
    1920 (Royal Cinque Ports, Deal)
        123
    1921 (St Andrews) 70–1, 144
    1923 (Troon) 2, 110
    1926 (Lytham and St Annes) 186
    1927 (St Andrews) 150
    1934 (Royal St George's) 143
Open Meetings 20, 39
Oppenheimer, Raymond 128
Orange Blossom Circuit 21
Orcutt, Maureen 139, 161, 166, 167,
    185
Ottawa 179
Ouimet, Francis 51, 71, 129
    US and Canada exhibition tour
        (1935) 173, 174
Oxford and Cambridge Golf Society
    66

Palm Beach 88–9
Pankhurst, Emmeline 26, 40, 60
Park, Doris 166
Parker, Mrs Willard 52
Pasatiempo in Santa Cruz 133, 163,
    179, 205
Pau in France 12, 13, 14
Paul, Alice 60
Pearson, Issette ('Czar') 42, 131,
    157
    death of (1941) 200
    'despotism' in pursuit of progress
        22–3
    forward looking nature of 158
    hegemony of men, satisfaction in
        women challenging 184
    improvement through playing with
        men, support for 67
    ladies golf, development beyond
        dreams of 93–4

Ladies' Golf Union, foresight in
    formation of 16–17
Ladies' Golf Union and 13, 16
Leitch sisters, keeping an eye on
    37–8
Leitch sisters, tireless support for
    39–40
Mabel Stringer and, effect of duo
    on women's golf 18–22
marriage to Thomas Miller and
    relinquishment of
    secretaryship of LGU 64
memorial for wartime nurse
    Margaret Fraser, promotion of
    cause for 58–9
men vs women at Claygare Club,
    participation in (1898) 124–5
pivotal in history of women's golf
    9–14, 31, 38
seasoning Cecil Leitch, eligibility
    rules and 43–4
suffragettes and 27
Pearson, John 76
Pearson, Thomas and Mary 9
Pebble Beach on Monterey Peninsula
    132, 179
The Perfect Golfer (Wethered, H.N.)
    186–8
Phelps, Marjorie 34
Philadelphia Ladies' Golf Association
    (1897) 21
Pickford, Mary 133
Pinehurst, North Carolina 52,
    139–40, 184
Plant, Henry 21
Point Judith Country Club in
    Narragansett, Rhode Island
    175, 189–90
political rights, womens' demands for
    25–6
Portrush 42, 108, 112
    see also Royal Portrush
Postage Stamp at Troon 107, 109
Pressler, Leona 154, 167
Prince's 112

Professional Golfers' Association 83
Purves, Dr William Laidlaw 9,
    10–11, 13

Raceabout, Mercer 121
Ramsden, Omar 200
Ranelah 44
Ravenscroft, Gladys 43, 44, 53–4, 65,
    111, 138, 158
    Ladies Amateur Open at
        Hunstanton (1914), fall to
        Leitch at 45–6
    Ladies Amateur Open at Troon
        (1925), demolition by
        Wethered in 183
    marriage to Temple Bell 63
Ray, Ted 51
Raynor, Seth 129, 132
Read's Weekly Journal 5
Red Cross 50, 59–60, 82
Renouf, Tommy 37
Rhode Island Amateur 89
Rhode Island Championship (1918)
    83
Rhode Island Ladies' Golf Association
    (1914) 21
Rhodes, Hal 144, 188
Rice, Grantland 90, 123, 178, 184,
    188–9
Richardson, William D. 123, 126
Rivermead 71, 75–6, 120, 180
Riverview Golf Club, Montgomery,
    Alabama 54
Road Hole 34
Road Hole at St Andrews 149
Roaring Twenties in America 93, 135,
    194
Robert Cox Trophy 76, 162, 181
Roehampton Golf Club 26–7
Rosenthal, Elaine 50, 55, 60, 71–2,
    82, 83, 87–8, 89
Ross, Donald 54, 88, 153–4
Royal and Ancient Golf Club 6, 11,
    32
Royal Liverpool Golf Club 10, 182

Royal Melbourne Golf Club 13
Royal Musselburgh Golf Club
    competition among fishwives at 6
Royal North Devon (Westward Ho!)
    8, 28, 42–3, 196
Royal Portrush 27–8, 29, 98–9, 105,
    115, 142, 159
Royal St David's in Wales 116
Royal St George's at Sandwich 10,
    106, 107, 132
Royal West Norfolk 197
Royal Wimbledon 10
Rusack's Hotel, St Andrews 6, 145
Ryder Cup (debut 1927) 158, 159

Sacramento Union 153
St Andrews 2–4, 8, 10, 11, 183–4
    British Ladies' Championship at
        (1929) 2–4
    Children's Golf Club in 7–8
    Himalayas putting green at 6
    ladies' putting at (1860s) 6
    Ladies' Putting Club at 7–8
    Old Course at 2–4, 134, 136, 137
    Swilcan Burn 33, 35 at
St Andrews (1929) 186
St Andrews Citizen 7
St Andrews Gazette 7
St Andrews Golf Club in Yonkers 14,
    15, 132
St Andrews University 38
St Annes *see* Lytham and St Annes
St George's 117
St Louis Country Club 184
San Francisco Golf Club 179
San Joaquin Valley 133
Sander, Anne Quast 141
Sarazen, Gene 110, 130, 184–5, 188
    US and Canada exhibition tour
        (1935) 173, 174, 175–6,
        178–9
Schloss Mittersill sports and shooting
    club in Austria 135
Scot brothers (Denys, Osmond and
    Michael) 12

The Scotsman 7, 161
Scott, Lady Margaret 12–13, 16, 27,
    28, 157, 187
Scott, Michael 128
Scottish Ladies' Golf Union (1902)
    20
Scottish Women's Hospital in Serbia
    58
Seignious, Hope 191
Sessions, Sally 192
Shaw, Dorothy 172–3, 176
Shennecossett Country Club in
    Connecticut 84, 85, 88, 119
Sheringham 62, 68–70
Sherman, General William Tecumseh
    59
Sherwood, Rosamond 64
Shinnecock Hills Golf Club on Long
    Island 15–16
Silloth 33, 35, 36, 37, 39, 41, 42,
    44
Silloth on Solway Golf Club 36
Simpson, Edith 197
Simpson, Tom 134–5, 197
Simpson & Co. 135, 136
Smith, Alex 84–5, 88, 92, 119, 139
Smith, Archibald 37
Smith, Horston 173, 178
Smith, Marilynn 192
Smith, Willie 84–5
Southern Amateur Ladies'
    Championships 47, 52, 53,
    54, 71
Spokane Athletic Round Table 192
Spork, Shirley 192
The Sportsman magazine 175
Stetson, Mrs G. Henry 140
Stewart, John Wood 14
Stewart, Laura Safford 14, 15
Stifel, Fritzi 119–20
Stirling, Alexa 89, 100, 101, 107,
    124, 157, 173, 183, 185
    association with Bobby Jones 51,
        54–5, 60, 84
    birth and early life 47–8

INDEX

Bobby Jones as childhood companion 49
British Ladies (1921), 'she's coming over for' 70–4
Collett's admiration for 82–3, 154
Collett's tip on swing from 88
Collett/Stirling v Hagen/Sarazen, Westchester-Biltmore Country Club (1923) 130
domination of women's golf by likes of 87
early years at East Lake with Bobby Jones 49–50
East Lake, family relocation to 48
exhibition golf, wartime pursuit of 59–60
father's code for life 50
final years in Canada, death in 1977 and 205–06
first competition with Bobby Jones 49–50
gifted musician, Atlanta Symphony Orchestra and 48
Hurd on battle between Stirling and Vanderbeck (1915) 52–3
idolisation for 192
impact on women's golf, transformational nature of 187–8
inspiration for new generations of women golfers 47–8
Leitch-Stirling match at Turnberry (1921), Helme's comment on 72–3
lifetime changes for, marriage and 120
matches against
  Hollins at Hollywood G.C. (1921) 131
  Leitch at Turnberry (1921) 138
  Wethered and, exhibition tour matches between 178–80
new challengers having grown up inspired by 139

seminal change in women's game, Stirling and 53–8
Stewart Maiden, influence on 49
Stoke Poges, loss to Reymond de Montmorency at 125
tournaments
  US Amateur Ladies' Championship, Belmont Springs, Boston (1916) 54–8
  US Amateur Ladies' Championship, Greenbriar G.C. (1922) 91
  US Amateur Ladies' Championship, Hollywood G.C. (1921), loss to Hollins at 131
  US Women's Amateur at St Louis Country Club (1925), 'greatest championship' 119–20, 141
  US Women's Amateur Championship (1914), golfing arrival at 47
trailblazing golf of 93
wartime experiences 59–60
women in golf and 61
Stirling, Dr Alexander William 48
Stirling, Nora 48
Stoke Poges 41–2, 108, 125, 184, 188
  men v ladies at (1935) 172
Storey, S.F. 125
The Story of American Golf (Wind, H.W.) 189
Strath, Davie 152
Stringer, Henry and Harriet 19
Stringer, Mabel ('Auntie Mabel') 52, 58, 65, 69, 127, 184
  coverage of Lietch's sparkling debut at St Andrews (1908) 38
  death of (1958) 200–201
  golfing dress, musing on 'outrageous' nature of 24
  on hardships of striking miners' families (1921) 72

Issette Pearson and, effect of duo on women's golf 18–22, 25
'ladies clubhouses,' perspective on 23–4
Leitch's defeat by Wethered in 1922, emotional reaction to 79
Littlestone Ladies' Golf Club, captaincy of 18–19
men vs women at Claygate Club (1898), memories of 124–5
Old Links at St Annes, 'delightful' postwar reunion on (1919) 62–3
on problems for early lady golfers 23–4
retirement (at 55) from golfing coverage (1923) 96
St Andrews Championship in 1908, epoch-making nature for 32–5
women's rights, belief in cause of 27
Stringer, Michael 32–3, 35, 38
Stuart, William Leitch 38
suffragettes, golf as target for 26–7
Suggs, Louise 184–5, 185, 194
founder member, WPGA 192
Sunningdale Foursomes (1935) 172
Sunningdale Golf Club 40, 41, 158, 159–62
Suttie, Elsie Grant 45, 59
S.W. Straus & Co. of Chicago 120
Swandon, Bernard 181–2
Sweetser, Jess 110, 126, 129, 143, 175–6, 185
Sydney Golf Club 13

Tacoma Golf and Country Club 141
Tait, Edith 8
Tait, Freddie 152
Tait, Frederick Guthrie 8
Tam O'Shanter tournament in Chicago 192
Tampa 88
Taylor, John Henry 42, 188
Teacher, Frances 44
Tennessee, Susan B. Anthony Amendment in (1920) 60
Texas Public Links Championship (1934) 193
Thirty Years of Championship Golf (Sarazen, G.) 185
Thomas Jr, George 156
Tigbourne Court, in Godalming 66–7, 170
Tillinghast, A.W. 176
The Times 3, 62, 66, 70, 112, 128, 147, 148, 152, 170
Tinkler, Basil Ashton 75–6, 160
Titleholders Championship (1954) 194
Titleholders tournament in Augusta 191
Titterton, Maud 33–5
Tolley, Cyril 42, 67, 125, 128, 133, 143, 155
Toronto 179
Torrance, Tony 128, 155
Tracy, Spencer 133
Travers, Jerome 51, 84
Travis, Walter 148
Troon 1–2, 169, 183, 184, 191
Postage Stamp at 107, 109
Turnberry 72–3, 97–8, 138

United Kingdom
Home Internationals 159
womens' suffrage, Representation of the People Act (1918) 60
United States
Army Medical Corps 59
Canada and, exhibition tour in (1935) 173–8, 178–80
star-spangled foursome for 174
Wethered to New York for 172–3
Wethered tour de force on 173–8, 178–80

INDEX

Constitution, womens' suffrage in 19th Amendment (1919) 60
global sisterhood, development of 14–15
United States Golf Association (USGA) 15, 16, 22, 51
 Collett's service to 202–3
 Jameson's interview with (at nearly 73) 193–4
 offer of cup for international competition (1909) 158
 Women's Committee 159, 202
US Amateur Championship 28, 107
 1922 (Brookline Country Club) 129
 1926 (Merion Cricket Club) 137, 139
 results of (1895-1935) 123–4
US Open
 1913 51
 1915 51
 1916 51
US Women's Amateur Championships 76, 137, 141
 1896 (Morris County G.C.) 16
 1913 (Wilmington Country Club) 158
 1914 (Nassau Country Club) 47
 1915 (Onwentsia Club) 52–3, 55
 1916 (Belmont Springs) 54–8
 1919 (Shawnee on Delaware) 87
 1920 (Mayfield Club, Cleveland) 88
 1921 (Hollywood Golf Club) 89, 131
 1922 (Greenbrier in White Sulphur Springs) 91–2, 190
 1923 (Westchester Country Club) 100, 101
 1924 (Rhode Island Country Club) 102, 103–04, 105
 1925 (St Louis Country Club) 119, 120–1
 1928 (Hot Springs, Virginia) 123, 140
 1929 (Oakland Hills Country Club) 153–4
 1934 (Whitemarsh Valley Country Club) 181
 1935 (Interlachen Country Club) 181–2
 results (1895-1935) 123–4
US Women's Open
 1946 (Spokane Country Club) 184
 2024 (Lancaster Country Club) 108
 launch of (1946) 192

Vagliano Cup 163
Van Wie, Virginia 139, 140, 141, 157, 166, 181, 185, 206
Vanderbeck, Florence 52–3, 55, 64, 71, 72, 89, 101
Vanderbilt, Alfred Gwynne 133
Vanderbilt, William K. 131
Vardon, Harry 29–30, 51, 68, 143, 171–2, 180, 187, 188
Vare, Edwin H. (Glenna Collett's son) 163, 175, 190, 203
Vare Trophy honouring Glenna Collett (1954) 194
Versailles, La Boulie in 45–6, 117
Victoria, Princess 27
Victoria, Queen 196
Voigt, George 155
Voluntary Aid Detachments 136
Von Elm, George 155

Walker Cup 144, 160, 161
 debut tournament (1922) 158, 159
 at Royal St George's (1930) 155
Walton Heath 40–41
 Open Meeting at (1908) 39
Wanamaker Department Store, Philadelphia 171, 173
Wannamoisett Golf Club 82
Watson, Charlotte 166
Wattles, Peggy 157
Wellesley, Massachusetts 14
Welsh Ladies' Golf Union (1904) 20

Wentworth Golf Club 164–8
West Lancashire Golf Club 39
Westbrook Golf Club 132
Westchester-Biltmore Country Club 100, 130, 139
Western Amateur Ladies' Championship 52, 191
Wethered, Elizabeth 197
Wethered, Herbert Newton 66–7, 85–6, 186–8
Wethered, Joyce 38, 41, 62, 73–5, 87, 154–5
   Babe Didrikson and 178–80
   birth and early life of 66–7
   Bobby Jones outclassed by 155–6
   in California with Marion Hollins 178–9
   change of heart for 141–5
   Christian Science, devotion to 199
   classically powerful swing of, Bobby Jones and 143–4
   Collett and, 'golf beyond mere mortals,' Helme's view 104–05
   Collett and, greatest women golfers 94
   Collett and, leviathans at Troon (1925) 108, 109, 110
   Darwin on Collett and, matchless at St Andrews (1929) 147–9, 150, 152
   death at Knightshayes (1997) 202
   departure of, opportunity for final bow for Leitch on 115, 116, 118, 121
   dominance of Wethered over Leitch (1925) 111
   and Edith Cummings at British Ladies (1923) 95–6
   'Empress of Golf' 1, 2–4
   enduring legacy 183–94
   engagement to Major Hutchinson 170–1
   exhibition tour of US and Canada (1935), swan song for 169–70, 171, 172–3, 173–8, 178–80, 18082
   final years and death at 96 of 200, 202
   flawless golf at Troon (1925) from, Darwin on 184
   'golf beyond mere mortals' 104–05
   Golf Illustrated, prominent feature on (1921) 104–5
   golf on television, later life fondness for 201–02
   greatest champion of all 20
   'Greatest Women's Match Ever Played' (St Andrews, 1929) 153
   Hagen on Wethered's strength and style (1934) 185
   Helme on Wethered at British Ladies (1923) 95, 96
   Helme on Wethered's 'glorious game' 69
   Howard on Leitch and Wethered at British Ladies (1922) 77–8
   idolisation for 192
   idolisation of Bobby Jones 68, 116, 144–5, 155
   inaugural Curtis Cup (1932) 163–8
   influences on 67–8
   international matches, attitude to 127–8, 163
   Ladies' Golf Association President (1951) 199
   Ladies' Golf Union, relationship with 160, 164
   Leitch and, four national championships for each 157
   Leitch and, leviathans at Troon (1925) 112–13, 114
   Leitch or Wethered, Helme's comparison between 98
   Leitch's defeat in 1922 by, Stringer's emotional reaction to 79
   life after golf for 196–202, 203, 204–05, 208

INDEX

magic at St Andrews (1929), surpassing greatness 145–52, 153
marriage to Sir John Heathcot-Amory 197–9
matches against
 Alexa Stirling, exhibition tour matches between 178–80
 Cecil Leitch at Troon (1925), Darwin on 112–15, 184
 Glenna Collet at Troon (1925) 1–2, 106–10
 Glenna Collett at St Andrews (1929) 2–4, 144–52, 153
mystery player in Surrey side, 'glowing accounts' about 65, 66
New York for exhibition tour (1935) 172–3
perfect swing, pursuit of 143–5
professional golf, lack of interest in 192–3
return to championship golf, St Andrews (1929) and 137, 140, 141–5, 145–52
Scottish golf, love for 67
stepping away 115–16
team competitions, attitude to 163–4
tour de force in US and Canada (1935) 173–8, 178–80
tournaments
 British Ladies' Championship at Portrush (1924) 98–9
 British Ladies' Championship at St Andrews (1929) 2–4
 English Amateur at Cooden Beach (1924), rematch with Leitch in 99–100
 English Amateur at Ganton, Scarborough (1923) 97–8
 English Amateur Championship at Sheringham (1920) 68–70
 epic Collett/Wethered final at St Andrews (1929), Darwin's comments of 3–4
 Ladies Amateur Open at Prince's (1922), victory over Leitch in 77–9, 93
 Ladies Amateur Open at St Andrews (1929), surpassing greatness with Collett 137, 140, 141–5, 145–52
 Ladies Amateur Open at Troon (1925), demolition of Ravenscroft in 183
 Ladies Amateur Open at Troon (1925), Leitch's narrow loss to Wethered in 112–15, 151
 Ladies v Men at Stoke Poges (1921), loss to Bernard Darwin 125–6
Victoria Medal of Royal Horticultural Society award for 196, 198
witness to new champion, Helme on Wethered's performance at Prince's (1922) 79
women gaining on men, Helme on Wethered and (1925) 123–4
World Golf Hall of Fame, induction into 201
'world's greatest lady golfer' 99–100
Wethered, Marion 66–7
Wethered, Newton 169–70
Wethered, Roger 66, 143, 155, 160, 170, 186, 197
 Amateur Championship, victory in (1923) 96–7
 Golf from Both Sides, new concept with Joyce 66
 influence on sister Joyce 67–8
 Walker Cup captaincy (1930) 144
 Worplesdon Mixed Foursomes wins for (1922–1936) 128
White, Eustace 40
White Sulphur Springs, Virginia 190
Whitemarsh Valley Country Club 193
Whitney, Harry Payne 133

Whyte-Melville, John 6
Wigham, Sybil 27–8, 30
Willock-Pollen, 2nd Lt. Henry 59
Wilshire Country Club in Los Angeles 179
Wilson, Enid 160, 161, 162, 166, 167
Wilson, President Woodrow 26
Wilson, Virginia 137, 140
Wilson Sporting Goods 191, 192
Wimbledon Ladies' Golf Club 10, 11
Wimbledon tennis 25
Winged Foot Golf Club in Mamaroneck 175–6
Woking Golf Club 28
Wolfe-Murray, Mrs James 6
Women's Amateur at Mayfield Country Club in Cleveland (1920) 71–2
Women's Amateur at Shawnee on Delaware (1919) 71
women's golf
  Bruntsfield Links golf on (1738) 5
  championship, launch of (1893) 3
  early embrace of international competition 158–9
  eternal problem, women competing with men 39–40, 122–36, 207–8
  firsts for, 1920s and 60–1
  mens' clubs, women joining 133–6
  mixed foursomes 127–30
  rubber-cored ball, boost for 28
  singles matches, progress against men and 127
  trailblazers for 131–3
Women's National Golf and Tennis Club 132, 174–8, 178–80
Women's Political and Social Union 26
Women's Professional Golf Association (WPGA) 191–2
Women's Southern Golf Association 52
Women's Texas Open 191
Worplesdon Golf Club 118
  Mixed Foursomes at 127–8, 129, 143, 199, 200
Wragg, Mabel 138
Wright, Mickey 189
Wright & Ditson sporting goods 60

Yates, Charlie 176–7
YMCA 201

Zaharias, George 179